D0200660

# The
# DEVIL
## Can
# RIDE

# The
# DEVIL
# Can
# RIDE

## The World's Best
## Motorcycle Writing

### Edited by Lee Klancher

motorbooks

First published in 2010 by Motorbooks, an imprint of MBI Publishing Company, 400 First Avenue North, Suite 300, Minneapolis, MN 55401 USA

Motorbooks titles are also available at discounts in bulk quantity for industrial or sales-promotional use. For details write to Special Sales Manager at MBI Publishing Company, 400 First Avenue North, Suite 300, Minneapolis, MN 55401 USA.

To find out more about our books, join us online at www.motorbooks.com.

ISBN-13: 978-0-7603-3477-5

On the cover: Pasko Maksim/Shutterstock

Icons from pages: 18, 26, 33, 132, 148, 186, 211, 216, 264 by iStockphoto; pages: 38, 44, 56, 77, 95, 106, 124, 144, 162, 169, 177, 202, 230, 238, 260, 272 by Shutterstock pages: 2, 52, 111, 288 by OILSHOCK!® designs

On the back cover: Copyright © OILSHOCK!® designs

Printed in the United States of America

To Joan Hughes.

# Contents

## Introduction 8

## I, Motorcycle

## The Motorcycle Life

## On the Fringe

## Journeys

## Turning Points

# Introduction

I READ *RUNAWAY RALPH* a minimum of 572 times at age eight. While I loved to read and would have consumed books voraciously wherever I grew up, my habits were compounded by the fact that I lived in rural northern Wisconsin three miles outside of a town of 50 people and there wasn't much else to do, particularly when the thermometer read 60 degrees below zero, the narrow little gravel road to our house was snowed in from here to eternity, and the county plow trucks' first priority was to open up the roads to the seven bars in the township before the DTs killed their customers.

After a particularly long, cold winter, most of which I spent huddled under a blanket in our living room fixating on motorcycles and mice, my father dragged me away from my books long enough for me to fall desperately in lust. You see, my Dad cut wood to heat our little house, and he needed to get his chain saw sharpened at a shop a few miles from our home. That shop later housed the Three Little Pigs Restaurant and the Swine and Dine Saloon, a tiny bar-restaurant where art-deco wall hangings, slumming south Minneapolis granola sorts, stoned hipsters, and local farmers with manure stains on their cuffed Levi's intermingled in Leinenkugel-fueled harmony.

That was later, when the outside world started to creep into the North Woods. Before the onslaught of chain restaurants, radio syndication, and cable television, the place was a proper greasy little shop that repaired the locals' hacked-out small equipment for pennies and sold chain saws, power ice augers, worms, fish hooks, milk, and Indian motorcycles in order to pay their astronomical heating bills.

My first terminal case of showroom lust was caused by one of those Indian motorcycles, a machine built for Indian by Italjet with a chrome tank, motocross bars, and a loop frame. I loved that bike and would sit on it and beg mercilessly for one. My parents were both teachers, and Dad had just enough cash on him to pay the $1.50 to sharpen the saw chain. Plus Dad considered it exorbitant to pay more than 20 bucks for a family meal, a hotel room, or a set of tires. He was not opposed to spending slightly more than that sum on rototillers, purebred beagles, and shotguns, but a new motorcycle was not and never would be part of Dad's fiscal priorities, means, or intentions.

Exactly why I had such an intense interest in the machine was a complete mystery to my father. He was a baseball player with a deep love for the game, and we spent hours playing catch and practicing batting in our yard. Despite the early exposure to the game (and perhaps because my skills at the game were sorely lacking), I never took on my father's passion for baseball.

Dad had no interest in motorcycles or cars, and I can't remember any of his friends showing up on motorcycles until I was much older. I believe Beverly Cleary is to blame for sparking my lust for that chrome-tanked motorcycle. As the years passed, I continued to read voraciously and beg in vain for a motorcycle.

In the summer of 1977, my entire family packed up into the family's pickup truck and took the great American summer road trip through the West. After the mandatory stops at Mt. Rushmore, Yellowstone, and the Corn Palace (and never paying more than 20 bucks for a campsite, much less a hotel), we crossed the Great Salt Lake and spent a week with my Mom's sister's family in a Sacramento suburb. Tucked away in the back of my uncle's garage was a Honda CT70. During one of Uncle Jim and my Dad's beer and B.S. sessions in his backyard, Uncle Jim offered to sell the Honda to Dad for $25. To my great shock, Dad eventually agreed to pay the lavish sum, and the bike and I rode together in the back of our Ford truck all the way to Wisconsin.

On the way home, I added motorcycle magazines to the stacks of science fiction, mystery, and spy novels in my room. Reading-wise, my taste ran toward Heinlein and Ludlum as a teenager, although I read anything I found on the shelves in our house or the local library. I read *1984* several times because my parents had a copy, and I read a host of Reader's Digest condensed books for the same reason (and came to despise them).

I ground the CT70 into bits riding it in the fields and trails near our house. When the CT70 died, Dad bought me an XL100 in nearly perfect condition. To this day, I consider that act proof of how deeply he cared for his children because I suspect he didn't quite understand the allure of motorcycles, and I know he didn't believe spending $400 on one to be a wise use of his limited resources.

The rest of the machines of my youth I bought with my own money, and I worked and rode as much as I could through high school, devoting all of my earnings to motorcycles, movie-and-burger dates, and library fines.

In journalism school at the University of Minnesota, I was introduced to literary journalism (also known as narrative nonfiction) by Professor George Hage, a wonderful man who incessantly railed on me about my grammar and read my work out loud in his class. The writing form appealed to me tremendously, blending my interest in drama with my desire to read extensively on a topic as intriguing to me as intelligent robots, sexually aware aliens, or secret agents with mysterious pasts. As I became a semi-adult (an ongoing process that my wife assures me regularly is far from complete), I was increasingly drawn to nonfiction writers who used the dramatic techniques of fiction writers.

Tom Wolfe, Tracy Kidder, and John McPhee became (and remain) three of my favorite writers. I could read their books in the journalism school library without having to hide them under the covers of *Harper's* or the *Minnesota Daily*, plus the topics these writers covered—astronauts and roadkill-eating naturalists, for example—hit the sweet spot of my literary sophistication.

Shortly after college, I went to work for Motorbooks as an acquisitions editor and became immersed in the world of motorcycle literature. Reading motorcycle magazines became part of my job, and knowing who did what well was a key component to being a good editor. I read and learned and also had the good fortune to work with a few of the better writers in the field.

When I set out to do this book, I wanted to combine some of the great short pieces and book excerpts from mainstream writers who delved into motorcycles with meaningful things written by writers from the motorcycle magazine industry. I also intended to include pieces from interesting motorcyclists who had something to say but weren't necessarily paid writers.

The writers in this collection all have something to say about the role motorcycles play in personal lives as well as society. Unfortunately, none of them write about sex-absorbed aliens. But I still found material that related to what I know well, which is riding motorcycles and reading dramatic narratives.

Surprisingly, I only just discovered most of these pieces while doing research for this book. I knew I wanted something from Pirsig, of course. I had imagined I would use his opening 20 paragraphs or so, but I found chapter 5 a bit more interesting and thought that it offered a glimpse into the depth and genius of this great book.

*Song of the Sausage Creature* was a no-brainer. Hunter S. Thompson is one of the finest writers of our time, and this is, in my opinion, his best work ever. So I knew that Hunter would need to be in this book.

*The Racer as Tourist* I read while putting together a compilation of Kevin Cameron's work, and I liked it tremendously. I had several pieces in mind written by Peter Egan but found that a short piece of his about first-time riders was a better fit for the collection and just as strong as some of his longer work.

Jamie Elvidge's award-winning article about her travels in Africa was another piece I had in mind before I started. I was a freelance contributor with Jamie on the short-lived magazine *Motorcycle Escape* and am a fan of her work.

The last piece I knew had to be in there was one that I read while traveling with Jamie on a story assignment for *Escape* in Alaska. Darwin Holmstrom, an editor I worked with at Motorbooks, had submitted a piece to her just before the trip. We read snippets in the funkiest B&B imaginable in Anchorage. Jamie was never able to find a spot for it in the magazine, and the piece went through the same life-and-death cycle at one of the chopper magazines. Happily, Darwin agreed to include it here.

While I didn't have a lot of specific articles in mind, I had a long list of writers to consider. I started collecting them several years ago, and the list included 146 writers last I looked. I quit adding to that list several months ago and am certain I could add another 50 that I have since discovered who had something significant to say about motorcycling.

I then began rereading and digging. I went to the library, read online, and begged rare books off of friends. As I began setting aside pieces I liked, I found that the pieces I chose grouped themselves into several themes.

The first chapter's selections are all pieces about how motorcycles define people. For some motorcyclists, being a motorcyclist is an augmentation or accentuation. I've always been alternately fascinated and turned off by this factor, but it is a part of the motorcycling scene. Hunter Thompson famously wrote about this in his Sausage Creature piece in *Cycle World*, while Singer did so with less flash and more understated humor in "King of All Kings." Dave Nichols talks about how the motorcycle fills a void and draws a certain brand of person into motorcycle culture. Peter Egan does what he does almost every month—writes about a fundamental truth of motorcycling so naturally that you read it and think that you've always known this very fact to be true when it never occurred to you before.

The second chapter is a counterpoint to the first. The writers and subjects of the articles are people who are living the life of a motorcyclist but are not necessarily defined by the machine. That might mean a racer's relation to his favorite tool, a biker's dedication to his club, a crazy collector on the loose in Russia, or a guy writing humorously about getting his learner's permit. Note that many of these writers are the real deal. Kevin Cameron was a motorcycle tuner before he became one of the industry's best writers. Tom Cotter and Kris Palmer are both passionate car enthusiasts. John Hall is a wonderful writer with hardcore cred. Gallese is the dilettante, but he did at least go to the DMV and apply for his learner's permit.

The next section speaks to how motorcycles in America are a symbol more than a tool. The qualities embodied by the American motorcyclist might be marketable, but they are not typically desirable. Bikers carry around the stain of an overblown weekend of hedonistic behavior in Hollister, California. That image was immortalized by a sensationalistic *Life* photographer, transformed into caricature by an army of cheesy films, and given a lethal edge by truly badass biker gangs who rose to power in the 1960s.

That dark knight image was a check cashed by Harley-Davidson, whose marketing geniuses figured out how to sell dentists the half-baked idea that $25,000 of steel and chrome V-twin and a leather-studded Harley-badged uniform transformed suburban dweebs into badasses.

The pieces I chose focus on explorations of bikers by writers who earned their stripes with serious investigative reporting or blood on their hands.

Mark Singer appears again in this section, and his portrait of more garden-variety bikers is much more innocent and offbeat than terrible. Bill Hayes is a biker who writes powerfully from the first-person perspective. Stevenson gives us an evocative portrait of an American hero who personified motorcycles in an exciting way without the immoral underpinnings carried by the motorcycle gangs. Scalzo and Walsh are impish deviants whose tastes lead them beyond traditional social mores but not so far out that they should be placed in jail (for long, anyway).

The next section is all about motorcycle travel. Left to my own devices, the entire book would be motorcycle travel stories. Observant readers will note that a good portion of the book is devoted to travel, and that's because this is my weakness. I think a motorcycle is the perfect traveling device, a vehicle perfectly suited to exploring new places. Selecting favorite pieces here was difficult because so much of this genre is interesting. I included some favorites from writers I know and a couple of pieces from adventurers who rode into the bowels of hell.

Pirsig's piece defines the last section, which describes turning points that take place in (or around) two wheels. Pirsig's book merges his past history of mental illness with his present reality on a motorcycle journey. His book was embraced for providing insight and understanding into mental illness and the dangers of electroshock therapy, and it is also a telling look at the idiosyncrasies of machines and the people who struggle to understand them. If Pirsig's thought-provoking themes are more than you want to chew on, simply relish the author's knack for capturing evocative motorcycle journey detail, such as the ratty three-dollar leather gloves he wears on this chilling early morning ride.

Choosing a piece from this complex and wonderful book was difficult to say the least, both because there are so many incredible passages and also because much of the book is hard to grasp when taken in context and impenetrable when excerpted. I selected this passage for the dead-on description of the inevitable weather-induced highs and lows of a motorcycle journey, the insight into the lives of the techno-challenged, and the closing paragraph's beautifully concise description of the draw of the open road.

Following Pirsig is a nearly impossible act, but the rest of the crew does a fine job of it. Michael Dregni takes us back to the British Invasion, Jack Lewis comes home from the war to his motorcycle, Steven L. Thompson captures the joy of motorcycling through the lens of age, Michelle Ann Duff writes eloquently about racing, and Darwin Holmstrom (with some effort) gets laid.

If you think I missed some great literature, you are probably correct. I was not able to read everything written on the topic, plus these pieces were selected by a man whose favorite works include a bit about a guy who holds the world record for stuffing weasels down his pants. Hungry ones.

So if you want to suggest some piece of motorcycle writing you believe is worth considering for another collection, email me at lklancher@mac.com.

There is certainly room for another book like this at some point down the road, plus I'm always up for an interesting read.

I hope you enjoy the book, and be sure to take your nose out of it once in a while to go down to your local chain saw shop or motorcycle store and fall in lust. Better yet, go riding.

Cheers,
Lee Klancher
August 2009

# Chapter 1 I, Motorcycle

**"WARNING: IF YOU VALUE YOUR LIFE AS MUCH AS I VALUE THIS BIKE, DON'T MESS WITH IT."**

—Mark Singer, King of All Kings

# King of All Kings

## By Mark Singer

JOHN BENJAMIN ALFRED REDMAN, who is the sole owner and chief executive of V.I.P. Sewer Cleaning, a plumbing enterprise with headquarters in Brooklyn, prefers to be called Johnny Redd. When you come equipped with Johnny Redd's range of talents, you're entitled. Not many plumbers double as private investigators, but Johnny Redd does. Along with a partner, he owns and manages Verify Investigation & Protection Services. V.I.P. Sewer Cleaning has a slogan: "Try Us . . . You'll Like Us!" Verify Investigation & Protection Services' slogan is "Investigations Throughout the World." Although Johnny Redd possesses licenses and legal permits to operate a car and a motorcycle, to own a pistol, a shotgun, and a mobile phone, and to do private investigating and general contracting, when he beholds his plastic-sheathed plumbing license he says, "I prize this license over any other license I got. You could become a doctor or a lawyer much easier than a plumber." About three-quarters of Johnny Redd's working time is devoted to plumbing, the remainder to private investigating. Verify Investigation & Protection Services offers clients criminal-industrial undercover work, executive protection, armed bonded couriers, electronic security equipment, chauffeur service, armed escorts, missing-person searches, and a few other conveniences. When Johnny Redd is asked how he manages two such disparate businesses, he says, "Easy. Rockefeller did it. Paul Getty did it. You just got to have key people in key positions. The trick is to get the right people—remember that—in any business."

Johnny Redd is tall, black, muscular, and physically forthright. He has a round face, straight reddish-brown hair that would reach his shoulders if he didn't keep it tied on top of his head, an ample supply of vanity, and a fondness for bright-colored, metal-studded clothing. He doesn't like to discuss his age, but he looks about forty. He is a graduate of Automotive

*Lee Klancher*

High School, an ex-marine, a veteran of the New York Police Department, and an enthusiastic Republican. "I used to be in law enforcement, and then I realized that wasn't for me," he says. "I'm very law-abiding, but I got the hell out. That was just a stepping stone. I'm a Republican because I'm strictly for people earning their living. It's terrible what's going on in this country. I'm against these people wantin' something for nothin'. You know, in Japan they don't even have holidays. That's how they got the jump on us."

On Waverly Avenue, in the Clinton Hill section of Brooklyn, Johnny Redd lives in the house he grew up in—a three-story row house that has pink metal awnings and a façade of pink and white stones, which give it a vaguely Mediterranean and vaguely Miami Beach appearance, and has a "BEWARE OF DOG" sign in the front window, which indirectly refers to a lot of nice stuff inside, including, Johnny Redd says, a basement "as elegant as a night club, with a water fountain in the ceiling." Like any busy chief executive, Johnny Redd moves around a lot. Sometimes you might call him at home early in the morning and make an appointment and he might say, "Come on by in an hour, and make sure you come." But then by the time you got to his place of business—it's a garage fifty feet from the house, directly opposite P.S. 11, the Purvis J. Behan School—something else might have come up. Someone who owes Johnny Redd a bunch of money might have unexpectedly got in the mood to pay up, or he might have suddenly had to run out to a big sprinkler job in Queens, so when you arrived he was unavailable for consultation. When this happens, it's comforting if someone else in the Johnny Redd organization is available for consultation.

The other morning, Darryl Walton, whose nickname is Mr. T., and whom Johnny Redd has referred to as "one of my lieutenants, a very loyal, dedicated employee in a key position," was situated in a key position on the floor of the garage on Waverly Avenue. Specifically, he was lying on an oil-stained rug ministering to Johnny Redd's motorcycle. The motorcycle is another manifestation of Johnny Redd's talent. Although Johnny Redd owns a silver 1965 Rolls-Royce (Silver Cloud), a red 1972 Cadillac Eldorado convertible with a vanity plate that says, "VIP REDD," a white 1976 Continental Mark V, and a fleet of blue Chevrolet trucks, none of these come as close to the core of Johnny Redd's being as his motorcycle. No other vehicle on earth resembles Johnny Redd's motorcycle. In one hand Darryl Walton held a tube of glue, and in the other a strand of red rhinestones. Three times a week, Darryl Walton replaces any rhinestones that have fallen off the motorcycle. Rhinestones, chrome, and gold are essential elements of the Johnny Redd aesthetic. They have made it possible for Johnny Redd's motorcycle, which started life as a simple Harley-Davidson Electra Glide, to look now as if it were wearing a chrome Oscar de la Renta ball gown.

An overlay of scrolled chrome filigree has been applied to most of the metallic surfaces. The eagle atop the front fender is gold-plated. So are the diamond-sign-shaped, rhinestone-studded hubcap covers and the crown that is fastened to the backrest. The front fender looks as if it came from Rolls-Royce, and so does the chromed radiator grille. Johnny Redd refers to the chrome Rolls-Royce emblem atop the grille as "the naked lady in front." He says, "That's my sweetheart." There is a plane of black leather between the grille and the windshield. Half of a chrome-plated .357 Magnum revolver has been welded to the right side of the gas tank, and an AM/FM quadraphonic radio and tape deck have been built into the dashboard. An aquatic diorama has been countersunk into the red leather cargo compartment. There is an on-board computer. Red rhinestones on the dashboard spell, "JOHNNY." The oil-pressure and voltage gauges look as if they were wearing red Dynel wigs. The running board is illuminated with red lights. "JOHNNY REDD" is spelled out in rhinestones on the backrest, and the gold-plated crown that is built into the backrest is studded with diamond chips that spell "KING OF ALL KINGS."

A sticker on the windshield shows a frontal view of a revolver and says, "NEVER MIND THE DOG. BEWARE OF THE OWNER." Three other stickers on the windshield say, "WARNING! IF YOU VALUE YOUR LIFE AS MUCH AS I VALUE THIS BIKE, DON'T MESS IT." Some delicate floral patterns have been etched into the windshield and the standards that hold the rearview mirrors. Each mirror has an imprint of Johnny Redd's name in red script. The mirror mounts have rhinestone-studded, gold-plated dollar signs. There is also a big chrome-and-rhinestone dollar sign on the cargo compartment. A five-inch portable color television set used to ride inside the cargo compartment, but Johnny Redd removed it a while back to give himself more storage room. Black leather fringe hangs from the cargo compartment and the driver's seat. The fringe goes nicely with the metal-studded, black leather gloves that Johnny Redd wears when he rides. He also wears a medieval-looking helmet with a snakeskin bill, feathers, chrome filigree, and a crest made with broom bristles. If Johnny Redd doesn't feel like wearing that helmet, he wears one with a chrome crest and a black ponytail of human hair. He acquired these from a member of the New Breed Motorcycle Club when that organization folded a few years ago. The previous owner of the helmets didn't want to sell them, but Johnny Redd shrewdly approached him in a weak moment, when he needed the money.

Johnny Redd doesn't belong to any formal motorcycle club himself, but he has a certificate from the Pythons Motorcycle Club confirming that he has ridden in its Annual Bike Blessing Service and Parade. The certificate has been signed by all the officers of the Pythons, including Mr. Big Stuff, president; Crasher, vice-president; Sweet Andy, treasurer; Baby Huey, business manager; Run Joe, road captain; Beddie, road captain No. 2; Killer Joe, sergeant at arms; and Mr. T. (a different Mr. T.), second sergeant at arms.

One recent morning, Johnny Redd happened not to be occupied with other business and was therefore available for consultation. He cordially consented to extol the motorcycle's mechanical prowess. "I've owned three different show bikes, but this one surpasses them all," he said. "It took ten people five years to get this bike to look this good. It took me five years to pay for it. And what you're looking at in beauty, I had just as much put into the engine and operation of the bike. With all that jazz on it, I thought I needed the extra power. It's too powerful, really. Yeah, very, *very* powerful. It pulls up a hill like it's nothin'. Very powerful. Plus I had special gearing put in it. See, nobody ever went this far on a motorcycle, so I figured I might have trouble with it. So I had all that performance work done."

An attractive woman passed by the entrance of Johnny Redd's garage as he was explaining this. He greeted her by saying, "Are you looking for me?" It turned out she wasn't. Even the most beautiful woman in the world would not be allowed to take the motorcycle around the block for a solo spin. No matter how much you admire Johnny Redd's bike, he won't let you drive it. He'll let you sit on it, but that's all. He let a blond actress ride *with* him when they appeared together in a movie called *Satan Studs*, but he did the driving. Johnny Redd gets a little sheepish when he talks about his experience. "It wasn't what you would call a Class One picture," he said. "It wasn't a *Rambo* or nothing." Once, two women were sitting on the motorcycle, "buck naked," but Johnny Redd doesn't recall all the details. Graciously, he has allowed two couples to get married on the motorcycle— not simultaneously—but, of course, they weren't able to borrow it for their honeymoons. Muhammad Ali sat on it once and asked to drive it, but Johnny Redd told him no way. On a number of occasions, Johnny has worked for Ali as a bodyguard. He has done the same thing for Larry Holmes, Rocky Graziano, Mick Jagger, and Telly Savalas, and he has auto-graphed photographs to prove it. He also has a letter from Jimmy Carter. "I spent a weekend in the White House with Jimmy Carter," he said. "Henry Jackson, the senator from Washington—Squirt Jackson—arranged it. He saw me on the street in New York with my motorcycle and said the President would like to see it. So I went down there for the weekend, and then Jimmy Carter sent me a letter to thank me for coming. Malcolm Forbes was interested in me, too. He wanted me to go on a cruise and then a motorcycle trip through China with him. But I couldn't leave my business." Johnny Redd admires all his luminary acquaintances, but he still won't let them drive the motorcycle. Rules are rules.

A red-and-white painted sign inside the garage enumerates some of the other rules that Johnny Redd lives by. If you lose a tool and it turns up

*Lee Klancher*

later, that costs you five dollars. Losing it permanently costs you a bundle. Forgetting to put the keys to one of Johnny's five trucks back on the proper nail sets you back five dollars, and so does failing to call headquarters when you're supposed to. Forgetting to leave a V.I.P. Sewer Cleaning fluorescent sticker at a job site when you finish a job—a fiver. No employee is permitted to throw out garbage without Johnny Redd's approval. Rule No. 15 says, "Do Not Work for Any Attorney Unless Instructed to Do So." Another "Beware of Dog" sign is conspicuously displayed. This apparently refers to King, a Doberman pinscher who spends some of his time gnawing a rawhide bone the size of a rhinoceros femur and the rest of his time emphatically resting his paws on the shoulders of anyone who steps within the radius of his leash.

Whenever Johnny Redd rides the motorcycle, he takes with him several photographs of it. These he gives to doormen and security guards so they will know to report a serious theft if they should happen to see anyone other than Johnny Redd cruising by on it. Johnny Redd hates to dwell upon the misfortunes that might befall his motorcycle. If you ask whether he has ever had a flat tire or a mechanical breakdown, he says, "Don't even mention it. Let's face it, I can't afford for that bike to break down nowhere. If I got to make a phone call, when I come back things ain't gonna be the same. I keep the bike in tip-top shape. I park it wherever I want to park it, but I don't stay away from it too long."

Usually, wherever Johnny Redd parks the motorcycle, it draws a crowd. Sometimes he hangs out at the Caliente Cab Company, on Seventh Avenue South, sometimes at the Spring Street Bar, in Soho. He has also spent a lot of time at the Cat Club, in the East Village. At the Cat Club not long ago, Johnny Redd became friendly with some people in a rock band called Kill Me. Someone named Randy is in charge of the band, and he is arranging for a movie star named Dirty Hanky and a girl who is a movie star, too, to pose with the motorcycle for a rock video. Randy has already arranged to have some T-shirts imprinted with a photograph of the motorcycle.

"They put the bike on a T-shirt, and the bike looks beautiful," Johnny Redd said. "But they also put the name of the band on the shirt. So when I wear the shirt I'm going around with a shirt that says, 'Kill Me.' Everybody be laughing when they see me in that shirt. I'm trying to spray-paint off the 'Kill Me' part. Why do I want to wear something that says, 'Kill Me?' I got too much to live for. Me and the bike, we're supposed to be on *Miami Vice*. We already did some shooting at the heliport and at the Water Club. You know who else I used to let ride on my bike? Miss Rheingold. I met her at the Spring Street Bar. Everybody who sees the bike falls in love with it. Hey, I've done a lot of things with that motorcycle. I'm an interesting guy, right?"

# Song of the Sausage Creature

## By Hunter S. Thompson

*Cycle World*

March 1995

THERE ARE SOME THINGS nobody needs in this world, and a bright-red, hunchback, warp-speed, 900cc café racer is one of them—but I want one anyway, and on some days I actually believe I need one. That is why they are dangerous.

Everybody has fast motorcycles these days. Some people go 150 miles an hour on two-lane blacktop roads, but not often. There are too many oncoming trucks and too many radar cops and too many stupid animals in the way. You have to be a little crazy to ride these super-torque, high-speed crotch rockets anywhere except a racetrack—and even there, they will scare the whimpering shit out of you. There is, after all, not a pig's eye worth of difference between going head-on into a Peterbilt or sideways into the bleachers. On some days you get what you want, and on others, you get what you need.

When *Cycle World* called me to ask if I would road-test the new Harley Road King, I got uppity and said I'd rather have a Ducati superbike. It seemed like a chic decision at the time, and my friends on the superbike circuit got very excited. "Hot damn," they said. "We will take it to the track and blow the bastards away."

"Balls," I said. "Never mind the track. The track is for punks. We are Road People. We are Café Racers."

The Café Racer is a different breed, and we have our own situations. Pure speed in sixth gear on a 5,000-foot straightaway is one thing, but pure speed in third gear on a gravel-strewn downhill ess-turn is quite another.

But we like it. A thoroughbred Café Racer will ride all night through a fog storm in freeway traffic to put himself into what somebody told him was the ugliest and tightest decreasing-radius turn since Genghis Khan invented the corkscrew.

Café Racing is mainly a matter of taste. It is an atavistic mentality, a peculiar mix of low style, high speed, pure dumbness, and overweening commitment to the Café Life and all its dangerous pleasures. I am a Café Racer myself, on some days—and it is one of my finest addictions.

I am not without scars on my brain and my body, but I can live with them. I still feel a shudder in my spine every time I see a picture of a Vincent Black Shadow, or when I walk into a public restroom and hear crippled men whispering about the terrifying Kawasaki Triple. I have visions of compound femur fractures and large black men in white hospital suits holding me down on a gurney while a nurse called "Bess" sews the flaps of my scalp together with a stitching drill.

Ho, ho. Thank God for these flashbacks. The brain is such a wonderful instrument (until God sinks his teeth into it). Some people hear Tiny Tim singing when they go under, and some others hear the song of the Sausage Creature.

When the Ducati turned up in my driveway, nobody knew what to do with it. I was in New York, covering a polo tournament, and people had threatened my life. My lawyer said I should give myself up and enroll in the Federal Witness Protection Program. Other people said it had something to do with the polo crowd.

The motorcycle business was the last straw. It had to be the work of my enemies, or people who wanted to hurt me. It was the vilest kind of bait, and they knew I would go for it.

Of course. You want to cripple the bastard? Send him a 130-mile-per-hour café racer. And include some license plates, he'll think it's a streetbike. He's queer for anything fast.

Which is true. I have been a connoisseur of fast motorcycles all my life. I bought a brand-new 650 BSA Lightning when it was billed as "the fastest motorcycle ever tested by *Hot Rod* magazine." I have ridden a 500-pound Vincent through traffic on the Ventura Freeway with burning oil on my legs and run the Kawa 750 Triple through Beverly Hills at night with a head full of acid. I have ridden with Sonny Barger and smoked weed in biker bars with Jack Nicholson, Grace Slick, Ron Zigler, and my infamous old friend, Ken Kesey, a legendary Café Racer.

Some people will tell you that slow is good—and it may be, on some days—but I am here to tell you that fast is better. I've always believed this, in spite of the trouble it's caused me. Being shot out of a cannon will always be better than being squeezed out of a tube. That is why God made fast motorcycles, Bubba.

So when I got back from New York and found a fiery red rocket-style bike in my garage, I realized I was back in the road-testing business.

The brand-new Ducati 900 Campione del Mundo Desmodue Supersport double-barreled magnum Café Racer filled me with feelings of lust every time I looked at it. Others felt the same way. My garage quickly became a magnet for drooling superbike groupies. They quarreled and bitched at each other about who would be the first to help me evaluate my new toy. And I did, of course, need a certain spectrum of opinions, besides my own, to properly judge this motorcycle. The Woody Creek Perverse Environmental Testing Facility is a long way from Daytona or even top-fuel challenge-sprints on the Pacific Coast Highway, where teams of big-bore Kawasakis and Yamahas are said to race head-on against each other in death-defying games of "chicken" at 100 miles an hour.

No. Not everybody who buys a high-dollar torque-brute yearns to go out in a ball of fire on a public street in L.A. Some of us are decent people who want to stay out of the emergency room but still blast through neo-gridlock traffic in residential districts whenever we feel like it. For that we need Fine Machinery.

Which we had—no doubt about that. The Ducati people in New Jersey had opted, for some reasons of their own, to send me the 900SS-SP for testing—rather than their 916 crazy-fast, state-of-the-art superbike track-racer. It was far too fast, they said—and prohibitively expensive—to farm out for testing to a gang of half-mad Colorado cowboys who think they're world-class Café Racers.

The Ducati 900 is a finely engineered machine. My neighbors called it beautiful and admired its racing lines. The nasty little bugger looked like it was going 90 miles an hour when it was standing still in my garage.

Taking it on the road, though, was a genuinely terrifying experience. I had no sense of speed until I was going 90 and coming up fast on a bunch of pickup trucks going into a wet curve along the river. I went for both brakes, but only the front one worked, and I almost went end over end. I was out of control staring at the tailpipe of a U.S. Mail truck, still stabbing frantically at my rear brake pedal, which I just couldn't find. I am too tall for these new-age road-racers; they are not built for any rider taller than five-nine, and the rear-set brake pedal was not where I thought it would be. Midsize Italian pimps who like to race from one café to another on the boulevards of Rome in a flat-line prone position might like this, but I do not.

I was hunched over the tank like a person diving into a pool that got emptied yesterday. Whacko! Bashed on the concrete bottom, flesh ripped off, a Sausage Creature with no teeth, fucked-up for the rest of its life.

We all love Torque, and some of us have taken it straight over the high side from time to time—and there is always Pain in that. But there is also Fun, the deadly element, and Fun is what you get when you screw this monster on. BOOM! Instant take-off, no screeching or squawking around like a fool with your teeth clamping down on your tongue and your mind completely empty of everything but fear.

No. This bugger digs right in and shoots you straight down the pipe, for good or ill.

On my first take-off, I hit second gear and went through the speed limit on a two-lane blacktop highway full of ranch traffic. By the time I went up to third, I was going 75 and the tach was barely above 4,000 rpm.

And that's when it got its second wind. From 4,000 to 6,000 in third will take you from 75 miles per hour to 95 in two seconds—and after that, Bubba, you still have fourth, fifth, and sixth. Ho, ho.

I never got to sixth gear, and I didn't get deep into fifth. This is a shameful admission for a full-bore Café Racer, but let me tell you something, old sport: This motorcycle is simply too goddamn fast to ride at speed in any kind of normal road traffic unless you're ready to go straight down the centerline with your nuts on fire and a silent scream in your throat.

When aimed in the right direction at high speed, though, it has unnatural capabilities. This I unwittingly discovered as I made my approach to a sharp turn across some railroad tracks, saw that I was going way too fast and that my only chance was to veer right and screw it on totally, in a desperate attempt to leapfrog the curve by going airborne.

It was a bold and reckless move, but it was necessary. And it worked: I felt like Evel Knievel as I soared across the tracks with the rain in my eyes and my jaws clamped together in fear. I tried to spit down on the tracks as I passed them, but my mouth was too dry. I landed hard on the edge of the road and lost my grip for a moment as the Ducati began fishtailing crazily into oncoming traffic. For two or three seconds I came face to face with the Sausage Creature.

But somehow the brute straightened out. I passed a school bus on the right and got the bike under control long enough to gear down and pull off into an abandoned gravel driveway where I stopped and turned off the engine. My hands had seized up like claws, and the rest of my body was numb. I felt nauseous, and I cried for my mama, but nobody heard, then I went into a trance for 30 or 40 seconds until I was finally able to light a cigarette and calm down enough to ride home. I was too hysterical to shift gears, so I went the whole way in first at 40 miles an hour.

Whoops! What am I saying? Tall stories, ho, ho. We are motorcycle people; we walk tall, and we laugh at whatever's funny. We shit on the chests of the Weird.

But when we ride very fast motorcycles, we ride with immaculate sanity. We might abuse a substance here and there, but only when it's right. The final measure of any rider's skill is the inverse ratio of his preferred Traveling Speed to the number of bad scars on his body. It is that simple: If you ride fast and crash, you are a bad rider. And if you are a bad rider, you should not ride motorcycles.

The emergence of the superbike has heightened this equation drastically. Motorcycle technology has made such a great leap forward. Take the Ducati. You want optimum cruising speed on this bugger? Try 90 miles per hour in fifth at 5,500 rpm—and just then, you see a bull moose in the middle of the road. WHACKO. Meet the Sausage Creature.

Or maybe not: The Ducati 900 is so finely engineered and balanced and torqued that you *can* do 90 miles per hour in fifth through a 35-mile-per-hour zone and get away with it. The bike is not just fast—it is *extremely* quick and responsive, and it *will* do amazing things. It is like riding a Vincent Black Shadow, which would outrun an F-86 jet fighter on the take-off runway, but at the end, the F-86 would go airborne and the Vincent would not, and there was no point in trying to turn it. WHAMO! The Sausage Creature strikes again.

There is a fundamental difference, however, between the old Vincents and the new breed of superbikes. If you rode the Black Shadow at top speed for any length of time, you would almost certainly die. That is why there are not many life members of the Vincent Black Shadow Society. The Vincent was like a bullet that went straight; the Ducati is like the magic bullet in Dallas that went sideways and hit JFK and the governor of Texas at the same time.

It was impossible. But so was my terrifying sideways leap across the railroad tracks on the 900sp. The bike did it easily with the grace of a fleeing tomcat. The landing was so easy I remember thinking, goddamnit, if I had screwed it on a little more I could have gone a lot farther.

Maybe this is the new Café Racer macho. My bike is so much faster than yours that I dare you to ride it, you lame little turd. Do you have the balls to ride this BOTTOMLESS PIT OF TORQUE?

That is the attitude of the new-age superbike freak, and I am one of them. On some days they are about the most fun you can have with your clothes on. The Vincent just killed you a lot faster than a superbike will. A fool couldn't ride the Vincent Black Shadow more than once, but a fool can ride a Ducati 900 many times, and it will always be a bloodcurdling kind of fun. That is the Curse of Speed that has plagued me all my life. I am a slave to it. On my tombstone they will carve, "IT NEVER GOT FAST ENOUGH FOR ME."

# The Seeds
# of Rebellion

## By Dave Nichols

*One Percenter*

Motorbooks, November 2007

I T HAS BEEN SAID that bikers are born bikers, not made into bikers. Rebellion is often the result of not fitting in with others. Children can be some of the cruelest people on earth. If a playmate doesn't fit in because he or she is too tall or too short, too fat or too skinny, has crooked teeth or big ears, or any number of perceived differences, children can be downright brutal in their ability to bully or abuse.

I didn't fit in during my school years because I had no interest in sports whatsoever. I didn't fit into any of the usual school cliques: I wasn't a social climber or a fashion trendsetter. I wasn't in the chess club or computer club. Sports just seemed like a waste of time to me. But motorcycles . . . they were something different. I loved motorcycles and rushed out to get my learner's permit at the tender age of 15. In Florida, where I grew up, you could ride a small motorcycle under a certain brake horsepower at that age.

I had watched every episode of NBC's *Then Came Bronson* TV series in 1969 and was drawn to the character of laconic drifter Jim Bronson, as played by Michael Parks. I was also drawn to the little red Harley-Davidson Sportster that transported him to each new adventure. The bike was the conveyance of choice for this free spirit. He would ride into a small town every week, get a job, and make a few bucks to buy beef jerky and gasoline, which was apparently all a gypsy biker needed on the road to adventure.

Most memorable was the show's opening, in which we would see Bronson pull up to a red light next to a family station wagon. The weary, work-worn driver of the wagon would look longingly at Bronson's Sportster before asking, "Where you headed?"

"Wherever I end up, I guess," was Bronson's reply.

"Man," the straight citizen would lament, "I sure wish I were you."

"Well," Bronson would grin before roaring off, "Hang in there."

*Lee Klancher*

Yeah, hang in there you poor son-of-a-bitch. I knew right then and there which of those two guys I wanted to be, and it sure as hell wasn't the poor slob in the rusty station wagon, with a clock to punch and a mortgage to pay. And I wasn't alone. The summer after *Then Came Bronson* debuted, more people went out and bought street bikes than in any summer before.

Harley-Davidson picked up on this trend and even came out with a special Sportster in Bronson Red.

Also in the summer of 1969, the film *Easy Rider* premiered in theaters all across America. I had to beg my parents to take me to the film because of its R rating. I'll never forget how embarrassed I was to have my timid mother sit through that movie with its nudity, foul language, and drug use. I thought I was going to crawl under the sticky theater seat when John Kay of Steppenwolf began screaming "God Damn the Pusher" over and over again. My face still gets red when I remember that moment. Yet I came out of the movie house a convert to the two-wheeled lifestyle. I wanted a chopper. I wanted to put on a leather jacket and roar across the country, flipping off the squares and laughing at the uptight society that raised me. I wanted to *be* Peter Fonda because, to me, he was the embodiment of cool.

During one of the druggy campfire scenes in the film, Peter Fonda takes a toke of marijuana and asks Luke Askew and Dennis Hopper, "Have you ever wanted to be anyone else?"

Luke Askew squints in the pot smoke and slurs, "I'd like to try Porky Pig."

Hopper giggles, and Fonda just nods. "I never wanted to be anybody else." Well, of course you never wanted to be anybody else; you're Captain America, you're Peter friggin' Fonda, the standard by which all coolness is measured. In that moment, my friends, the die was cast, and the rebel in me found a voice. Without ever having thrown my leg over a motorcycle, I knew that there was something about riding one that had to do with freedom, with the feeling of the wind in your hair and bugs in your teeth. By whatever name that feeling went, I wanted it.

As it turns out, I was right. Few things I've found in life give me the same sense of freedom I feel while blasting down the road on a motorcycle, especially if it's a custom chopper.

What makes one child a quiet computer geek and another a football hero? What makes a kid a rebel? It's been said that you can tell which kid is going to grow up to be a social outcast just by watching them in kindergarten. Are bikers born with the need to turn up their collars and sit in the corner of the classroom, listening for the sound of a Harley passing by? Someone once told me that the biker-to-be is the kid who won't just follow along and take orders. He won't be bullied either. He is the kid who pushes back, he might not win every fight, but he won't put up with any crap. The rebel apparently has a very low tolerance for bullshit of any kind. The lone wolf listens to the tune of a different drummer all right; it's the thump of a big V-twin motor that gets his pulse pounding.

How far back would we have to go to trace our rebel roots? Could the origin of rebellion and search for personal freedom go all the way back to the cave dweller? Imagine a tribe of Neanderthals huddled in their cave, gnawing on the bones of some slow-moving mammal, hoping that they can figure out that "fire thing" pretty soon because sushi might work for fish, but raw badger sucks! The cavewomen are squashing some kind of berries into a paste, a couple of the men are arguing over the score of the sloth toss regionals, and several furry kids are having a contest to see who can land on their heads hardest and live.

Out in front of the cave squats Zog, carving the first wheel out of stone. He sips a strange brew of hops and water from a gourd and gazes across the valley toward the setting sun. You just know he's thinking, "If I can carve another one of these round things, I'm gonna ride the hell away from these losers."

Let's leave Zog with his thoughts (mainly because there's no way to prove that the first rebel outlaw was a caveman) and take a look at the history of those who turned away from society and convention to forge their own path. Who were the forerunners of the outlaw biker? There is no doubt that there have been select tribes throughout history that have left their bloody marks on the human psyche, scars that are still borne by the outlaw bikers of our time. The outlaw biker subculture borrows many elements of its lifestyle from ancient warriors of many lands and times. Ever notice that biker tattoos include images of savage Vikings, Celtic weaves, or piratical skull and crossbones? Well, there's a reason for this. You see, one percenters provide vessels through which the warrior outlaw spirit lives today. They are among the few remaining tribes that still embody the spirit of freedom.

# *That Critical First Ride*

### By Peter Egan

*Cycle World*

May 1994

TRUE STORY. When my boyhood friend Pat Donnelly was in his early teens, he was invited to a birthday party on the family farm of his classmate, Conrad Shaker. Conrad had a horse and saddled him up so all the kids at the party could take a ride. Pat, who had never been on a horse before, climbed into the saddle and gave the horse a gentle prod with his heels. The horse took exactly two steps forward, exhaled loudly, fell over on its side, and died.

Pat, who was wearing a brand-new pair of extremely cool engineer boots just like James Dean's in *Rebel Without a Cause*, had his leg and boot trapped under the horse, but both were eventually extricated with minimal damage. The party was over. Pat gave up on horses and two years later bought his first motorcycle.

Usually it works the other way around.

A more typical first ride story comes from my good friend Lyman Lyons, who grew up in Louisiana. A buddy of Lyman's had saved up all his paper-route money for several years and bought himself a new scooter, a Cushman Eagle. The friend insisted Lyman "take a spin," and Lyman complied with a display that only the masterful Buster Keaton could have orchestrated. He whacked open the throttle, froze at the controls (forgetting which way to twist the grip), rocketed across several front lawns, and finally blasted through a thick hedge, which probably saved his life by slowing him down before he hit the inevitable tree.

The brilliance of this physical comedy was lost on the Cushman owner, who quietly examined the crushed front fender and bent fork and simply said, "My scooter . . . " over and over again.

Lyman, needless to say, did not rush right down to the Cushman dealer and plunk money down on his own two-wheeled fun machine. He was somewhat abashed and never really recovered his full measure of youthful enthusiasm for scooters—or motorcycles.

*Lee Klancher*

I have now lived long enough to have heard at least a hundred of these first-ride disaster stories, and I'm sorry to say that most of them involve motorcycles rather than horses.

Tell a group of people at a party you ride a motorcycle, and at least one person in the crowd can produce a richly detailed, moment-by-moment account of catastrophe on a first bike ride. Usually the tale is quite similar to Lyman's and ends in a vow never to ride again, or to "stick with four wheels."

As nearly as I can tell, a typical sequence of events in most of these mishaps seems to be: (1) surprise at the abruptness or speed of forward motion combined with a poor sense of twist-grip modulation; (2) growing panic in realizing that the technique for stopping safely has not been adequately rehearsed; and (3) a total loss of steering control as the unnatural instinct to countersteer is replaced, through terror, by an attempt to physically turn the handlebars in the direction you want to go (which is effective only at very low speed), causing the rider to hit the very object he or she had hoped to avoid.

When you think how many times this has happened to first-time motorcycle riders, and how many of them have gone away dazed and confused, the minutes of simple training might have eliminated many of these accidents, and a course from the Motorcycle Safety Foundation would prevent just about all of them.

Those few first rides are clearly the most dangerous—as are the few first months of riding—so I'm all in favor of as much training as possible.

And yet . . . when I listen to these stories, there is a side of me that says perhaps not everyone is cut out to be a motorcyclist. My own first ride, for instance, was not a lot better than Lyman's, yet the effect was quite different.

I was trying to buy an old Harley 45 from a guy who ran a local gas station. I was 15 and could not legally ride on the street, so he let me take it for a short ride in the pasture behind the station. I chuffed around successfully for a while, mastering (?) the foot clutch and tank shift, and all was well until I returned to the station. I looked down at the clutch pedal as I came to a stop and ran into a bunch of trash barrels full of scrap metal and old oil filters. The bike and barrels tipped over with lots of noise but no real damage. I quickly scrambled up and got the bike on its stand, just as the other owner came around the corner, wearing a flipped-up arc welder's mask.

"No problem," I said. "Just bumped into some cans."

He scowled and went back to work, welding.

A week later, when I turned up with the money ($100) he told me he'd decided to keep the bike. So I made a down payment on a brand-new Bridgestone Sport 50.

Strangely, it never occurred to me to shy away from motorcycling because I'd dumped the Harley on its side. I would no more have given up the idea of owning a motorcycle than Lyman—who is a good baseball player—would have given up baseball because he struck out his first time at bat. The incident was a small setback but not a trauma. All the defense mechanisms in my brain closed ranks, made their excuses, and the event was quickly paved over, seamlessly, almost as if it had never happened.

The difference here, of course, is simply a matter of commitment. Lyman was merely curious, while I was absolutely fanatical. I had to have a bike, and nothing else would do. Most of us will accept a lot of hard knocks to fulfill some personal dream but are turned away rather quickly if we take a bruising of a merely marginal pursuit.

Maybe that first ride is just a filter, a means to separate those of us who have to ride a motorcycle—or horses—from those who don't.

# Chapter 2 The Motorcycle Life

"Before you go home and pop *Easy Rider* in your DVD player, first learn how to stay on your bike **without falling off** while in the Target **parking lot**."

—Sebastian Gallese,
*McSweeney's*

# TD1: A Personal Remembrance

By Kevin Cameron

*Cycle World*

July 1984

NNOCENT EVENTS SOMETIMES punch through time into the past, leaving us fascinated, surrounding us with the vapors of forgotten feelings. On my way back from Daytona this spring I picked up a 1965 TD1-B Yamaha production road racer—the ancestor of the sophisticated TZ250 Yamahas that dominate 250 racing. I ran a B-model many years ago, and my friends all had them too. I've half-wished to find and restore such a machine, but it was no big thing or I'd have done it long ago, right?

New England mud season greeted me at home, and the old Avons on the bike left wet grooves in the soggy lawn. It was a hard push to the shop, where I leaned the tattered machine against a bench still strewn with Daytona preparations. Then I carried in three sets of exhaust pipes and several moldy boxes of parts. One of the boxes broke, spreading pieces everywhere. Never mind—I'd deal with it later. My Daytona coverage beckoned from the typewriter inside the house, setting me firmly back in 1984 with its watercooling and radial tires and 180-mile-per-hour speeds. In the evening I told my wife, "I have to go up to the shop to check on a part." This is something I say often. With the wet earth threatening to suck my shoes off, I trudged toward the TD1—it was the real reason for the excursion. I turned on the shop lights and looked at the mess, then squatted down to pick up the pieces from the burst box. I began to recognize them. This little slotted brass slug is part of the throttle cable junction box. This is a remote-float Mikuni M-type carburetor—they didn't release the superior VM center-float carbs until late 1967, and then only to factory teams. M-types flooded under braking and, conversely, leaned out under acceleration. Seizures. As I hunkered over the parts pile, I remembered all the schemes for preventing this, schemes we had hatched and coveted and later shared 17 years ago. What difference did it make now? This junk is obsolete.

*Lee Klancher*

Mikuni would be embarrassed even at the mention of these zinc hazards to navigation.

All the same, my mind hurtled back through time. I stood up and looked over the other boxes of parts. I might as well spread this stuff out and go through it, I thought. An hour later I was still pawing through the mess, setting grimy pieces in little piles. Each part had a nature and a story, and I remembered them all. These linen-and-varnish-insulated magneto coils used to short across to the rotor, leaving little black spots and then quitting. The sand-cast, vertically split cases required a special Yamaha jack to separate them. These forks had what we had called "joke damping" and would blow the seals in two or three races. Replacing them was a machine-shop operation, requiring the drilling out of steel pegs, the pulling of a bushing, the making and fitting of oversized pegs, or the use of Allen set-screws. Warm up the engine too fast, and the cast-iron piston rings would break, in turn chipping the chrome off the cylinder walls above the exhaust ports. I remembered waiting at the parts counter with needs that didn't help the dealer one bit. Waking up in the van after an all-night, 600-mile trip from Boston to Harewood Acres in southern Ontario, hearing the rumble of a Manx Norton started by an early bird intent on having his oil hot before breakfast. Cold-water shaving in the van's side mirror. Standing stiff and hungry in the sign-up line.

We left Boston after dinner on Friday nights, having loaded the van with bikes, parts, and tools. Everyone put $10 into the gas kitty. Somewhere on the way, maybe on the New York Thruway or 95 South to Virginia, we were transformed in the sweep and glare of interstate headlights. That morning we had been nameless big-city working stiffs, but now we were motorcycle racers. Perfect trip-timing would put us at sign-up with no time for a nap. The adrenaline rush that had sustained us through all the driving could continue unbroken right through Saturday practice. Pure energy, pure enthusiasm. It was fine.

This was the dying time for the lightweight racing four-stroke. The special Ducatis of Charles Ingram, the Motobis of Amol Precision, the Sprint H-Ds of the national circuit all had to bow under the terrible pressure of the maturing two-stroke. Yamaha had found ways to stop the constant seizures of the TD1-A and had broadcast the message in hundreds of AMA-legal production racers, bringing this awful truth to every racetrack. The four-strokes were still very good—light, responsive, and highly developed—but the Yamaha powerplant was steadily squeezing the life out of them all. The B-model was the turning point.

My friends with TD1s urged me to prepare my racing rivals properly; pull up in the four-stroke's draft, flick out to pass, sit up, and pretend to adjust my goggles while riding one-handed.

Our Boston-area TD1 stars, Frank Camillieri and Andres Lascoutx, had other humiliations for their opponents. Frank would roll out of his truck on practice morning, slide a kickstart lever on his bike, and start it *with his hand.* Lascoutx was always first onto the false grid and first out to practice. He won everything in 1966. In those days you could enter your 250 in the 350, 500, and open classes in club racing. Camillieri won them all one year, and the big-bike riders went out on strike; we won't race any more unless *he* is out of here. They compromised: Camillieri could ride but would not be scored except in 250. After that, he would build up a big lead and stop out on the course, waiting for the big four-strokes to come toiling around. He would pull out after them from a standing start and catch and pass them down the straight. Or he would build up a half-minute lead and wait playfully a few feet short of the finish line on the last lap. When the smoking, bored-out Triumphs and Nortons came wobbling into view, he would grin at them and push across the line—first.

Why so vindictive? Before the Yamahas came, you had to belong to a clique to win races—a clique centered around one of the specialty shops that did secret porting and could (most important of all) put needle bearings in your rocker arms. You couldn't just *buy* this work—that would be too crass. You had to *qualify* for it, and that meant spending hours, weeks, and years hanging out at these shops, buying lunch, and hoping, in time, to be accepted as one of the elect. Then they might take your money and put the all-important needle bearings in your rocker arms.

The Yamaha was the great equalizer in racing. To win, all you needed was the ability to ride and $1,147 plus destination and setup. No more rocker arms. No more buying lunch.

At this point I had been standing in my shop, staring at the piles of parts, for quite some time. I was startled by my wife's voice: "How *is* that part, Kevin? Did you know it's dinnertime?" Yes, it's not 1967 any more. I drifted back to the house.

I had surprised myself. I have never been able to understand the "vintage" or retro-fashion impulse. I'm not interested in repeating my own mistakes no matter what the style. But here I was, backsliding in the same way. Somewhere in that pile of parts was a catalyst, acting mutely to send me back 17 years. Would I become foolish like those fellows in their perfect 1968 Camaros, antique Motown blowing out of the eight-tracks, while both their drivers' licenses and their hairlines say they are all 40 years old? Our lives are here in 1984, aren't they?

But I still have my pale-green Okuda-Kohi points checker. I could sit right down to worship my TD1 with it as I did back then—cross-legged at the right side of the engine, rocking the crank with a 12mm open-end, watching the needle, tapping on the points arm. I know these crank-mounted clutches—you have to service them after every fast start, or they will slip next time. Save time by flopping the bike on its right side so the oil falls away from the clutch. Pull the cover, pull the clutch, compress it, pull the snap-ring, and you have hot, warped clutch plates in your hand. Slick. Also obsolete nonsense. Yamaha made those crank-speed clutches small because they had only one-third the torque to transmit. Seems like a neat idea until experience teaches that clutches must be sized not so much for the torque but for the heat of slippage.

Events floated into mind. We did a double weekend—Mosport up in Canada and Nelson's Ledges in Ohio, leaving after the Mosport final, tired zombies, humming through evening into dark with our eyelid hooks in place, changing drivers often and pouring much coffee. It seemed to take a long time getting to Buffalo, and when at last we saw the sign, "Bridge to USA Ahead," it didn't look right. It wasn't. This was Detroit, not Buffalo. Following the white line like robots, we had missed the turn, driving an extra 180 miles west. Rugged racers, stupid but tough. The famous Detroit riots began shortly after we had whistled through the empty early-morning tunnels and vacant interchanges.

The following week, I had collected everyone's magneto rotors to have them re-magnetized. When I failed to return one rider's rotor on time, I found a poem on my bench.

*Urban uproar, Black ghetto*
*I care only for my magnetto.*

My TD1 never started well, and I never figured it out, although in the process I learned to rebuild cranks, port cylinders, and do other fancy things that didn't help either. My worst start was at Mosport. No doubt my calves bulged in my $100 Lewis leathers as I pressed forward against the locked front brake, looking at the starter's flag. Push-starts were still in vogue then. The flag was up! I lunged hard, heaving the 236-pound machine ahead, dropping the clutch on the third step. There was no answer from the motor. I heaved, clutched, and heaved again. Riders streamed by me on both sides as I tried to keep from falling over my bike in my struggle. No reaction from the engine as I spun it over. Push! Now I was the last rider, for even the most recalcitrant Ducati had fired and left. I could hear the hollow EEEEOOOOEEEOOO of my intakes as I searched unavailingly for that perfect throttle opening, the one that would bring the engine up with a shriek. At a faint pop-pop-pop I snatched the clutch in with hope. But the noise died away. My legs were very tired now, and I noticed a great need for air. I began to worry about being ridden down by the riders coming around the circuit behind me. Lapped in 200 yards! How long had I been pushing? Long, I was sure. Turn one, where the track turns downhill—gravity will help me now. As I pushed out of sight around turn one, a ragged cheer went up from the few spectators there.

That was humiliating, but worse was to come. I sold that machine to a Vespa mechanic who saw instantly what I had overlooked—two different needles in the carburetors.

It wasn't all like that, or I never would have continued. There were fine moments. My best race centered around a lecture I gave myself. I had just fitted a set of 1967's latest tires, Dunlop Triangulars, and I engaged in this self-directed monologue: "I am a novice, my corner speeds are slow, but now I have these fine tires. At such speeds, on these tires, I am as safe as if at home in bed. Just snap open the throttle in turns and nothing will happen except I will go faster." In the event, I followed a Ducati 250 into Gunnery Corner, a long right-hander, and I opened up. I closed on him quickly (the throttle is a great thing, isn't it?), and he, hearing the crack of my exhaust, tried to escape. Accelerating, he leaned over farther and farther, but I pulled up easily on my lovely tires. Presently his peg struck a long stream of red sparks from the tar and then dug in. He slid and tumbled off the course while I continued, elated and confused at the same time. Certainly my idea about the tires had been proven, which was nice.

Overcoming fear is valuable. I had passed one of the highly touted Ducatis in a corner, and that was nice, too. There was also something else more valuable—I had felt that sudden elation and clarity of mind spoken of by mountain climbers, motor racers, soldiers in battle, that state of grace in which it seems you have become perfect and cannot possibly make any error, cannot be touched by events. I had, for a moment, become a perfectly relaxed passenger in the back of my own skull, looking out with calm detachment as my actions unfolded. It was a tremendous feeling. It was also a dangerous one, as any drunk on his way home from a party well knows.

I gave up racing at the end of that year, turning to working on other people's machines instead.

Now here is this old TD1-B in my shop, asking me to find the missing parts, to sandblast and paint, to renew bearings, to re-create. It has already paid me well for these services by turning my thoughts back to the big, gnarled roots of my enthusiasm for this sport, back to the silly romantic notions, the elations, the round-the-clock enthusiasms. I think it's a fair deal.

# Welcome to Texas Motorcycle Safety School

## By Sebastian Gallese

*McSweeney's*

I PLAN ON TEACHING YOU automatic-car-driving sissies how to not kill yourself on the road. You can call me Mr. King if you would like, but I prefer you just call me King. Since I already introduced myself, I would also like to inform you this is no "ride my Vespa from Starbucks to the office by 9" course. After rigorous drills of swerving, dynamic braking, and emergency maneuvers, God help me if you think you can join Hells Angels. Maybe you will be able to pedal that 5cc toy you mistake for a bike to the park for a Sunday picnic while I ride downtown to pick up some real women.

First, hop on your bike. I said get on the bike, no ballet dance required. OK, now turn the fuel-injection switch to "On." Turn the ignition. Can't find it? Let me guess, your Lexus has remoteless key start? Switch the kill button, put the choke on, and press the electric starter, and did you just try to start the bike from second gear? If we didn't have to wear helmets out here, I swear certification would solve itself.

Now let's begin our first exercise. I call this the West Texas roll. Maneuver in the first-gear friction zone between the orange cones and then shift to second gear on the straightaway and through the turn marked by the green cones. Act like you own this practice parking lot. I want a little James Dean look on your face, but not too much. You aren't ready for that much cool yet. There you go, downshift to first and stop the bike. You actually might not be mistaken for a man with a midlife crisis if you keep this up.

Before you go home and pop *Easy Rider* in your DVD player, first learn how to stay on your bike without falling off while in the Target parking lot. Not much to a tight U-turn, just a little counterweight steering while looking behind you. Excuse me! Don't go Euro on me and pretend you're making courier deliveries on your Stella. Roll back on the throttle before entering the curves!

*Lee Klancher*

You see that bike over there, that 1,000cc of man with all of society's sensitivity stripped from his metal body? (Apologies to the ladies in the group, but we just didn't have your kind when this machine was invented.) He doesn't pay child support, he doesn't go to Alcoholics Anonymous meetings, and he doesn't take crap from his boss. He just knows how to ride. I hope someday you will release yourself to this untamed beast. But before that happens, you have to first learn to not crap your pants just admiring his beauty.

Your final test, ladies and gentlemen: the supercourse. First, you will tightly weave the lime-green cones while using the clutch. Then, you will enter a large turn with the slow-look-roll method (without the clutch!) and finish off the straight with a quick-stop brake (if you even think about dropping that rear braking foot to the pavement, your certification paper is mine). The easy part is done. Now, I want you to do two U-turns in a figure-eight fashion through those cones. May God have mercy on your bike-riding abilities.

You showed a little gusto out there today. I judged you folks wrong. I am not going to hold it back: It makes me somewhat teary-eyed to see so many qualified cyclists in one place. It reminds me a little of my family reunion. Or the county prison. I want you to remember that what you learned today can not only save your life but, more important, can keep you from looking stupid on your bike. Let's ride.

# *Memorial Day Weekend 1967*

## By John Hall

*Riding on the Edge: A Motorcycle Outlaw's Tale*

Motorbooks, September 2008

*People with courage and character always seem sinister to the rest.*
— Hermann Hesse, *Demian*

THE WEATHERMAN had predicted clear blue skies over the entire East Coast. And he was right; it was already hot when we rolled out early Saturday morning.

Like the Dark Legions of Muspell, we rolled out of the damp, wooden, dirt-floor garages in Maspeth and Greenpoint, Long Island. Out of the parking lots of all-night neon truck-stop diners on U.S. 1 in Rahway and Linden, New Jersey. Out of the dying corrugated steel and mining towns beside the quiet rivers in the rolling mountains of Pennsylvania. Out of the moonshine hollows of West Virginia and the second-floor crash pads over waterfront bars in Baltimore. Out of the mist-shrouded oak and hemlock forests of the Blue Ridge and Allegheny Mountains, down the wide-open asphalt highways of the great Shenandoah Valley of Virginia, and even down the quiet Saturday-morning streets of the nation's capital.

The Pagans were on the run.

The Pagans, with names like Big Dutch, Apple, Satan, and Little Jesus. Indian Joe, Renegade, Crazy Joey, Pappy, German, and the Whiteknight. Sweet William and Saint Thomas. Chuck, Blackie, Wild Flea, and Amish. Animal, Stoop, Dizzy, Ozark, and Oakie. J. P. Soul, the Preacher, and the Rabbi. Tom Thumb, Friar Fuck, Baby Huey, Righteous Fuckin' Elroy, and the Galloping Guinea.

The leather-clad Teutonic knights were on the run, their pony-tailed Guineveres clinging to their backs. First in small bands of five or six, they rode down the quiet morning streets of sleepy little American towns and cities, where the roar of their unmuffled straight pipes rattled the window panes of small, wooden-frame houses. Then in larger packs, they roared down the highways, flying past wary motorists and puzzled cops, who sat dunking donuts in paper cups and spilling coffee on their laps. By evening, the packs had formed a caravan, an army of bearded barbarians on souped-up, chopped-down, raked-out hogs, gleaming chrome tailpipes, well-worn black leather jackets, and greasy denim vests with the image of Dark Surt grinning on their backs.

Their destination: Reading, Pennsylvania, where 12,000 straight motorcyclists were gathered for the Grand National 12-Mile races. A month earlier, when the same Reading Fairgrounds had been the site of the Billy Huber Memorial Races, the Pagans had been just one of many East Coast outlaw clubs, along with the Heathens of Reading.

The outlaw motorcycle club was a monster spawned unintentionally by the American Motorcycle Association (AMA), which claimed to represent 99 percent of the motorcycle owners in America. In 1965 the AMA published a pamphlet proclaiming that 99 percent of all the motorcycle riders in America were hard-working, God-fearing, tax-paying, flag-waving, church-going, milk-sipping, cookie-eating, law-abiding citizens and that the average American had nothing to fear from these people when they rode past on Sunday afternoons. It was the criminal element, the AMA claimed, the shit-kicking, beer-guzzling, gang-banging, ass-stomping, rock-'n'-roll-playing, hell-raising heathens and devil-worshiping hooligans who belonged to "outlaw clubs," which were not affiliated with the AMA. *Outlaw clubs*, the AMA again claimed, accounted for less than 1 percent of the people who rode motorcycles but accounted for 99 percent of all the crime, mayhem, and bad publicity that the public associated with motorcycles.

But the AMA had it all wrong. In the first place, I saw plenty of AMA motorcyclists raising hell, for which outlaw bikers later took the heat. Besides there was a lot more to it than what the AMA claimed. It was part of what was beginning to be called the generation gap. Older motorcyclists belonged to the AMA clubs. They could remember when Marlon Brando made *The Wild One* and hamburgers cost a nickel. They wore black leather caps and '50s-style emblems, which they painted on the back of their black leather jackets along with club names like Mercury Riders. They rode "garbage wagons," full-dress Harley-Davidsons equipped with windshields, saddlebags, *sesselfurzer* seats the size of living room chairs, and even radios and electric starters.

Outlaws were younger and leaner, longhaired rednecks and badass white boys with attitude. Many were Vietnam vets who still loved their country but no longer trusted the government. Outlaws and criminals are not the same thing, as the AMA seemed to think. Criminals are crooks who manipulate the system to get rich. Outlaws simply don't give a shit. Al Capone was a criminal who died in bed a rich old man, his brain and wiener rotten with syphilis. John Dillinger was an outlaw. He died in a hail of bullets outside the Biograph Theater with his girlfriend on his arm. People came from all around Chicago with handkerchiefs to mop up his blood in the street like he was an American saint. That says it all about the difference between real outlaws and mere criminals. Outlaws like John Dillinger and Jesse James get cut down in the street but rise up from the dirt to live on as American legends, while the memories of wise guys and mere criminals rot with their bodies in their expensive, satin-lined coffins.

Outlaw bikers scorned helmets and Japanese motorcycles. We rode American, British, and German bikes with tiny bicycle seats and chopped-down fenders, stripped of all unnecessary accessories like windshields, saddlebags, mirrors, and front brakes. We souped-up the engines and raked-out the front ends. We wore our emblems and club names on sleeve-less denim vests. That way we could wear the denim vest over our black leather jackets to proclaim our presence by "flying colors" (as we called it), or slip the denim vests under our leather jackets to avoid police detection. We reveled in our status as outlaws and began wearing swastikas just to piss off the world. And after the AMA published its pamphlet, we outlaws began wearing "1%" patches on the front of our jackets to disassociate ourselves from what we considered the "candy-ass" AMA riders.

Eventually the diamond-shaped one-percenter patches came to stand for everything the outlaw biker lived for and believed in. We guarded our patches with pride, and getting one ripped off was tantamount to castration. Not every club was allowed to wear them. On the West Coast only a handful of clubs wore them by mutual agreement. The Midwest, from the western foothills of the Alleghenies to the eastern foothills of the Rockies, was completely under the control of a Chicago-based outfit called simply the Outlaws, chromed cavaliers who rode across the great prairies of the Heartland with a pair of crossed pistons and a grinning chrome skull named Charlie on their backs. But the East Coast was like a bunch of

Lee Klancher

feudal baronies. Each town was dominated by a different club that went around ripping one-percenter patches off other clubs that it considered too candy-ass to wear them.

In 1966, the Maryland-based Pagans decided to change all that by building an East Coast outlaw empire. On December 23, 1966, the club rented an entire hotel in a dilapidated section of Newark, New Jersey, for a giant, old-fashioned Yuletide celebration; and it invited every respectable outlaw club on the East Coast. It was a good party, as outlaw parties go, and eventually the cops were called in. While the rest of the country prepared for the arrival of Saint Nick with visions of sugar plums dancing in their heads, the cops and the outlaws punched out each other in the halls and threw each other down the stairs for an hour. When it was all over, the cops had to commandeer a half-dozen buses from the local school district and drive the outlaws away handcuffed to the seats.

In an age when internet porn, rap lyrics, and pedophile priests have become everyday news items, it is hard to remember just how uptight and impressionable the country was back in the mid-1960s. Imagine what it must have been like for average depression-born and World War II–bred Americans as they sat at the breakfast table in their new robes and slippers on Christmas morning, eating toast and sipping eggnog, while looking down at the barbaric images of long-haired redneck bikers and bandaged-up cops staring back at them from the pages of the Sunday paper. For an entire week, even the ultra-establishment *New York Times* treated it as a major cultural earthquake. On the pages of the *Washington Post*, one even detects a sense of municipal pride in Maryland's own infamous outlaw motorcycle club, as *Post* reporters actually hunted down and interviewed the Pagans for their account, which, not surprisingly, blamed the whole riot on the police.

The donnybrook apparently began about 1 a.m. when the hotel manager and Special Police Officer James Robinson began to get antsy. The manager suggested that Robinson pull the plug on the band and tell the merrymakers to go home, which Robinson did.

"That's when they started emptying beer on me," Robinson later claimed, "and I called for help."

Help arrived in the form of two Newark police officers, who found Robinson "covered with beer" and surrounded by a crowd of shaggy revelers who were shouting "Heil Hitler!" at him. Someone draped a sheet over the shoulders of one of the cops as a joke, causing his partner to fly down the stairs and shout into his car radio: "Send everything!"

"Everything" turned out to be a phalanx of three dozen club-swinging cops charging up the stairs, and that's when the Yuletide festivities degenerated into a full-blown riot, which Newark Police Sergeant Roy Lane called "one of the most dangerous I have ever seen." The Pagans were driven off to the police station where, the newspapers reported, they were "stripped" of their iron crosses and "swastika charms," and "forced to take showers."

But perhaps the best performance was reserved for a buffoon of a person named James Del Mauro, Newark's chief magistrate, who, later in the week, seemed more concerned with matters of hygiene than justice, as he dressed down the Pagans in a courtroom cordoned off by 35 plainclothes detectives.

"Never set foot in Newark again for any reason," he told the defendants. "This city doesn't want people like you." Then, in language reminiscent of how a red-faced Irish customs agent might have described Del Mauro's own people as they arrived at Ellis Island a half-century earlier, the judge continued: "You are the filthiest people I have ever seen. I look at you and wonder what has happened to the youth of today. I have been taught that there is nothing cheaper than soap and water to clean yourself with."

He best described his sentiments after the initial arraignment, when a "shocked" Del Mauro told reporters, "I just don't understand these people."

The party may have ended in a bust, but for the Pagans it was a boom. The story was smeared all over the front page of the New York tabloids, and by the next afternoon, the Pagans were the biggest name in the East Coast motorcycle world. The site of the party, right across the river from Manhattan, had been deliberately chosen to antagonize the Pagans' biggest rivals, the Aliens. This club had resisted all offers to merge with the Pagans and considered the metropolitan New York area to be its exclusive fiefdom. For two years the Aliens had successfully ripped the one-percenter patches off every other club that tried to fly them in the metropolitan New York area.

At the party the Pagans announced that they had formed clubs in New York and New Jersey, as well as other cities like Bethlehem and Lancaster.

By the next year, they claimed, the Pagans would be the only one-percenter club on the East Coast. Instead of fighting them, the Pagans invited the other clubs to join them in building an outlaw empire from the frozen and snow-covered wastelands of northern Quebec to the swampy Everglades of Florida.

Starting a new club is one thing, but getting an established club to throw down its colors and patch over to your club is quite another. The Pagans were already negotiating with the big clubs in Baltimore, Wilmington, and Pittsburgh, but the Heathens of Reading were the big piece missing from the puzzle.

In those days Reading was still a hard-ass, blue-collar town. It was also a mob town. At one time it was the third largest motorcycle manufacturing town in America. Its association with motorcycles continued, as every year it hosted races at the old Reading Fairgrounds. In the 1960s Pennsylvania had more motorcycles per capita than any state in the country, including California. Reading was centrally located between the big East Coast cities: New York, Philadelphia, Baltimore, Washington, and Pittsburgh. And while the local Heathens may not have been the biggest club on the East Coast, it was one of the most respected, thanks to the leadership of a former paratrooper named Chuck Ginder.

The Heathens was a large club, and Chuck ran Reading like a feudal warlord. He had the cops scared, he had the mob scared, and he had the citizenry scared. Independent motorcyclists avoided riding in packs through his town, and they never wore denim jackets with cut-off sleeves, much less one-percenter patches, because they knew this was an invitation to getting hit in the head with a chain while sitting at a stop light.

Chuck was a legend on the East Coast, and every club admired the way he had the town locked up. I even saw him stop ROTC cadets from Albright College and make them kneel down and unblouse their pants right on Penn Street. Sometimes I thought that as a former paratrooper he got madder at the bloused pants on college kids than at unauthorized one-percenter patches on motorcyclists. "At least they fuckin' ride motor-cycles," he used to say. "Half these kids never even been on a plane, much less jumped out of one."

A month before the Memorial Day races, ambassadors from the Pagans had come to the Reading Fairgrounds for the Billy Huber Memorial races.

They negotiated a deal with Chuck where his club members would become Pagans but would be allowed to continue wearing small Heathen patches over their hearts. The week before Memorial Day, Satan rode up from Maryland with the new Pagan patches, which he handed over to Chuck in the editorial office of the *Berks County Record*. And the moment was recorded for posterity on the front page of the May 25th edition with banner headlines:

"Outlaw Motorcyclists En Route to Race"

"Reading Set for Grand National 12 Mile Contest"

"Local 'Heathens' Accepted as a 'Pagan' Chapter"

These headlines were followed by a half-page photo of three of the swastika-covered cavaliers, which ran the caption:

Heathens Join Pagans—It was quite an occasion last week in the Record office when several motorcycle buffs dropped in to join forces. For the "Heathens" cyclists of Reading, it meant being granted a Pagan chapter locally. Witnessing the transaction is "Big Jim" as "Pagan's" Satan, right, hands over the colors to "Chuck," president of the local group.

With the Heathens firmly in the pack, the Pagans were now ready for their first big show as the number one one-percenter club on the East Coast. We left New York early, rode down the dilapidated skyway they call the Brooklyn–Queens Expressway, over the Williamsburg Bridge, through Manhattan and the Holland Tunnel, then over the Newark Skyway and into the marshy New Jersey Meadowlands, where we met the Jersey Pagans at an old dilapidated bar stuck back in the high, swampy marsh weeds.

When we pulled up, the Jersey brothers were coming through the door with their hands full of brown bottles of Rheingold beer. As they shoved them in our hands, we could feel that they were cold and covered with sweat. The swampy Meadowlands were already lush and green, but it would be another month before they started to stink. So we just sat on our bikes, sucking down the beer and fresh spring air. We exchanged the traditional outlaw greeting: a bear hug and a peck on the lips. Then after an outlaw breakfast of pickled eggs, dried beef jerky, and salted peanuts, we were off.

Like old-fashioned cavalry brigades, outlaw motorcycle packs were followed by baggage trains, which were made up of pickup trucks, panel trucks, and cars with trailers. While it was mandatory that you show up for a run, it was not mandatory that you show up on a motorcycle. You just had to get there. Bikes got wrecked or were impounded by the police. Brothers had just gotten out of jail, others were in casts.

These grounded brothers were condemned to riding in the baggage train. The old '60s outlaws would do almost anything for a brother, but hauling one around on the backseat of his machine was not one of them. So the grounded brothers were condemned to riding in the car with tools, stray women, citizen hangers-on, and the weekend supply of beer. If a grounded brother could not ride, he could at least get drunk.

Almost inevitably, Sweet William Parker rode in the baggage train, relentlessly sucking down one bottle of beer after another and titillating a party of ladies that he had picked up the night before. Sweet William found himself in the baggage train more often than not because he rode a motorcycle the way he drank beer and did everything else: to wretched excess. We used to tell him that he didn't need a throttle on his motorcycle—just an on-off switch. That's because the carburetor was either cranked wide open with the throttle nearly ripped off in his hand, or else he was standing on the brake pedal, all 230 pounds of him, trying to lock up the drum brakes and bring the screaming machine to a halt before he blew a red light and broad-sided a tractor trailer.

He blew head gaskets and burned valve seats, or just wrecked the thing and mangled it up like some dirt bike. Fortunately he had a Beeser, a British bike similar to a Triumph, manufactured by Birmingham Small Arms (BSA), and like Triumphs they were easy to repair and handled well. Had he tried some of his circus stunts on a hog, he would have wrecked a lot more often. It seemed his bike was in an almost constant state of repair—in someone else's garage. That's because we never let Willie work on his own bike. He had no mechanical ability whatsoever, and he fixed bikes, like everything else, to wretched excess. He could apply enough torque to rip the head off a boar hog; 1/4-inch aluminum bolts stood no chance against him. Eventually Geoff "PW" Quinn just told him, "Don't touch the fuckin' thing. Just bring it over here right away. It's easier to fix it before you go fuckin' everything up."

After a few breakdowns we arrived covered with grease and sweat at the rusty old steel bridge that spanned the Delaware River between Phillipsburg, New Jersey, and Easton, Pennsylvania. The Whiteknight was waiting for us there with a contingent of Bethlehem Pagans drinking Horlacher beer from cans. The Whiteknight was a big Pennsylvania Dutch steelworker with tremendous tattooed biceps, a ruddy face, and brushed-back sandy-red hair. He was a competitive weight lifter, an easygoing kinda guy, but strong enough to pick up a Sportster by himself and stick it in the back of a truck.

The Whiteknight gave us a hearty welcome and then led us to the clubhouse, which was sandwiched in a row of wood-frame company houses on a high hill overlooking the giant Bethlehem Steel mill. We got off our bikes and stretched. Car doors opened, and brothers got out and cursed, while Willie staggered out and gave a wild yell. The Bethlehem brothers began throwing us cans of Horlacher from the porch. We opened them up, and the beer spritzed all over the place. Then we stood in the street awhile, drank beer, and talked. There were spring green mountains in the background, but down in the valley it was all grease and grime with the legendary mill stretching like the smoldering carcass of a dragon with red-brick scales. Steel and smoke, redneck bars, and country roads. The Pagans were in their element.

All three clubs—New York, Jersey, and Bethlehem—had strict orders not to go into Reading. The Mother Club did not want bands of drunken Pagans staggering around town getting into fights and getting arrested. It wanted every available member to show up at the fairgrounds, not half the club in jail for the races on Sunday morning.

The Whiteknight had been told to wait for a phone call, at which time we would be told how to go to Reading. In the meantime he told two prospective members to wait at the clubhouse for the call, and we collected the drunks who had staggered out to the cars and put them to sleep on couches. Then we rode in a pack to a Polack bar by the mill.

It was a classic Pennsylvania mill town bar—slightly greenish off-white paint, the color of old hard-boiled eggs. A couple of Phillies and a couple of Mets posters scattered between other posters with American flags and sentiments like "Bomb Hanoi Now" and "America, Love It or Leave It." A yellow, cracking photograph of General Douglas MacArthur decorated the

*Lee Klancher*

front end of the back bar, and the back end was watched over by a photo of the former middleweight champion of the world, Tony Zale (whose real name was Tony Zaleski), the hardest piece of steel ever to roll out of Gary, Indiana—another hard-ass American town like Bethlehem and Reading.

There were old guys in beat-up caps with union buttons on them sitting at the bar drinking shots of rye whiskey. In the back room a bunch of younger guys were shooting pool. When we walked in, the older guys looked a little worried, especially the owner, a middle-aged guy, who was tending bar. In fact, he looked like he'd just seen the angel of death walking through his door. The Whiteknight walked up to the bar with the Jersey and New York leaders and told him we were just there for a couple of beers and no trouble.

Actually, the Pagans rarely did have trouble in places like this. A lot of us were Teamster truck drivers, steelworkers, and longshoremen who had grown up around places like this. Trouble usually seemed to come from Italian mob wannabes in creased pants and patent-leather shoes, college jocks—especially football players on steroids—and smartass, middle-class mallrats who had not been smacked around enough when they were young. But in places like this, we were all forged out of ore from the same mine shaft, and soon everybody was pouring beer out of pitchers and shooting pool together. Then the phone rang, and the owner handed it to the Whiteknight. "Let's go," he shouted as he handed it back to the owner.

The place emptied quicker than a courtroom after a not-guilty verdict. Outside, brothers were jumping on their kick-starters and revving their engines. We rode back in a pack to the house on the hill, where there were more guys from Bethlehem and Allentown waiting for us. By the time we arrived, there were about 75 bikes all over the street in front of the house.

The Whiteknight came out of the house with Sleepy from New York and Updegraff from New Jersey. He held up his hands as a sign to shut off our engines. Dozens of engines shut off at once, and our ears rang from the silence.

Then the Whiteknight spoke: "We are going to meet the rest of the club just north of Reading. We are going to ride in a pack. Stay in twos. Do not pass anyone. If a light turns red, do not stop. If a cop tries to pull you over, ignore him too. Stare straight ahead. Make him go to the front and pull over the entire pack."

Then he yelled, "Let's go."

First a few loud sputters, then a few roars, then the shit-kicking thunder of about 75 internal combustion engines, a total of about 5,000 cubic inches of steel-lined cylinders, all roaring at once, each one revving at a different rate, each one bellowing through different lengths of tail pipe—some of which were swept up 4 feet in the air. It was like mechanical thunder roaring through every pipe of a Bach organ at once. Goose bumps would rise on your neck, and your hair would try to stand straight up on your head. The only experience that ever came close was listening to the sound of thousands of Irish drums and war pipes coming up New York's Fifth Avenue on St. Patrick's Day.

We pulled out and rode double file down old Route 222 through Kutztown, where people ran out on the porch to stare as if we were an army of invading Huns. Just north of Reading, near a town called Moselem Springs, there was a large parking lot. Some of the old Heathens were already there. Others had gone to meet the Maryland and Virginia people and would be there in an hour. It was the gathering of the clan—the most Pagans ever assembled in one place at the same time. And this is where I first met the old Heathens, who for the past week had been the Reading Pagans.

There was Blackie, tall and lean, sitting on a raked hog with a chrome sissy bar. Half Sicilian and half Pennsylvania Dutch, he was dressed all in black, as was his bike. Even his hair and long, pointed beard were black, as black and shiny as the hand rubbed lacquer on his gas tank. On his forearm he had a topless bikini girl tattooed over the word "Honolulu," a souvenir from his army days.

Behind him sat his wife, Baby, a Mexican girl from Fresno. He had brought her back as a souvenir from his California days. She was as tall and lean as him—same height, same weight, same black hair. In fact if they had been mules, they would have been a matched pair.

Next to him was Righteous Fuckin' Elroy, a Mennonite farm boy from Leola, a Pennsylvania Dutch town in Lancaster County. Like Blackie, he was tall and lean but with large hands and big bones, typical of the large component of Swiss and Alsatian blood in the Pennsylvania Dutch stock. He had dark-brown hair swept back in a mane like a wolf man and deep-set, dark eyes.

Then there was Bob Rayel, or "Rayels," as he was called, Chuck's prime minister and number-two man in the Reading club. He wore a helmet, not one designed for safety, but a steel Nazi helmet with red swastikas emblazoned on the sides. It was the only kind of helmet an outlaw ever wore back in those days.

But the most impressive thing about him was sitting behind him—his wife. She had auburn brown hair, cut in bangs and falling in clean waves over her shoulders. She was only 20 at the time, yet she had two kids already out of diapers. Still, with her soft green eyes and pouting mouth, she looked like a little Pennsylvania Dutch teen-angel herself. Sweet 16 and Queen of the Hop. The two of them contrasted each other's appearance as much as Blackie and his wife complemented each other. I remember I made a point to check out the handle on her name patch as we waited in the cool night air for the rest of the pack. It just said "Jane."

This was the beginning of the golden summer of '67. The Pagans then looked nothing like today's popular media-generated stereotype of the biker image: some middle-aged graybeard loon with a big belly who goes around sounding like a cross between Burl Ives and your standard New York City homeless-rights advocate, calling everyone "Bro."

The Pagans milling around the parking lot that night were much leaner and younger. Members approaching 30 like Pappy, the Irishman from Jersey with the big Teamster truck-driver beer-belly, were exceptions. Their hair was long but pushed back and greasy, and their beards were trimmed. It was obvious that they spent more time listening to Johnny Cash and Patsy Cline than to Bob Dylan and Joan Baez. But the beards would grow shaggier and the hair more unkempt. In a few years, when the country scene moved from Nashville to Austin, the outlaw biker would replace the cowboy as the fashion model for a new generation of longhaired, redneck country singers, and the motorcycle would replace the horse as one of the redneck's three most prized possessions, along with his dog and his gun.

Many of these guys were also veterans with their own brand of patriotism. They wore swastikas, but they would stomp anyone in a minute for burning an American flag. Most of them hated George Rockwell's neo-Nazis as much as they hated war protesters. There were no ethnic or outside group loyalties in the club. You were either a Pagan or you were not. In a group of 200 Pagans, you might find two with some obvious African ancestry, or maybe two Puerto Ricans or two Jews. But at this time you could safely say that 99 percent of the collective ancestors of your one percenters, clear back to the Stone Age, had lived north of the Alps and east of the Danube River. In other words, the outlaw bikers of the '60s descended from the same Celts, Hunkies, and Germans who terrorized the shit out of the Greeks and Romans 2,000 years ago, with their long hair, tattoos, outlandish attire, and hard-drinking violent behavior.

In the dim, mist-shrouded past of history, these people had worshipped the swastika as a symbol of the raw, violent, creative, and masculine side of the divine force behind the universe. It was the symbol of a god who rode on the wings of the wind and hurled thunderbolts from the heavens. As such, they could not have chosen a more appropriate symbol.

And then there were our women.

There were no women members, as such, and no women rode their own bikes in the pack. Remember, these were the days of mule-headed carburetors and defiant kick-starters that could toss you over the handlebars in a heartbeat. And like the Pennsylvania Dutch religious sects, the behavior that the club expected from male and female members was radically different. Here again, these women had nothing in common with the popular media-generated image of the loud-mouthed biker bitch.

These were country girls who grew up in the valleys attending church on Sunday, but during the rest of the week they listened to songs like "He's a Rebel" and "The Leader of the Pack." After school, they drifted into town and either got pregnant or went to work in the mills, where the only air conditioning was an open window. As they bent over their machines and the sweat poured from their brows, they dreamed about cold lager, the smell of well-worn leather jackets, and riding through the cool night air with their arms wrapped tightly around a bearded barbarian with tattooed biceps.

Just after dark, another pack rode up. At the head of it rode Chuck Ginder, leader of the Reading Pagans, and behind him sat Sweet Pea, his eight-months-pregnant wife. Next to him, his long greasy hair blowing in the night breeze, rode Fred "Big Dutch" Burhans, Grandmaster of the entire Pagan nation, the man who turned a loose confederation of rebel clubs from Maryland and Virginia into an outlaw empire. Behind them rode the Maryland and Virginia Pagans. The Southrons wore as much Confederate as Nazi paraphernalia, thus proudly embracing their Southern birthright at a time when pragmatic and ambitious Southern white boys like Al Gore and Bill Clinton were trying to run as far away from that heritage as they could.

After a brief huddle with the Mother Club, the individual club leaders called their brothers together and explained the rules. Our man Sleepy was a squat little guy with a Dean Martin hairdo and sunglasses who walked with the wobbly gait of a slow-moving gas station attendant. After he wobbled over, he pushed his Dean Martin sunglasses up over his forehead and explained the rules to us: "We are going to ride through Reading in a pack. There's 10,000 citizen bikers in town from all over the country. They're all going to be downtown. And we are going to ride from one end of town to the other. We are not going to stop. Chuck and Dutch are going to ride at the head of the pack."

Then he added that we would not be partying in Reading. The club didn't want any hassles with citizens the night before the big races. The Reading people had rented a cornfield out on the Lancaster County line, and it was there that we were going to party. There would be guys flying patches from other clubs, and every one of them was in the process of becoming a Pagan. They were all to be treated just like brothers, and anyone starting a hassle would get his colors yanked right on the spot.

Then Chuck gave us the word and we started our bikes—over 500 of them—in a deafening roar like the coming of Ragnarok. Chuck and Dutch pulled out at the head of the pack, and the rest followed. Before us lay one of the oldest cities in America, where over 12,000 straight motorcyclists were already in town for the Grand National races.

Reading sits at the foot of Mount Penn, on the Schuylkill River, and along the old railroad line that connects Philadelphia with the old anthracite coal region. It was originally a Pennsylvania Dutch market town, and by the Civil War it was the capital of German-speaking America. But by 1900 it was becoming an industrial town with a large influx of immigrants from Eastern and Southern Europe. With the advent of Prohibition, it became the beer capital of America, as beer-baron Max Hassel continued to operate all five of Reading's breweries illegally but at full capacity.

Hassel, a 19-year-old immigrant at the time the Eighteenth Amendment was passed, had the vision to see that the law would never work. He formed a real estate company and bought up all five of Reading's breweries, as well as night clubs and bars, which he operated as speakeasies. Under Hassel's reign, Reading became Sin City, with wide-open prostitution and gambling in the alleys off Penn Street. High rollers and revelers rolled in from New York, Philadelphia, Baltimore, and Washington. Night life in the clubs on Penn Street hummed, and at one time the city was home to the biggest floating craps game in the world.

By the mid-1960s a reform government had cleaned up most of that. There was still gambling and prostitution, but the high rollers were gone. Many residents now considered the night life dull and were looking for something to put some spice back into the town. Also, because of the proximity to New York and Philadelphia, some of the country boys were starting to feel rebellious and sporting a longhaired redneck image. Eventually they found their way into the Heathens, which became one of the largest and most respected outlaw clubs on the East Coast.

Now they were all Pagans. And for the next couple of years they would provide the locals with the excitement the town was looking for, until the locals decided that the Pagans were too hot and tried to clean them up like they had cleaned up the mob—but that was later. On this Saturday night of Memorial Day weekend 1967, the Pagans were about to burst into Reading as the undisputed outlaw kings of the East Coast.

The pack rode in from the north, out of the shadow of the Blaubarrick (Blue Mountain), past the silent graves of the Charles Evans Cemetery and the idle coal cars in the quiet railroad yards, all the way up to City Park where Penn Street begins at the base of Mount Penn. Then, while the town was warming up to the sound of country swing bands with names like Dottie and the Dukes, and Curly Smith and the Spadesmen, the Pagans descended down Penn Street. Two abreast, in a dark line of chain whips, earrings, gleaming chrome, straight exhaust pipes, and swastikas, with our women clinging to our backs, the bearded barbarians rode through town like a wave of thunder.

Today Laurie Hartmann is a Little League coach who lives in Central Pennsylvania where her husband drives a mail truck, but she remembers that night well: "I was only 10 years old at the time," she says, "but we only lived a half block off Penn Street. I could hear them coming from the other end of town, and I remember sitting up in my bed watching them go by on Penn Street. All the kids in the neighborhood talked about it for years."

The adults talked about it for years too. The Pagans had put some spice back into the town on that warm spring night in 1967, when a band of guys, many who had not known each other a year earlier, suddenly found themselves banded together in the number one one-percenter club on the East Coast.

The pack rode down to the end of Penn Street, where it crossed the Schuylkill River Bridge under the big yellow letters of the Sunshine Brewery sign. Then we rode out Route 222 for the Lancaster County line, to the party that was on a farm they had rented. The fields had just been plowed, so everyone had to stay on the perimeter. We parked our bikes in the mud and cursed as the cars and trucks got stuck and had to be pushed out of ruts. Soon the spring mud was up to the tops of our boots. But finally everyone got parked and we settled down to party. There were hundreds of Pagans, as well as the other clubs that were about to become Pagans, clubs from Pittsburgh, Baltimore, and Wilmington.

Sleepy walked up to me with a can of Old Dutch beer in each hand, his slow-moving gas station attendant walk rendered even more ridiculous by the fact that he now had to suck his foot out of the mud with each step. Finally, huffing and puffing, he made it over to me and shoved one of the beer cans in my hand.

"Fuckin' shithole," he mumbled.

"I was thinkin' the same thing," I said. We sat down on the bumper of a truck.

"I mean," he said, "these guys come to New York, we take them out and show them the bars and clubs, and they can party and get laid."

"That's right," I said, "We don't take 'em to the garbage dumps in Greenpoint or the cemeteries in Maspeth."

"A whole fuckin' city with 12,000 scooter-jockeys in town," he mumbled, "just 10 miles up the road, and we gotta sit here in some fuckin' cornfield, where there ain't even a decent place to take a shit."

And so there we sat, two Brooklynites in Pennsylvania. A Dutchman from Ridgewood and Wop from Williamsburg, drinking beer we had never heard of and without even a decent place to take a shit, as Sleepy had put it. We had passed over the Aliens and instead joined an upstart rebel club, and here we now were sitting in a cornfield on the bumper of a truck, in Lancaster County, Pennsylvania, slowly allowing ourselves to be absorbed into the great rural Redneck Republic of America.

We sat quietly, resting for a while and absorbing the whole thing. Then Sleepy turned to me, slapped me on the arm, and said, "But you know what? I wouldn't have it any other way. I really like these guys. It's just this feeling I got in my bones that this is a great thing we got goin' here."

And he was right. I was thinking the same thing: it was a great thing. Thirty years later, the widow of one Pagan described it this way: "I remember we had this club called the Heathens, and then we became Pagans back in '67. And then suddenly all you guys started showing up from New York, Jersey, Maryland, and Virginia, guys who had never seen each other before. But you were all acting like you had known each other all your lives. You were just like brothers. I never saw anything like it in my life, except maybe for the Mennonites."

I never heard it better put. The Pagans were a one-percenter outlaw motorcycle brotherhood, medieval and mystical, far more like the religious warrior brotherhood of Teutonic knights than some sort of modern criminal enterprise like the government and media were always trying to tell people it was.

The next day we arrived at the fairgrounds in a pack. It was hot and sunny. It was also the first year as a reporter for *Reading Eagle* columnist Joseph N. Farrell. He was one of the reporters assigned to cover the races. It was his first meeting with the Pagans, and he would later become an expert on them. Here is the way he remembers it:

> There's a picture that's been indelibly imprinted in my memory for 30 years now, of a hippie girl, a flower child in beads sitting at the feet of a stern state police commander in full riot gear, offering peace and love to those around her.
>
> None of whom was interested.
>
> The state police commander and his squadron were blocking the gates to the old Reading Fairgrounds racetrack against a horde of mounted Pagans, the "outlaw" motorcycle gang in full force.
>
> The Pagans wanted in, with their bikes, to the grandstand area, where hundreds or perhaps even thousands of respectable motorcycle enthusiasts were cheering on their professional motorcycle racers.
>
> It was the clean shaven 99 percent under siege by the greasy, bearded one percent, or Attila at the gates of Rome, and the state police were having none of it.
>
> The Pagans could go in, they were told, but not with their bikes—the cops feared, with good reason, the gang would literally ride roughshod over the clean-cut cyclists in the stands and create a riot.
>
> Whether or not the Pagans had that in mind—and let's face it, they probably did—what they told the police was that they would never leave their bikes outside, out of sight, to be mauled over by vandals or curious cops looking for serious infractions.
>
> It was in many ways a game no one could win. The Pagans never did get in, but the fear of future attempts put an end to motorcycle races at the Fairgrounds.
>
> *Reading Eagle*
> May 26, 1997

No one remembers who the flower girl was, but the state trooper standing over her was Harley Smith, an old-fashioned Pennsylvania Dutch cop, who was capable of drinking beer or swinging a truncheon as hard as any Pagan. It would not be his last run-in with the club, nor would it be Joe Farrell's.

When the Pagans disappeared out the other end of town, no one knew what to expect or where we would appear next. The locals had panicked and called out the riot police. Although the national guard would have been better, the riot police served our purpose. We could have left prospects—our term for wannabe members who were still on probation—to guard the bikes and then gone in without them. But had we done that, then everyone would have known what happened. This way no one knew what would have happened. They could only speculate.

At the time we didn't know all of this. All we knew is that we had rode all the way to Reading to hang out in a hot, dusty, gravel-covered parking lot for an hour, with dust flying all around us, pissing and moaning and cursing with no beer, only to break up into small packs and ride back to Bethlehem, where we sat on the wood-frame porch of the clubhouse all night drinking Horlacher and watching the lights in the mill.

But whether we guys from Long Island or the brothers from Bethlehem knew it or not, one thing was now certain. There were 12,000 motorcyclists inside the fairgrounds, and the riot police had been called out to protect them. How could other clubs now claim to be real outlaws when the riot police had to be called out to protect them from the Pagans?

That weekend a legend had been hatched in Reading from an egg laid in Muspell.

# You're Only Crazy Once

## By Tom Cotter

*The Vincent in the Barn*

Motorbooks, September 2009

"**WEAR YOUR OLDEST CLOTHES,**" Dick Fritz said to his colleagues. "And don't forget the Liquid Wrench."

Fritz and his friends Rich and Ben were packing for a trip overseas. Usually, old clothes and Liquid Wrench would never make it onto even the most casual tourist's packing list. But these three were about to embark on the barn-find adventure of a lifetime. In just a few hours, the trio would be on a Delta Airlines flight from New York's Kennedy Airport to the most unlikely destination of Sheremetyevo International Airport in Moscow, Russia.

They were on the hunt for the elusive armor-plated Mercedes 540K Aktion P.

Fritz had been a car guy his whole life. His first car was a 1939 Ford convertible that he purchased for $125 from a neighbor in 1956. His father warned him, "I wouldn't buy that car if I were you!" But Fritz did what teenaged boys are supposed to do, and he bought it anyway, explaining to his dad, "But you're not me. . . . "

It was in sad condition, with a ripped top and torn upholstery. But the money saved from mowing lawns enabled him to purchase a new top and install seat covers. Eventually he painted the car—using a small compressor he had used to paint model airplanes—and installed a 1953 Mercury V-8 with two carburetors and dual exhaust.

Eventually that car was sold, and a succession of Chevrolets followed, including a 1955 Chevy and a new 1963 fuel-injected Corvette.

It was motorcycles that left the first motor vehicle impression on young Fritz, who at six years old was already witnessing motorcycle circus tricks in his backyard.

"I grew up in a neighborhood near Nyack, New York, and behind us lived a real clown who had traveled with circuses around the world," said

Fritz, now 68. "He would have fellow circus performers visit, one of which would arrive pulling a travel trailer, and inside was a motorcycle that he used in his act.

"Even though my father would have killed him [if he knew], he would take me for rides when my father was at work."

As he got older, both cars and motorcycles took a backseat to education for Fritz. His intention was to pursue a degree in aeronautical engineering, but when the car bug bit, he changed his major to mechanical engineering and enrolled in the engineering program at Clarkston University in New York.

Enrolled in the same college was the son of a respected auto racing personality, Luigi Chinetti. Chinetti had been a champion race driver in Europe—having won the 24 Hours of Le Mans three times—before emigrating to America in 1940. Chinetti later became Ferrari's first North American importer. Chinetti's son, Luigi Jr., would invite Fritz to work on the racing team's pit crew at tracks such as Watkins Glen, Lime Rock, and Sebring.

"Soon after I graduated from college in 1962 I was called by Mr. Chinetti to come to work at the dealership," said Fritz. "I was 22—what did I know? But Mr. Chinetti said they needed a manager, so I took the job."

He remained there until 1978.

"I handled the importation, sold Ferraris, managed the Ferrari North American Racing Team, designed race car components, handled customer service, designed and installed the first automatic transmission in a Ferrari along with the first Ferrari air pollution control systems, and basically was involved in the whole business," he said.

The Ferrari business wasn't always as robust as the company has been in recent years. There were times, according to Fritz, when the company couldn't make payroll for its small office staff and mechanics.

"With Mr. Chinetti's permission, I opened up a company called Amerispec in 1976," he said. Amerispec was a company that specialized in the legalization of imported cars for use on U.S. roads. "The U.S. Ferrari business wasn't real good in 1975. All they imported to us was the 8-cylinder Dino 308 GT4 model, which not too many people seemed to want, so we legalized the 12-cylinder Boxer Berlinettas and 400 automatics."

"Mr. Chinetti was 75 years old and wanted to sell the business, but I knew I didn't want to work for whoever bought it, so I worked nights and weekends developing my own business in the meantime."

In time, Amerispec thrived as it federalized such cars as the Ferrari Boxer, the Porsche 959, and the McLaren F1 during the boom days of the 1980s. His customers included Jay Leno, Ralph Lauren, and David Letterman.

Then it all went bust as Amerispec tried to tread water during the economic downturn of the early 1990s.

Then one day the phone rang. "Hello," the caller said to Fritz. "Can you help me get my two cars I've imported from Russia out of a container and into this country legally?" Fritz was curious and asked the gentleman, who was obviously also from Russia, "What kind of cars are they?"

"A Mercedes and a Horch, which I hope to sell over here," the gentleman said. He continued, saying there were lots of valuable German cars in Russia to be found.

A light bulb went off in Fritz's head.

"There wasn't much exotic car business going on in 1992 with the recession and all," he said. "So instead of just sitting around the office waiting for the phone to ring, I thought it might be a profitable adventure."

He quickly called his friend Rich Reuter, whose family had owned a restoration business for three generations.

"Because they had restored so many Mercedes-Benzes, I thought of Rich first because he was an expert on the vintage models," said Fritz.

"And it just so happened that Rich had a friend in Moscow who was a writer and a literary guy who could possibly help us out. Then I mentioned it to a customer, Ben, who was instantly interested and said he would be willing to back us financially if we included him."

Suddenly it was a "go," and the three men were packing for a trip to Russia. Because they didn't want to stand out from the Russian population, they decided to wear old clothes and to bring containers of Liquid Wrench in case they needed to remove rusty bolts from any of the cars they were hoping to find.

Reuter knew just one Russian, but word soon began to spread even before they landed that three American car enthusiasts were coming to Russia in search of old cars. In addition, "agents" from Tennessee said they would be glad to show them rare Russian car collections that could be purchased once they landed.

"We brought over $30,000 or $40,000 in American cash, each of us taking a third of the pile of $100 bills," said Fritz. "We carried the cash in our jackets just in case they searched our checked luggage, which they never did. If they had, a less-than-honest customs agent might call his friends on the outside and you'd never be seen again.

"I must admit, though, that carrying around $40,000 cash was frightening, knowing that at the time tourists were being killed in Russia for as little as $200."

When they arrived in Moscow, they checked into a very nice hotel, which was owned by Lufthansa Airlines. It felt somewhat out of place at the very time when the economy of the Soviet Union was collapsing. The plan was to meet their Tennessee connections in the hotel lobby the next morning at 10 a.m.

By 11:30 a.m. they had not shown up.

So as Fritz, Reuter, and Ben waited and waited, an interpreter they had hired mentioned that he knew of a motorcycle collector nearby who might be interested in selling some bikes.

"Well, we weren't doing anything there in the hotel, so I said I would go look at them because the other two guys didn't know anything about motorcycles, and at least I knew a little," said Fritz.

Fritz and his interpreter drove across Moscow into an area crowded with apartment complexes. He was then asked by a young man to crawl through a 4-foot-tall window down under the sidewalk and into a dark basement. He didn't know if he would ever come out again.

He entered the 6-foot-tall basement, and it took a few minutes before his eyes could adjust to the dim light.

"The bikes he had down there were really neat," said Fritz. "There was a military Indian Model 741, which wasn't in very good shape. Then there was a military Harley-Davidson WLA 42, a Matchless, and a BMW R35. He also had several Russian motorcycles, but I wasn't really interested in those because there was really no market for them in the States."

Prior to the trip, Fritz had done some research about American motorcycles in Russia and discovered that the United States had given a couple of thousand Harleys and Indians to the Soviet government during

World War II to assist in fighting the Nazi Army. These bikes had been built to U.S. Army specifications but were basically street models that had some different details and were painted Olive Drab.

"I have no idea how he ever got the bikes down here, through that small opening next to the sidewalk," he said. "The owner was a young guy, probably between 25 and 28 years old. He was clean cut, good-looking, and calm. At this point in our trip, I didn't know who I could trust and who I couldn't trust, but dealing with this guy, I got the feeling that I could trust him."

Without consulting his colleagues, he decided to buy the bikes if they could be had for a fair price.

"I would never come up with a price first," he said. "I would always let the seller come up with a price and then say, 'That's way too much money.'

"Over time we realized that many of the Russians would start by asking $20,000 for a bike or car. When I'd tell them that was too much money, they'd say, 'OK, then how about $2,000?' We'd sometimes be able to negotiate down to $350."

Fritz's negotiation with the young fellow was much easier than most others they would experience, though. He paid about $200 for each bike, so he felt pretty good about his $800 investment when he joined his two colleagues back in the hotel lobby a little while later, who were still waiting for their Tennessee brokers.

"Hey, I think I just bought enough motorcycles to pay for our trip," he said. "I bought four of them."

Reuter was fine with the purchase, but the financier, Ben, was skeptical. "You bought motorcycles?" he asked. "What did you do that for?"

"I told him not to worry, we'd make money with them," said Fritz. "I figured they had to be worth at least $10,000, which would put this trip in the black."

Fritz had arranged with the bikes' owner to store them until shipping arrangements could be secured.

Their Tennessee brokers finally showed up the next morning, 24 hours after the appointed time. They led their fellow Yankees to a muddy, dirty field where a number of steel shipping containers were located that people used as garages. The steel doors had three locks on them so that the contents could not be stolen.

"They told us about this very rare four-wheel-drive Mercedes-Benz touring car that had been specially built for a Nazi field marshal," said Fritz. "It was something like a 1937 or '38 230 Mercedes.

"I looked at it and said to Rich, 'This is junk.' He said, 'I know.' " It was the body of a Mercedes mounted onto the chassis, suspension, and drivetrain from some sort of Soviet military truck. And he was trying to tell us that it was all original.

"We didn't want to say anything negative to this guy because who knows if he might turn up something worthwhile in the future."

The Tennessee brokers said they had an option to buy a rare Mercedes 770K and a Horch, but they were 900 miles away, and they needed to sell this Mercedes 4x4 before they could buy those cars. They also showed them photos of a Mercedes 500K and a Horch, which they said they had just sold and were on their way to America, and Fritz studied the photos carefully. He noticed a little red-and-blue sticker under the hood of the Horch and wondered what it might be for.

Fritz and his colleagues said they would be in touch and went searching for other cars in the Moscow area.

Their interpreter on this trip, Stash, was a sharp fellow, and he kept asking people throughout Moscow if they knew of any old cars that were for sale.

"We had seen so many cars, but most of them were junk," Fritz said. "Many had some sort of Russian engines adapted into them, were undesirable models, or were in such terrible condition that it didn't make any sense to ship them halfway around the world.

"But the motorcycles kept showing up."

Finally, after they had spent a week in Russia, they were preparing to go home, empty-handed except for the four vintage motorcycles they had secured on the first day they arrived. But clearly, it was rare old cars that would command a small fortune back home that they were after.

Then, at 10 p.m. the night before they had planned to leave, they got a call from Stash. He told them of a friend of his who had a bunch of valuable cars.

"OK, let's go," said Fritz.

So they drove to the outskirts of Moscow and met an interesting, neat older fellow who sported a full beard.

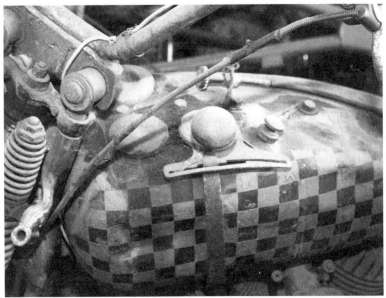

*Lee Klancher*

"He was apparently a famous artist in Russia. We talked with him for quite a while, then he invited us to see his cars and motorcycles he had in the barn," said Fritz.

"He had quite a few interesting cars and bikes, including a familiar Mercedes 540K and Horch. When he opened the Horch hood to show us the engine, I saw that red-and-blue sticker that I had seen in those photos from the Tennessee guys. I said to Rich, 'Those cars belong to this guy!' Reuter replied, 'I know.'"

The artist said he enjoyed inviting people to tour his collection and take photos, but he wasn't interested in selling any of them. That's when they realized their Tennessee friends were, in fact, con artists.

So Fritz, Reuter, and Ben returned home without having purchased any ultra-rare classics but secure in their purchase of the four vintage motorcycles.

"We went home without finding any real treasures, but we knew we'd be going back again soon," said Fritz.

A few weeks later, Reuter got word from a friend that a Swede named Peter had contacted her and said he had found an armor-plated

Mercedes 540K in Estonia that was for sale. That's all Fritz, Reuter, and Ben needed to hear; they made reservations and flew back to Moscow as soon as they could.

Once in Moscow, they boarded a train for the 11-hour trip to St. Petersburg, then another 11-hour trip to the former Soviet territory of Estonia. They rode in the second-class section so they wouldn't stand out as wealthy Americans. Once in their four-berth sleeping unit, Fritz took a metal clothes hanger he had packed to wire the two door levers shut from the inside so they couldn't be robbed while they slept.

Peter the Swede, a 40-something-year-old adventure-seeker who sported a ponytail and specialized in finding World War II vintage aircraft, met them at the train station. Because he was essentially a scavenger of old things, he said he would occasionally come upon cars and motorcycles as well. Peter, who had once spent prison time in Morocco, was very street-wise, according to Fritz, and had once worked for former race driver Bob Grossman's classic car shop in Southampton, New York.

Peter picked up the Americans at the train station with his 1979 Chevy Nova, making Fritz and his companions a little more comfortable in the foreign land. He informed his passengers that through his friends in the Old Car Club of Estonia, he had arranged for an afternoon visit to a man with an armor-plated Mercedes-Benz called the Aktion P.

Fritz had done research on the Aktion P cars, mostly through an excellent story that had appeared in Volume 28, Issue 1 of *Automobile Quarterly*, and discovered that the heavy-gauge steel plate used inside lightweight aluminum bodywork and the 1 1/2-inch-thick windshield and side glass made the car virtually bulletproof. The aluminum body, in addition to keeping the overall weight of the car lighter than a steel body, also prevented magnetic bombs from being planted on it, which was apparently a popular assassination technique at the time. The car also was built sans running boards to keep unwanted passengers from hitching a ride and threatening occupants. A total of 20 Aktion Ps were built in 1943 and used by Hitler and his top officials.

Of the 20 Aktion P armored cars produced, only one was known to exist; that lone survivor sat in a museum in Prague. The rest were reputedly destroyed by angry mobs after the war ended because they symbolized Nazi aggression.

At 4 p.m., Peter drove the Americans to a small farm outside of the city of Tallinn, the largest in Estonia. They looked inside the barn, which was beginning to fall in on itself, and saw piles of "stuff."

"There were old car parts, bicycles, all sorts of metal parts, just 7-foot-high unorganized piles of junk," said Fritz. "You couldn't even walk into the barn without climbing on the piles."

"There's no car in there," said Reuter.

There was a rope hanging from the rafters that Peter the Swede used to swing himself to the back of the barn, where he began looking around.

"Is there a car back there?" asked Reuter.

"Well, there are pieces of a car," answered Peter.

The aluminum body was here, the chassis was leaning against the wall over there, the fenders over there. Peter used a flashlight to read the chassis numbers to the Americans: "408377." This particular car had been assigned to the motor pool at the Third Reich Chancellery in Berlin, so it had been used by Adolf Hitler, Eva Braun, and virtually all the other Nazi high officials and generals.

Fritz and his colleagues had to control their enthusiasm, not wanting the car's owner to see their delight. Reuter later said that it was like winning the lottery. They had just discovered the only other surviving Aktion P.

The owner confirmed that other major components—the engine, rear axle, doors, and so on—were in five other barns in the area. The car was complete when he bought it many years earlier. He explained he had dismantled the car when his teenage daughter was very young because the KGB spy organization, the Estonian Old Car Club, and various other groups knew of the car and wanted it. At one point, the Russian Mafia had threatened to disfigure his young daughter if he didn't present them with the car. After taking it apart, he simply told those interested parties that he had sold it.

"He said he wanted something unique, and that's why he bought it," said Fritz. "He collected lots of things, including a vintage Cleveland motorcycle. He asked if we could stop by our local Cleveland dealership when we returned home and buy a repair manual and some parts for him. I had to explain that the original Cleveland company had been out of business for many years."

*Lee Klancher*

After they had dug out many of the parts, the three Americans huddled in the Nova to discuss their next move. "We wanted it," said Fritz. "We were prepared to pay $50,000, $100,000, $200,000, whatever it took to own that car."

They sent their translator to the car's owner to ask how much he wanted for the car. When the translator returned, they couldn't believe their ears; he wasn't interested in selling it!

"We said, 'What?' " said Fritz.

Not wanting to waste any more time, the Americans bid farewell and continued to follow up other cars and motorcycles in the Estonian countryside.

"We looked at some Maybachs, great big sedans, but they were missing too many parts or were too badly deteriorated," said Fritz. "One rare, custom-bodied Maybach we saw had been cut up into 2-foot-by-2-foot pieces and stored in an 8-foot-by-8-foot shed. It was a rare car, but you could never restore a car that was destroyed that badly."

They returned to Tallinn and tried for several days to buy the Aktion P. Having no success, they flew home with no valuable cars but had purchased four more motorcycles, leaving Peter and his two Estonian friends to try to pry the Aktion P from its owner.

After many phone calls to Peter they learned that maybe if they returned to Estonia they could buy the Mercedes. They first flew to Moscow and pursued several motorcycle leads. One address was on the fifth floor of an Estonian apartment complex. They walked into the young man's small apartment to see his Harley-Davidson WLA 42 in the living room. Another partially assembled motorcycle was leaning against the wall, and wheels, tires, gas tanks, and other parts were neatly stacked on top of cabinets and along the floor.

"We took the elevator up here," said Fritz. "It was about 3 feet square. How did you get these motorcycles up here?"

The young man, Victor, explained that he and a friend had carried them up 5 stories, 10 flights of stairs. He said the threat of theft from parking them on the street was too great.

"He started the motorcycle up right in his apartment just to prove it ran," said Fritz. "Luckily he was a young guy with no family. He actually spoke a few words of English because he watched American television programs."

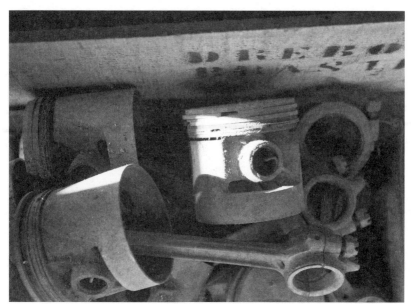

*Lee Klancher*

They bought the Harley for about $800 and arranged to keep the bike stored in the apartment until shipping could be arranged.

From there it was off to another motorcycle collector, this one a father and son who ran a semilegitimate repair and restoration shop in the basement of their building.

"The son would restore bikes to a pretty low quality, but at least he got them back on the road again," said Fritz. "They had a few Indians, but they had a strange method for negotiating the price. It was early evening, and they said we should go to the café to have a glass of vodka. At 3 a.m., we left the café, having consumed five bottles of vodka! But we bought a nice Indian 741 for about $1,200.

"We were in pretty bad shape the next day, though."

They also inspected another Indian, a 1919 model, in another fellow's apartment. Fritz said the bike was very nice for its age, at least what he could see of it.

"The guy hadn't paid his electric bill for his apartment, so the lights had been turned off," said Fritz. "I had to inspect the bike using a cigarette lighter as a flashlight.

"Even though we really wanted the bike, we could never come to an agreement on price, so we left his apartment empty-handed."

They also bought another rare BMW R75 complete with a sidecar. An interesting feature of that sidecar was that its wheel was driven with a driveshaft from the rear wheel of the motorcycle, making it two-wheel drive and excellent for the duty that model performed during General Rommel's assault on Africa.

After a busy three days, Fritz and Ben returned to Estonia to talk with the Aktion P owner. Another four days of talks failed to have the Mercedes in their hands, so Fritz packed for a flight to America the next morning. Reuter, who had stayed in Moscow to hunt for more cars, would meet Fritz at the airport the next day to fly back with him. But the Aktion P, the prize they had sought, still eluded them. Ben had decided to stay in Estonia to try to secure its purchase one more time. Fritz went to bed early, and Ben went to the owner's home in the countryside for more negotiations.

"At 5 in the morning, Ben comes bounding into the hotel room shouting, 'We got the car. We got the car. Get up! You have to figure out how to get the car to America,'" said Fritz. "I told him that if he was kidding me, I'd kill him."

Ben negotiated a complicated deal that included "a lot of cash," Fritz's old Mercedes station wagon, and an American boarding school education for the man's daughter.

"What?" Fritz asked, still in a slumber. But once Ben explained the deal, and that the man's daughter's education was his highest priority, it made sense. When Reuter arrived at the airport from Moscow to meet Fritz and he wasn't there, Reuter knew something was up and went to the motel where Fritz and Ben were staying.

The third trip a few weeks later was virtually dedicated to packing up the Aktion P in order to sneak it out of the country under the cover of darkness. The car's exit from Estonia was complicated but included two rented cargo planes, an 18-wheeler, several delivery vans, payments to the general manager of an airport, hush money, and a foggy night, making their escape that much more hazardous. But after several stressful days trying to stay out of the sight of undesirable Estonians, the car and its new owners escaped and were headed for America. Between the purchase of four motorcycles and the Aktion P, the third trip had been the charm.

The group, now energized from their daring purchase and escape, made a total of seven trips to the former Soviet Union, looking for cars, motorcycles, and even World War II aircraft.

"On one trip, Reuter, Peter the Swede, and I flew across Siberia to the Kuril Islands to see if there [were] any World War II American warplanes to be had," said Fritz. "It was somewhat frightening flying to Petropavlosk on the Komchatka peninsula across the 11 time zones of Russia, over the nothingness of Siberia.

"We took a two-hour helicopter ride to Seviro Kurilsk, a city of 4,500 on the third northernmost island, and drove to some of the old Japanese airbases that had existed there before the Russian occupation," said Fritz. "They did find a number of dismantled King Cobras, Japanese Zeros, and Betty bombers, as well as old tanks and military trucks, but we decided not to pursue them. There was just some bad feeling we had about the area, and we just didn't feel safe being there."

They returned to Moscow and St. Petersburg to search for more motorcycles. One gentleman they met invited them over to his large basement to see his collection. On the way there, he drove them on a piece of elevated roadway that was about 1,000 feet across and 6 or 7 miles long.

"He explained to us that underneath the road they were driving on was every type of military vehicle you could think of—trucks, tanks, airplanes— and about 1 million people," said Fritz. "This was the Memorial Highway that contained the remains of the city of Leningrad [St. Petersburg] after the Germans had attacked. That was a sobering experience.

"When we made it to his country house, he showed us a very nice Harley-Davidson and a nice Mercedes 170, both of which we purchased. But he was a tough negotiator because he never reduced his price but instead kept adding other items into the deal.

"As we were writing up the deal, he mentioned that it was a shame we weren't there six weeks earlier because he had just sold two Auto Union Grand Prix race cars.

"We said, 'What?' Then he showed us the photo of the two rear-engined cars in the basement and explained that he had just sold them six weeks earlier to a collector from Europe.

"Can you believe that? These are the priceless cars that Audi restored and displays today."

The Mercedes, which was purchased for $19,000, never made it to the States. Fritz figures the car was probably stolen before it reached the dock in what was probably an "inside job" among the shipping agents.

On another trip, the trio was invited into a barn that was loaded with old motorcycles and parts.

"This guy had a two-story building stacked with parts, and they were fairly neat and organized," said Fritz. "Upstairs he had gas tanks lined up, wheels, sidecars, fenders, handlebars, and frames. Downstairs he had complete bikes. It was an impressive collection, but his prices were very high, so we didn't buy anything from him."

A number of the bikes they looked at were sitting outside and too far gone to make good investments. One they did purchase was a BMW R75 with a sidecar that had been sitting in a field with grass growing through its frame and wheels.

In all, Fritz believes he inspected at least 100 motorcycles and purchased just 14. Only 3 of the 14 ran, but all of them were nearly 80 to 90 percent complete.

The least amount of money they paid for a motorcycle was $200, and the most they paid was $4,000 for a bright green Indian. They figured that if they could buy a motorcycle and have it transported to the United States for an average of $2,000 each, there would be a healthy profit when they were sold for $7,000 or $8,000 each.

Fritz wishes they had purchased more BMW R75s with sidecars. These turned out to be the most valuable and desirable to buyers in the United States.

"These were made for the Nazis fighting in the Sahara Desert, and they had a few special features to cope with the environment, such as supplemental air filters. The extra-large air cleaner looked like a Nazi helmet that sat on top of the gas tank," said Fritz. "Air would come up inside the helmet and then down through a tube through the center of the gas tank and into the carburetor.

"These bikes were built for the desert, but when Rommel was defeated, they were shipped to Russia for the German offensive against the Russians on the Eastern Front. When Germany was defeated, all those bikes were just left there.

"After the war, Russia took everything of value they could out of Germany, including the contents of the BMW factory. Soon, Russia was pumping out BMW clones, which they still continue to build versions of today.

"We sold the BMWs for between $8,000 and $10,000, when they were probably worth closer to $20,000."

And even though they didn't buy any of the spare parts they discovered, Fritz said that they did see piles of spare parts as well. "The most interesting was an Ariel Square Four engine and a sidecar with an opening in the front that looked like a jet plane," he said.

"We really didn't make any money on the bikes, but it did pay for our trips."

All 14 bikes were crated and packed into one 20-foot storage container that was put on a ship in Tallinn and arrived in New York a few weeks later. Total shipping cost was about $2,000.

Soon after the bike booty arrived at Fritz's Amerispec shop in Danbury, Connecticut, he brought a couple of his discovered motorcycles to the huge Super Sunday motorcycle rally held nearby. The bikes were a hit.

Instead of marketing the motorcycles in *Hemmings Motor News* or the *New York Times*, all the bikes were sold through word-of-mouth. Fritz said that they were satisfied with the profits their motorcycle sales generated but admits that today, with the extensive use of the Internet, he would utilize sites like eBay to generate a higher return.

Fritz has had many years to reflect since taking the most dynamic barn-finding expedition of a lifetime in 1992. First, he believes there are still places around the world that offer treasure hunters opportunities to search and buy long-forgotten vehicles.

"I think Africa probably still has World War II relics," he said, "especially if you were hunting for motorcycles like the BMW R75 and aircraft. Things certainly wouldn't rust very badly there. And I believe that treasures still exist in Russia."

Fritz believes that searching for cars in Russia would be safer now than it was 16 years ago.

Russians are good negotiators, said Fritz. "They are calculating, rational, and very intelligent," he said. "Remember, some of the best chess players in the world are Russians."

The most unusual negotiation Fritz was involved in was for a motorcycle. Negotiations had ended because Fritz thought the asking price was too high. "Then the seller pulled me aside and informed him that for this price, it included a Russian girl. I said, 'What do you mean a Russian girl?' The seller said, 'We have a lot of Russian girls here. If you want for one night, two nights, she's included in the price.'

"I said, 'No, thank you very much. All we are after is cars and motorcycles; we don't want to bring anything else home.'"

Fritz and his colleagues feel best about the boarding school education they were able to give to the daughter of the Estonian Aktion P owner. She attended two years at an exclusive private school in Massachusetts and, now in her early 30s and again living in Estonia, still stays in touch with them.

Now that Fritz is older and hopefully wiser, has he thought about making another Russian treasure hunt, knowing the risks involved?

"It does occur to me occasionally," he said. "But it's usually after a large meal where I've had too much to drink. In the middle of the night I wake up in a sweat having just dreamed about going back there.

"I've actually heard of a rare Mercedes 500 fastback called the Autobahn Carrier that is sitting in Iran. It was built to celebrate speed record runs on the Autobahn and once belonged to the Shah of Iran. I've seen pictures of it, but am I going there? No way! Maybe someday the conditions will exist to safely go over there and get that car, but I don't see that happening soon.

"With all the dangers we encountered—potential theft, kidnapping, death, Mafia, KGB, and disorganized crime—the modern-day treasure hunt was worthwhile only because of the Aktion P, which was quite valuable. I wouldn't relish being killed over a BMW motorcycle.

"Because you're only crazy once."

# Mechanical Minded

## By Kris Palmer

*Motorcycle Survivor*

*Tips and Tales in the Unrestored Realm*

Parker House Publishing, 2010

THE MECHANICAL MINDED—to those who are not—are people who know how things work. If you have this disease, you know its symptoms are more serious, no easier to shake off than measles or a broken arm. To the mechanical minded, an old device with gears, levers, and shafts is not just accessible. It's irresistible. Regardless of size, purpose, or value, it will stop you, seize you, draw the full band of your intellectual powers into its quirks and cleverness. You'll study it, learn its underlying necessity and invention, and send a mental nod across time to the craftsman who solved a problem with his hands and his wit.

When of this mind frame, you can't walk away from vintage handiwork without wishing you hadn't. Either you'll go back and study the creation or be haunted by the lost opportunity, the insight you might have gained and built upon with a little scrutiny.

The Chantlands have mechanical minds. Fascinating machines dominate their world, from the rare, the strange, the highly acclaimed, to objects as simple as a mousetrap, a pulley, or a hand-cranked butter slicer. How others value these devices is no concern to them—except that investment hunters make their lives more expensive. What matters is the genius, the passion, the skill, or the sense of humor that went into producing it.

Take Sid Chantland's storage shop. With a rifle sight, you couldn't pick a line from one end to the other without a dozen car, bike, or household curiosities getting in the way. If it's old, if it's cleverly built—and especially if it's unrestored—it belongs here. As he says of his bikes, "It doesn't have to be shiny for me to love it."

In his space, a Model A with 11,000 miles sits beside a 1948 Triumph Speed Twin with 50. Behind the Ford rests an original Excelsior whose early-style throttle and magneto linkage would delight Rube Goldberg— the straight portions of the handlebars twist, rotating flanges that move

*Jerry Lee*

sections of straight rod through ball joints and pivoting arms from the handgrips along the bars then down the headset and back along the top of the engine to the fuel and spark controls. This mechanical cable-precursor alone deserves a full minute of study. There are years of minutes here.

Five more steps and a 1916 Model T stops you cold. It wears hand-brushed black paint—now flaking—original folding top, and original seat leather, pleated, faded, and checked. A plate-glass windshield, top pane folded down, seems harmless enough, like stacked swords behind a paper screen. The only clue to its hazards is a long crack wandering across as it would on a picture window—no safety glass here, not in these original panes. Unrestored, un-"improved," this Ford is a freeze-frame of early automotive history.

In front of the untampered-with T is a creation no Chantland could resist: a homemade bike built from everything but motorcycle parts. The engine is 1928 Chevrolet, the frame rails Model T, the radiator a modified chicken-coop heater; the fenders are their automotive counterparts reshaped and riveted, while the handlebars are cut from tubular table legs. Wheels are motorcar, the rear, only, fitted with a band brake (plan your stops a day in advance). The headset is a Model T wheel hub; steering inputs run through extended Model T steering links connecting the handlebars to the homemade fork. Spanning the nose of this beast—mottled, tapered, dented, and beautiful in its hand-fabricated homeliness—is a long tank for coolant, not fuel. (The gas tank is at midship.) Nothing from *The Great Race* boasts more imagination than this bike, and it's fully functional. Sid has ridden it. He even has a photo of the farmer who created it in 1939.

Even the surrounding walls and ceiling deserve a look. Built in the early 1900s, Sid's building has served many purposes over the decades, including as a casting-pattern factory. As much of the original work and craftsmanship as can be saved, will be, and Sid goes old, not new, when looking for doors, windows, and details. Like his brother and father, he knows architectural salvage and antiques dealers as well as auctioneers.

All three Chantlands own old buildings. Rough-cut beams from old-growth trees, in widths and lengths unavailable today (back when a 2x4 really was 2 inches by 4 inches), have the right feel of home to this family. The lumber in their structures was hand-felled and hauled by horse teams. One plank with a sawmill's 100-year-old mark will catch a Chantland's eye—the same way they will find a pinstriper's random brush marks on the bottom of a motorcycle fuel tank where he made a few strokes to remove excess paint from the bristles before striping the visible surface.

The mechanical gene comes from Bob, who began tinkering as a child. His family had no money, so at age 12 or 13, he started building his own motorbikes, affixing Briggs & Stratton engines to bicycles. The first examples had a wooden pulley that rubbed on the rear tire—no clutch development at this young age. Bob also learned the bartering art, trading up from his homemade stuff to factory-built scooters and minibikes.

His first full-size motorcycle was a '48 Indian Chief that a friend of the owner's had wrecked trying to see how fast it would go. Bob was 16 and paid $45 or $50 for the bike, which was resting on its "belly"—bent fork removed—in a large, frozen puddle in a leaky shed. Bob and his father had to chisel it out and then straighten the fork, as well as possible, with a blowtorch and a sledgehammer. They freed stuck valves with a liberal soaking in Liquid Wrench, whose distinctive smell to this day immediately triggers Bob's memory of working on this bike. He got it on the road, then swapped it the following year for a '57 Mercury motor to go in his '56 Ford.

In 1965, Bob purchased his first brand-new bike, a Triumph Bonneville. He rode it on the street for a year before his interest in drag racing changed the way he looked at it. Out came the wrenches and off came all parts that weren't holding it together or making it go. Bob ran at the drag strip on that bike and others for about five years, doing as well as a guy can expect with no budget and no sponsors. Mainly, it was a thrill and a chance to bond with some other guys who loved motorcycles and a mechanical challenge.

For a while, Bob had a related business making aluminum barrel castings to convert 650 Triumph engines into 750s. Members of the go-fast crowd were interested, though not always in paying for them. "Racers wanted your stuff free," Bob remembers, "because they thought they were going to make you famous." He sold about 500 or 600 of them, a number much smaller than the potential market because he had a hard time getting quality castings. If he could have solved that problem, he figures he could have sold thousands.

Like his father, Sid got into bikes as a kid. He still has his Honda 50 MiniTrail. He spent a lot of time on dirt bikes, including trips to Mexico's Baja peninsula. In the mid-1980s, he was in the service stationed in Germany, where he capitalized on the chance to cover all of Europe by bike—a Honda XLV 750 R. Brother Scott likewise grew up with a set of handlebars never far from reach. Collecting bikes was a natural extension of riding them, and other stuff followed. Sid calls it "a hobby gone haywire" and attributes it to "bad genes," by which he means good genes. Their affliction serves motorcycle lovers past, present, and future.

Bob still has some of his racing stuff, or Sid does. Or Scott. One of Bob's old drag bikes is in Sid's building, but it might take a few seconds for them to remember who owns it. The Chantlands like the same sorts of things, and they buy and sell between themselves without necessarily moving anything. If you're fortunate enough to be exploring the collection with all three men, Bob might identify a bike, Scott will rattle off some interesting details, and Sid will announce that he recently found the receipt from when he, or Bob or Scott, bought it.

*Jerry Lee*

Their knowledge pool is amazing, both as to what the factories built and what they own themselves. Because they admire the same skills and ingenuity, they are equally fascinated by almost everything any of them has collected. When Sid mentions that he has a DKW from World War II, Bob says that a bullet hole passes right through the exhaust pipe. Scott adds that the slug is still lodged in the engine's cooling fins. Because a bike's history is part of what makes it interesting, having three minds storing cool details keeps the collection's facts and stories well preserved, particularly for the gems.

And there are gems.

Having the Chantlands as a chapter in an unrestored motorcycle book is silly in a way. Unrestored bikes could be a section in a book on the Chantlands and all the fascinating things they own and acquire. They have dozens of motorcycles still in their original paint with the original seats, motors, wheels, and mirrors. Some have their original tires. A few have the original battery, never filled. Bob has 1940s bikes new in their original crates, unridden, unassembled, parts still wrapped in paper at factories that no longer exist by workers no longer around.

One of Bob's great finds is his 1954 Vincent Black Shadow, which a schoolteacher bought new in the crate in 1956. The teacher had numerous motorcycles and was a huge literature collector. He'd write to manufacturers and ask them to send him their brochures. He also amassed thousands of magazines. When he passed away, his collection went to his brother, a farmer. A friend of Bob's who used to ride Vincents when he was younger put him on to it. Bob bought 10 to 15 bikes, plus the literature, about 25 years ago. The Black Shadow has clocked only 2,597 miles and is original and unrestored, right down to the tires. To the untrained eye, it looks like a new motorcycle.

There's another prize too. Bob says, "I get great pleasure out of saying the holy grail of antique American motorcycles isn't a Harley." It's a Cyclone, made in Saint Paul, Minnesota. A dozen or so are known to exist, but most of them are Cyclone engines in an Indian or other chassis. When bikes were scrapped in the early days (the company went under in 1916), the engine was often saved because farmers used them to run pumps and generators before electricity was widespread. Because Indian chassis are abundant and somewhat similar, they offer a means to build a Cyclone for

*Jerry Lee*

someone with an engine. Cyclones with their original frames are scarce, and only two are known with their original paint—Bob's and the bike once campaigned by Don Johns, a racer for the Cyclone factory.

Sid's sweet bikes include the Triumph above, a half dozen other rare and low-mileage Triumphs, the gorgeous original-paint early Rudge pictured here, old drag bikes, scooters, and many other treats. Even modest items can be unique, like the World War II–era scooter converted to steam power by some restless innovator looking to avoid gas rationing.

These bikes just scratch the surface of the Chantland collection, or collections, if you view them as separate entities. Bikes are just a portion of the total machinery. Sid probably has 100 mousetraps, some more than a century old, focusing mankind's creativity on a single ancient adversary. He has antique fans, too, and Scott has discovered a fondness for old refrigerators.

Together, their accumulated creations capture much of the ingenuity of the last 100-plus years. They might joke that they are captives of their sprawling possessions, but that's a modest, self-deprecating view. It's amazing what these men have amassed. If you could touch an object and travel back in time the years in its age, just imagine where this collection could take you. Touch a bike from 1910 and an 1895 mousetrap and you're back in George Washington's lifetime. Add Sid's building and Bob's and two bikes from the '40s, and Christopher Columbus still lives. But there are hundreds of bikes here, plus cars, furniture, lights, signs, castings, fans, mousetraps, and sweepers. The collective age of Bob's bikes alone extends back before the time of Christ. Add Sid's, just his bikes, and you can verify the sets in *Raiders of the Lost Ark* by viewing the real pharaohs at the height of their powers.

There's so much history here, so much creativity, artistry, and genius. Just a few hours of walking among these bikes makes you feel a little smarter, a little more in touch with the industrial age. Whether peculiar to you or as familiar as your own face in the mirror, the mechanical mind is a gift to all.

# Chapter 3 On the Fringe

"From the time I was eleven the **Hells Angels** were my **surrogate family.** As a homeless child on the streets of San Francisco, I was their little **mascot"**

—Adele Kubin, *Grease under the Angel's Wings*

# Grease under the Angel's Wings

By Adele Kubin

*International Journal of Motorcycle Studies*

March 2006

*The girls stood quietly in a group, wearing tight slacks, kerchiefs, and sleeveless blouses or sweaters, with boots and dark glasses, uplift bras, bright lipstick, and the weary expressions of half-bright souls turned mean and nervous from too much bitter wisdom in too few years.*
—Hunter Thompson, *Hells Angels*, 1966

NOT QUITE. Hunter never understood us girls, at least not all of us. That September night back in 1966 when he finally got his ass pounded, and his book ended, most of the Daly City chapter of the Angels were at the Top Hat Bar in Redwood City. Lisa and I were taking a powder when we heard the commotion. Guys came running in, craning necks over the crowd trying to figure out what happened. Simple story. Hunter had finally pissed off one of the guys enough to get his chops smacked and his welcome card revoked. End of Hunter's story. A few months back I had asked Thompson what he was doing hanging with the club. Writing a book about bikers, he said. I thought that was a crazy topic to pick, but the guys tolerated him for a while, kind of like an amusement, like a crazy person in a small village. They tolerated me too, but differently.

From the time I was eleven the Hells Angels were my surrogate family. As a homeless child on the streets of San Francisco, I was their little mascot. Contrary to popular belief, not all young girls were treated as chattel. The president of the Daly City chapter took me under his wing and protected me until I was fledged. Danny and I are still friends. I grew up with the club. During our time together they gave me encouragement and support, the know-how to build my own bike, and from that beginning, a chance to rebuild my life.

Midnight, January 20, 1979. I was riding with Danny and the boys headed to a party at Le Chateau, an old mansion turned nightclub on the summit of the California Coast Range above Santa Cruz. Route 280 made me nervous. Deer crossings were common, and the last thing I wanted to do on this stormy night was hit a deer with a motorcycle on a dark country road.

I tucked my chin into the collar of my leather jacket trying to hide from the half-frozen rain. The steady vibrato of the Harley engine reassured me. All of my life I had distrusted my own abilities. Things hadn't worked out as I hoped. I'd lost my family, my home, even my name. So I expected troubles from the cycle, too, and for some good reasons. My army surplus trike was built on a 35-year-old frame and a small budget with old tools and parts I'd scrounged from swap meets and out-of-the-way bike shops all over the West Coast. The smell of carburetor cleaner, fresh oil, and new paint reminded me that this was, after all, our maiden voyage. Something could indeed come loose, come out of adjustment, or fly apart. But it was my bike, and I wanted to ride.

More rain. I could hear the rumble of the other Harleys behind me. Once again I cursed the person whose idea it had been to put me at the head of the pack. Someone had decided that since I was the only female and with the slowest machine, I should be in front so they wouldn't lose me. I protested that I didn't know where the turn-off to Le Chateau was but to no avail.

I was concentrating on the deer-ridden road in front when I realized the noise behind had shifted direction. Damn! I looked back. The pack had turned off. They were dropping away on a diverging road now 10 feet below down a steep stone embankment. Without really thinking about the consequences I cranked the handlebars, twisted the throttle, and launched off the cliff. Into the air I went, flying, on a homebuilt, World War II, three-wheeled Harley-Davidson. Not many people ever have that sensation, or the next one. Crunch! I landed with enough force to knock the wind out of me, but still rolling, and right in front of the pack where I had started. I could hear the hollering and hurrahs above the wind and engine noise. When I turned around, everyone was waving hands and cheering. I was stunned. What a stupid thing to do, and it worked! I rode on, benumbed, a silly smile on my face.

Later, at the nightclub, amid the sounds of revving bikes and loud rock and roll, the boys offered praise: "We've never seen anyone with balls like that!" "You are one bad chick!" "That bike you put together stayed together!" They surrounded me, picked me up, carried me into the building, tried to buy me beers. I planted myself upon a table, leaned back against the wall, closed my eyes, and listened to the music. Here was peace. I was in the safest place among the safest company I could imagine. Beloved and admired by the guys, I was finally warm, and with my own motorcycle. Life was good.

Later, Danny and I sat in a darkened hallway, heads together so we could hear above the music, talking as we did whenever we got some privacy from the gang. "You're the best friend I've ever had," he told me. "How'll I ever find anyone else like you?" I was the only person who never wanted anything from him. He was Danny Reb, the Prez, a legend, the most respected member of the club. Outsiders, wannabes, and hangers-on who rode with us were constantly trying to impress and befriend him. I just liked him. I understood Danny. He was a good person, self-raised in a mean-streets world surviving the only ways he knew how. I'd been there, too. We shared empathy and affection. If anyone wanted his ear they spoke to me, knowing he'd listen to what I had to say.

"I've got to go now," I said. Danny understood me, too. Times were changing. On the margins, the club was being pulled down into organized crime, to drug dealing and violence directed by outsiders. Money was replacing loyalty; fear was replacing respect. I knew if I stayed much longer I'd have to do things I didn't want to, things that I could never forget or forgive. Danny knew it, too. "It's time for you to get out of here, go up to Oregon like you're always talking, start that gardening business." I've always loved the land: plants and soil and trees and open spaces. I always wanted to live by the work of my hands, making things grow, caring for nature. Now I'd try. "I want you to be careful up there," Danny offered. "It's hard for me to know you're somewhere I can't protect you." It was then I realized how much Danny cared and that he wanted the best for me. He was truly the best friend I ever had, willing to give me up, see me gone, just so I could have a chance to be happier, a chance he never would find. It was the most unselfish act anyone had ever done for me. I moved toward the door, the room now thick with booze and party noise. The guys gave me more hugs, friendly words, cheers. But they knew, too. I was leaving. Danny's friend, the lost kid on the slow trike, was headed out for the last time.

I walked out into the night. The rain had stopped. Moonbeams through the misty redwoods shone silver on the wet highway. Collar up, gloves and glasses on, I kicked the bike over, headed down the road. Gliding around curves, I thought about Danny and the boys and the changes that were happening to me. After all these years, on the streets, doubting, afraid, getting by, there was hope. With the help of good friends, biker friends, Hells Angels, I finally had the strength to choose a new life, find new roads to ride, and new things to do when I got there.

**Note:** As Thompson tells it in his book, his terminal trouncing took place a hundred miles north of here. Neither the guys nor I ever understood why.

# The Gang's All Here

## By Mark Singer

Hollister, California

WITHOUT PREJUDICE, I passed up the chance last month to buy a five-dollar copy of a panoramic photograph inscribed "Northern California Gypsy Tour, Bolado Park, Hollister, California, 1937." It depicted three hundred or so peaceable-looking citizens (motorcyclists, most of them minus their machines), plus several children—a clean-cut bunch, lounging on the grass, attired as if about to head off for some tennis. A charming enough artifact, I thought, but not one that offered any insight into what makes the present-day Hollister economy go ka-boom every Fourth of July weekend, when between eighty thousand and a hundred thousand bikers and gawkers descend upon the place.

Ten years after that photograph was taken, a far more memorable and consequential portrait was snapped, this time on San Benito Street, Hollister's main drag, in front of Johnny's Bar & Grill. That photograph is still the centerpiece of the behind-the-counter décor at Johnny's, framed along with the cover logo from the July 21, 1947, issue of *Life*, in which it was first published. It shows a heavyset fellow in a motoring cap, khakis, and leather boots straddling a motorcycle while clutching a beer bottle, with several empties lying in the foreground. A headline and subhead say, "CYCLISTS' HOLIDAY: HE AND FRIENDS TERRORIZE A TOWN," and a one-paragraph caption describes a Fourth of July debauch—how "4,000 members of a motorcycle club roared into Hollister . . . quickly tired of ordinary motorcycle thrills and turned to more exciting stunts." Traffic laws were flouted, vehicles were "rammed into restaurants and bars, breaking furniture and mirrors. . . . Police arrested many for drunkenness and indecent exposure but could not restore order."

No one in Hollister today minds—nor, it seems, did anyone protest in 1947—that this journalistic account was based upon a mostly fictitious premise. What actually materialized that Fourth of July was the equivalent of a couple of frat parties on steroids—an unseemly exhibition of drunken, uncouth behavior, perpetrated by a gathering of out-of-town motorcyclists who temporarily had the constabularies overmatched but who in the end paid their traffic fines and did their brief time in the pokey. The celebrated photograph was staged the day after the noise subsided. Instead of a terrorist invader, the loutish-looking beer guzzler was a photographer's prop—a poseur in a tableau that was lifelike up to a point, but above all *Life*-like, and basically bogus. Nevertheless, the episode proved, in the long run, to be extremely good for business.

In 1996, a year shy of the fiftieth anniversary of the *Life* photograph and whatever had led up to it, some biker-friendly Hollister boosters began envisioning the first Hollister Independence Rally. "A group got together and approached the city," Ellen Brown, the current executive director of the rally, told me. "But the city-government people were not holding their arms open. They didn't want a reenactment of 1947, as they understood it. They weren't looking forward to raping and pillaging." The group persevered, however, and the necessary permits were granted. Though many businesses boarded up for the weekend, the 1997 event proceeded without serious complications. "By the third year," Brown said, "we had won most people over."

Nowadays, the local establishment proudly proclaims Hollister "the birthplace of the American biker," mindful, no doubt, that the image commonly evoked by the term "American biker" is not the weekend hobbyist—the Orange County accountant or the San Fernando Valley dermatologist who gets his jollies riding his Harley-Davidson Road King to the golf course—but the hairy prole in greasy Levi's, the lineal descendant of the cowboy who has skipped several consecutive Saturday-night baths, the creature who would just as soon dismantle a small California town as overhaul an engine. Which is to say that Hollister has deliberately embraced a cliché whose provenance can be traced to Marlon Brando's performance as the alienated antihero of Stanley Kramer's 1954 movie *The Wild One*. For some reason, most bikers have been willing to overlook that *The Wild One*, in addition to being the first biker picture, was the first laughably awful biker picture. Hollister, in particular, has a proprietary fondness for the movie, a fondness rooted in the fact that

*The Wild One* was Hollywood's lame imagining of Hollister's mythical invasion of 1947.

Motorcyclists have been gravitating to Hollister (population thirty-five thousand, seat of San Benito County) at least since the nineteen-twenties, attracted by an oval dirt racetrack near downtown as well as by hills that offer ideal terrain for climbing competitions. Until the Hollister Independence Rally came along, the local economy was mainly dependent upon agriculture (apricots, cherries, apples, lettuce, peppers, onions), although the southern outskirts of Silicon Valley are within commuting distance. I arrived in Hollister a couple of days before the crowds gathered for this year's proceedings, and my first stop was the rally headquarters. As I chatted with Ellen Brown, a friendly, efficient woman in her early forties, a caller delivered the news that a banner that had been strung between utility poles on San Benito Street was welcoming visitors to, oops, the 2001 instead of the 2002 rally. "It's hard to find good free help," Brown said. "But if that's the biggest problem we have this week, we're doing pretty well." This was a not-very-oblique reference to the very real apprehension that this year something truly frightful might happen in Hollister.

Last April, during a motorcycle rally in Laughlin, Nevada, an early-morning gun battle and knife fight inside a casino left three people dead and a dozen wounded. Hours later and eighty miles away, on the shoulder of an interstate highway in California, police discovered the corpse of a biker with several bullet holes in his back. Three of the dead belonged to the Hells Angels, and the fourth was a member of the Mongols, a motorcycle clan that has grown rapidly in Southern California in recent years, largely by recruiting new members from Hispanic street gangs. A contingent of Hells Angels were staying at the same hotel as the Mongols, and the result was the bloodiest installment yet in a feud provoked by the Mongols' attempts to expand into the Angels' traditional territory, in Northern California.

Law-enforcement people who specialize in monitoring biker bad behavior said that they weren't surprised by the lethal jousting in Laughlin. Part of it was explainable in terms of a demographic shift: many of the older Angels are, well, old—Sonny Barger, for decades the Angels' equivalent of a capo di tutti capi, is now in his mid-sixties—and, until relatively recently, most local chapters haven't pushed aggressively to rejuvenate their ranks. Because the Fourth of July spectacle in Hollister was the next major event on the West Coast motorcycle-rally calendar, and because the Hells Angels have always made a conspicuous showing there, speculation immediately turned to whether the Mongols would come around for more action. As it happened, a couple of deputies from the San Benito County Sheriff's Department had been inside the casino in Laughlin, on an intelligence-gathering mission, but had gone to bed about an hour before they would have had to duck for cover. In the aftermath, Curtis Hill, the sheriff, told the *San Jose Mercury News*, "It's flat-out war. It will be interesting to see how many people die between now and when they call a peace to this thing."

When I left the rally headquarters and stopped by Sheriff Hill's office, he wasn't in, but his second-in-command, Lieutenant Mike Covell, was doing a fine job serving up meaty sound bites. "If there is violence, what's the nature of it going to be?" he said. "Is it gonna be knives, ball-peen hammers, guns? In Canada, they use rocket launchers."

The Hollister Police Department had enlisted forty extra cops for the weekend, and the F.B.I., the Bureau of Alcohol, Tobacco, and Firearms, and four separate California state law-enforcement agencies would be represented, in uniform and undercover. A sizable contingent of media folk were also standing by, ready to wring their hands in the event of bloodshed. I deeply empathized with the anxieties of my fellow Fourth Estaters, who, I suspected, feared an anticlimax even more than they did an outburst of fresh violence.

When I mentioned to one of my teenage sons that I would be attending a big motorcycle rally, he pleaded, "Dad, promise me that if you're going to be hanging with the Hells Angels you won't be wearing your usual polo shirt and chinos." He had a point, but, knowing that I'd be cruising into town behind the wheel of a Chevy Malibu or an Oldsmobile Alero from Avis, I couldn't see the advantage of investing in a leather vest, chaps, boots, gloves, skullcap, and three-hundred-dollar sunglasses. So most days in Hollister I wore Levi's, sandals, and a commemorative T-shirt from the Dan Quayle Center and Museum. (Bikers tend to lean politically to the right.) I calculated that after I had been sufficiently exposed to ninety-degree heat and the shirt had accumulated stains from deep-fried cuisine, it would get sufficiently gamy to enhance my street credibility. Another option—riding, say, a Harley Fat Boy with custom stretch handlebars, chrome Thunderstar wheels, shotgun exhaust pipes, and bullet-hole decals on the gas tank—wasn't really an option. For one thing, I don't have a motorcycle license. And one reason I don't is that the only time in my life I attempted to operate a two-wheeled motorized vehicle—a Vespa, slightly larger than a child's stroller—I was less than five seconds into a test drive, wearing shorts, when I crashed into two parked cars, an experience I relive every time I admire the conversation-piece scar on my right thigh. Anyway, I'd have no time for carefree recreation. I had a job to do: scoping out one percenters and urging them to share their thoughts and feelings.

The term *one percenter* derives from the American Motorcycle Association's defensive claim, during the nineteen-fifties, that only one percent of the bikes on the road belonged to criminally inclined social misfits. The Hells Angels and many other motorcycle clubs embraced the designation as a badge of pride—literally, by sewing "1%" patches on their vests. Sergeant Mike Rodrigues, of the San Benito County Sheriff's Department, told me to assume that all the one percenters who made appearances in Hollister—he mentioned the Red Devils, Hellbent, Molochs, Ghost Mountain Riders, Ancient Iron, Devil Dolls, Tophatters, Lonesome Fugitives, Solo Angels, Vagos, and Skeleton Crew motor-cycle clubs—were allied with the twelve Hells Angels chapters on hand. (Rodrigues also said that there was a lone Mongol living in Hollister, and a Mongol chapter with at least eighteen members in San Jose, less than an hour away. Conventional wisdom held that any Mongols who dared to show up wouldn't be dumb enough to wear their colors.)

A hundred and fifty or so non-one-percenter clubs were repre-sented, in varying numbers, and it didn't take long for all of them to blend together in my eyes and brainpan, like very, very loud wallpaper. Biker fashion, male and female, never mind age or club or gang-color distinctions, has such a narrow range of permutations—leather, metal, wraparound shades, bandannas or skullcaps, German-infantry-style helmets, Harley-Davidson logos, tattoos—that from half a block away an aggregation of bikers milling on the street, self-consciously checking each other out, looks no less like a unified army than a regiment of uniformed soldiers does. Up close, virtually every bike, proudly polished to an impeccable gleam, struck me as beautiful, especially when parked.

But even then there were so many to see that it was almost impossible to focus. Some ninety percent were Harley-Davidsons; the rest were Indians, BMWs, BMC Choppers, Yamahas, Suzukis, American Iron Horses, and a miscellany of customized hybrids. More than a hundred and fifty vendors had rented booths, from which they were flogging every conceivable sort of motorcycle accessory and personal gear, along with such optional merchandise as leather thongs, toe rings, Pig Snot Biker Wax, insulated bodysuits, knives, tank tops ("These Tits Are Real"), legal services, and in-your-face helmet and gas-tank stickers ("I Had a Wife Once but Her Husband Came and Got Her"; "Unless You Are Totally Nude Don't Lean on This Bike"; "The Beatings Will Continue Until Morale Improves"; "You're the Reason Our Kids Are Ugly"). The average rider had twenty-five thousand dollars invested in his or her machine. The ambience was nothing if not aspirational. For the right price, presumably, everything in town was for sale, which raised—or perhaps rendered moot—the metaphysical question of who (or what) was the genuine article and who was a wannabe.

On San Benito Street one afternoon, before the festivities hit full stride, I came across a bunch of credibly menacing-looking dudes hanging out in front of Johnny's Bar & Grill. These were members of the Boozefighters Motorcycle Club, the crew who, according to legend, caused all the ruckus in 1947. The Boozefighters regard Johnny's as hallowed ground for its historical significance and because the ashes of Wino Willie Forkner, one of the founding members, who died in 1997, six days before the inaugural Hollister Independence Rally, are displayed inside.

I had a cordial conversation with Carl "Big Daddy" Spotts, who owns a motorcycle-repair shop near Lake Tahoe. Spotts was tall and hefty, with a flowing gray beard, and he wore a leather vest, jeans, a wide belt with an oval Boozefighters buckle, and a green cap that identified him as the club's West Coast national representative. "I also belong to the Elks," he said, pointing to a membership pin on the cap. "And the Moose." He had a flaming-wheel tattoo on his right biceps and on his left, a Boozefighters logo that was a work in progress. "That's a cover-up," he said. "Originally, I had a skunk put on there when I was fifteen."

The standard Boozefighters regalia also included a vest patch that said "GB."

"There's disagreement as to what the 'GB' stands for," Spotts told me, "whether it's 'gag box' or 'gag bucket.' Either you had to bring a joke to each meeting or you partied till you puked."

I asked why they had come to Hollister in advance of the main event.

"It gets pretty rough," Spotts said. "You can hardly walk into the bar, it's so crowded."

He continued, "Some of our original forefathers are here tonight and tomorrow, so we came to party with them. There'll be about fifty or a hundred of us. Then we plan to drive up north of San Francisco about a hundred miles to visit Wino Willie's widow."

Three self-anointed Boozefighters had come from Norway, provoking an internecine debate about their legitimacy. "We're working on that," Spotts said. "They just have to join the national. Norway's a long ways from here. We'll straighten it out. They're good guys. We just can't afford to have guys who aren't Boozefighters running around with our badge on. If they get in trouble, it reflects on us. We try to keep our image clean."

A passing Harley Electra Glide backfired loudly, and Spotts clutched his chest. "I'm on heart medication already," he said. "I don't need that."

Later, I wondered what nutritional advice Spotts might have received from his doctors, given that the staples of a rally diet are corn dogs, nachos, funnel cakes, Polish sausages, onion rings, and beer. That, at any rate, was what sustained me as I waited for a bloody biker battle to break out. In the absence of hand-to-hand combat, I decided that the prudent journalistic strategy was to studiously witness, and thus be in a position to capitalize on the dramatic potential of the tattoo contest, the beauty pageant, the arm-wrestling tournament, and the "bike games," which would feature such tests of skill as the weenie bite—in which teams made up of a male biker and his female rider pass through a wood-frame portal from which a thickly mustarded hot dog dangles vertically, at eye level, on a string. (Big trophy to whoever—no hands allowed—snatches the biggest bite with her teeth.) "At other rallies, they have outhouse races, where the gal sits on the can, which is on skids, while her partner pulls her with his bike," Ellen Brown told me. "But we don't go in for that sort of thing. No wet-T-shirt contests, either. We favor family-oriented competitions."

At four in the afternoon on the Fourth of July, ten adventurous women and a modest crowd of witnesses and moral supporters gathered at Hollister's only bowling alley for a preliminary round of the Hollister Independence Rally pageant. Similar sessions had been held a few weeks earlier in two neighboring towns, yielding six finalists, and Niessa Bauder-Guaracha, a clothing designer, who had volunteered to be the pageant coordinator, was hoping to come up with four more. The proceedings were late getting started, so I went outside and surveyed the venders in the bowling-alley parking lot. In one booth, a guy in his 30s, with straw-colored hair and a handlebar mustache, accompanied by his eleven-year-old son, an up-and-comer who wore Oakley shades and a camouflage bandanna, was trying to decide which sew-on American flag to display on the back of his black leather vest. He was tempted to buy one that included the message "Try Burnin' This One . . . Asshole!"

"You definitely want the 'asshole' on there," the vender said.

"You're right. Matter of fact, make that a double 'asshole!' "

Back inside, the pageant candidates, who had been instructed to wear biker gear, were lining up to pose with a Harley-Davidson Softail Springer that was doing double duty: it was also the first prize in a raffle. "Biker gear" evidently was a synonym for "not very much." Bauder-Guaracha had told me that the judges would evaluate physical appearance, personality and poise, and marketability. It took me no time to spot a potential winner. She had long, straight, brunette hair and long, blue fingernails, and she wore a leather unitard cut so that it gave maximum exposure to her long, tanned, fat-free legs. She also wore lace-up, black, vinyl-and-leather boots with three-inch platform soles and stiletto heels, and amber-tinted wrap-arounds. Her name, I sensed, was also Amber, but in fact it turned out to be Melissa Crowley.

"You seemed so relaxed posing on that bike," I told her. "What kind of motorcycle do you ride?"

"I'm not a biker," she said. "What's holding me back? I need a bike. Or somebody to drive it, maybe."

Before I had a chance to reconsider my deep misgivings about riding a hog, Melissa introduced me to her husband, Ryan, who explained that he'd never owned one himself because his father, back in Boston, was a nurse who warned him, "Before you get a motorcycle, you've got to come to the hospital and see all the guys in traction." Melissa and Ryan, who were in their early thirties, had moved to California five years earlier; he worked in advertising, she was an assistant manager at a health club, and she'd entered the pageant more or less for the hell of it. The prize money—a thousand dollars for first place and merchandise prizes to the first two runners-up—wasn't really on their minds, even though Ryan did mention, in passing, his mortgage. "I told Melissa two weeks ago, 'If you're gonna take this seriously, you're not doing it,' " he said. "First place will go to some twenty-one-year-old. Second will go to the niece of someone on the committee. The best we can do is third."

It soon became apparent that Melissa would indeed be advancing. An official came over and handed her four patches bearing the logos of Miller Lite and Harley-Davidson, along with instructions to display them on her bathing suit. "I don't know how that's going to work," Ryan said. "There's more material there than there is on your bikini."

I was accurately forewarned that the crowd would peak on Saturday, and I had to park my car half a mile from the center of the action. This inconvenience generated an immediate dividend: as I walked past the headquarters of the San Benito County Sheriff's Department, Sheriff Hill happened to be standing out front. I introduced myself, and he invited me inside. "We arrested five Hells Angels last night," he said, as we sat in his office. "Two on illegal-weapons charges—a knife and a loaded revolver. Another guy was flanking the cops while they were dealing with the first two guys, they told him to back off and he didn't, so he was arrested, too.

"Today, I'm hearing information that this is the day when something's supposed to happen—all completely unsubstantiated, but I've got a number of people chasing that down. And you've got these one percenters out there surveilling and countersurveilling each other. That creates a tremendous amount of tension. The Angels are barely paying attention to the police because we're not the big threat. They're actively looking for something downtown. You see that look. There's all this posturing. It's a big dance being choreographed by all the one percenters."

Half an hour later, on San Benito Street, caught in a crowd that reminded me of Rockefeller Center during Christmas-tree-gazing time, I met three Angels from Merced, California. They seemed to be staring intently at the passing parade, so I decided to test Sheriff Hill's theory that they were doing surveillance. "I see you guys looking around," I said. "What are you looking for?"

"What are we lookin' at? Just lookin.' "

"Looking for pussy. Check it out. This is the time of year to look, when they're not wearing much."

Around the corner, milling next to a booth that the Daly City chapter had rented for the weekend, was a contingent of about forty Angels—Budweiser-drinking, bear-hugging, N.F.L.-linebacker-size specimens. The Sonoma County chapter president wore what looked like clean, pressed Levi's, but there was no one I felt eager to introduce to my mother or to interrogate about the status of the war with the Mongols.

A block away, at the booth operated by the Devil Dolls Motorcycle Club—adjacent to one stocked with Sonny Barger trademark merchandise—a woman named Mickey was pushing Devil Dolls pinup calendars. Barger was in town to promote his most recent book, *Ridin' High, Livin' Free*, Mickey said, and I could probably find him at the factory showroom of Corbin, a manufacturer of motorcycle seats and accessories. She called him on her cell phone, and he agreed to speak with me.

It took me fifteen minutes to get there, for an interview that lasted about ninety seconds. Barger, who made his name in Oakland but now lives near Phoenix, was seated behind a table piled with books, accompanied by comrades from the Cave Creek, Arizona, chapter. Before we got started, his cell phone rang, and whoever was calling immediately irritated him. "I'll tell you why we've got a problem," he was saying. "Because you keep fucking with me. And if you don't stop fucking with me it's gonna be a bigger problem." For someone whose speech was impeded by a hole in his throat— he lost his vocal cords to cancer twenty years ago—Barger articulated quite well. I wanted to discuss the Mongols, of course, and thought I'd ease into it by explaining that I felt that the media's general approach to the subject had been . . . I was going to say "hysterical," but he beat me to the punch with "like vultures." I mentioned that I already owned a copy of *Ridin' High, Livin' Free* and was sorry that I'd left it in my hotel room. But it was too late; gravity had taken hold.

"I can see where you're coming from," Barger said. "The interview's over." His Cave Creek colleagues rose from their chairs to emphasize the point.

Recalling the closing pages of Hunter Thompson's classic *Hell's Angel*—specifically, the scene in which the hardworking journalist is suddenly set upon, severely beaten, and stomped—I figured why push it. Besides, I'd already had a brush with possible bodily harm that morning, during breakfast in my hotel. I had approached the coffee urn at the same moment as a burly, gray-bearded biker with a long ponytail. "Go ahead," I said, deferentially.

"Goathead!" he said. "Why you callin' me Goathead?"

"No. I said, 'Go ahead.'"

"I thought I heard 'Goathead.'"

"Believe me, I wouldn't call you Goathead," I assured him. Then, when his back was turned, I heard myself whisper, "But somebody else might."

My printed schedule promised a Sunday-morning service at the Hollister United Methodist Church, led by members of the evangelical Christian Motorcycle Association. Walking to the church, I heard birds chirping in the magnolias, an experience that hadn't been available for days. I wandered past the spot where, the day before, I'd witnessed the large gathering of Hells Angels and saw that during the night they had dismantled their booth. Wisely, the Mongols had been no-shows, and it now seemed clear that the threat of violence, however real it had been, had passed.

As the day progressed, I experienced an odd sensation of community (not to be mistaken for a sense of belonging). I'd hung around long enough for certain faces to become familiar, certain vectors to intersect. In church, I recognized Bobby Bible (née Robert Engel, a.k.a. Bobby Biblestein), a refinery worker from Los Angeles whom I'd seen a couple of days earlier, at the tattoo contest, where he was showing off a crucifix on his chest. After the service, I discovered that we had had comparable face time with Sonny Barger. Bible had been in Laughlin and had run across Barger a few hours before the shoot-out.

"I saw him at the Flamingo Hotel," he said. "Sonny was signing books. So I felt led by the Holy Spirit to go up to him. I leaned over the table, looked him right in the eye. I said, 'Sonny, I'm gonna ask you one question. Do you believe in Jesus Christ as your personal savior?' He said, 'No, I don't.' Not angrily, just matter-of-factly. I said, 'Sonny, you know, you're gonna go to Hell when you die. O.K.?' He looked back at me with that biker look, that get-out-of-my-face-you're-pissing-me-off look. So I picked up on that right away. All of his buddies were standing there. And I exited left."

The previous afternoon, at the Hollister Independence Rally pageant finals, caught in a crush of several hundred hooting and hollering guys (and a much smaller number of gals, none of whom appeared to be exercising absolute free will), I found myself standing next to Dallas Roberts, from San Diego. I'd also met Roberts at the tattoo contest, where he won first prize in the "flaming" category. He had red hair under a red bandanna, a sunburned face, and a few days of stubble, and he wore a T-shirt promoting a microbrew called Arrogant Bastard Ale, which he'd got Sonny Barger to autograph during a visit to the Corbin showroom. The pageant itself was a repudiation of my powers of prognostication; Melissa Crowley finished out of the money. The winner, as Ryan Crowley had predicted, was a twenty-one-year-old blond surfer-girl type named Tara Rice. During Tara's first stroll down the runway, I realized I'd seen her several times already—at the California Glamour Girls booth, where, for nine or twelve or fifteen dollars a pop, anyone could pose for a Polaroid portrait with one or two or three young women wearing blossom-print pink bikinis and fixed smiles.

I even had a return engagement of sorts with Goathead. I didn't feel like sticking around for all the bike games, but I did catch the weenie bite, where the winners were an oddly matched couple named Sandy Williams and Russ Wood. Sandy was a slender grandmother who told me she'd already started training her two-year-old granddaughter for the weenie bite. Russ, who was about the size of a telephone booth, had such masterly control of his Harley-Davidson Softail that this was his and Sandy's fourth weenie-bite first place in the past three years, one of forty trophies that they'd collected overall. Clearly, justice had been served—though not the weenies themselves; those got spit out—and I knew that it was time to rev up my Chevy Malibu and bid Hollister farewell. I drove out of town, rolling past the apricot and apple orchards for a couple of miles, until I came to a stop sign at an intersection. Four motorcyclists pulled up next to me, and the leader of the pack, hulking over his Harley Dyna Low Rider, was Goathead himself. I thought about giving him a fellow-biker's wave, but that wouldn't have been appropriate. I also considered giving him the finger, just to keep things interesting. But I nodded and smiled instead, and, gratifyingly, Goathead did the same. Then we both headed west, into the sunset, or some other destination.

# Grandfather's
# Milk

## By Bill Hayes

*The Original Wild Ones*

Motorbooks, August 2005

FIVE-YEAR-OLD GIRLS usually observe the world in a slightly different light than a grizzled old biker.

Usually.

"Grandpa, why do you have that bottle of milk on the back of your vest?"

Old 'n' grizzled wasn't about to begin a long, morally tinged ramble about the difference between milk and moonshine, which one's good for you, which one's not, and why. Instead he answered with a smile and a kidlike shrug that simply said, "Just because." And to a little girl that was OK, that was reason enough. Her grandpa is a member of the original wild ones: the Boozefighters Motorcycle Club. The "bottle" is the centerpiece of the patch, a sacred green icon that symbolizes a brotherhood and a heritage that few are ever fortunate enough to experience. Is it actually supposed to be a bottle of *milk*? Probably not. But that really is left up to the imagination. The Peter Pan eye-of-the-beholder that is the fanciful essence of an innocent five-year-old is, in many ways, what also fuels the Boozefighters.

The truth is that the founding fathers of the original wild ones were really just big kids themselves, simply trying to recapture some of the youthful fun they lost out on due to the innocence-destroying interruption of a very adult evil known as World War II.

There were no excuses, no laments, no protests. The country needed young soldiers. They went. War changes everyone. And every-*thing*. When young vets like Willie Forkner, Robert Burns, and George Manker returned home, it was difficult to forget the horrors of what they had seen. It was hard to shake off the ingrained military regimentation. It was impossible to shed some of the cold-sweat guilt that comes with surviving while so many others did not. And there was an unnerving restlessness in trying to adapt to the calmness and serenity of "normal" living after drowning in chaos. It was easy, however, to adopt an "I don't fit in" kind of attitude. It was easy for returning vets to feel more comfortable with one another than with those from "the outside."

The recipe had been written. The mix was almost complete. All that was needed was the addition of a potent ingredient to spice up the social soup. Something like, say, racing fast motorcycles. The races and rally organized by the American Motorcyclist Association Gypsy Tour in 1947 boiled the soup into a fiery jalapeño-laced stew.

The green stitched bottle that the five-year-old asked her old gramps about was very different from the *real* bottles that were gathered from the streets of Hollister by an energized photojournalist during that infamous weekend. The image on that patch is very different from the horde of *broken* and empty bottles that were carefully arranged around the seemingly drunk and woozy non-Boozefighter (identified as Eddie Davenport or Don Middleton, depending on the source) by *San Francisco Chronicle* photographer Barney Peterson.

The resulting picture was not exactly a work of art that might have emerged from the all-American portfolios of Ansel Adams, Norman Rockwell, or Grant Wood. No. Instead, we were treated to an urban-ugly portrait of the tipsy "model," astride a "nasty, fire-breathing, Milwaukee-steel dragon," viciously framed by those stale-smelling empties and jagged glass shards.

When that twisted version of *American Gothic* leaped out at the sophisticated readers of *Life* magazine's July 21, 1947, issue, a frightening chill blew through the calm kingdom air. Some of the common village folk wanted to head for the hills, and some wanted to take up pitchforks, sickles, and torches against the strange new beast.

Some wanted to tell the whole story. Sort of. Filmmaker Stanley Kramer produced *The Wild One* six years later, and the snarling cat was out of the bag. The question is, of course, just how sharp were that cat's claws really?

In the year 2046 the Boozefighters MC will celebrate its 100th anniversary. Some members are already planning for the party. Members of the surviving "originals" will range in age from 120 to 129. Some current members will attend at a much more spry 107.

But more than a half-century has *already* passed, and the legend has grown. The embroidered green bottles went on in 1946, Hollister swept up all that busted brown glass in 1947, *The Wild One* rolled out on black-and-white celluloid at the end of 1953, and the always colorful stories, tales, and traditions have never stopped.

Some of the members accept, reluctantly, that there is a slight chance that they might not quite make the club's 100th anniversary bash, but they're more concerned with carrying on the most important Boozefighter tradition of all: Having fun. One of the early members, Jack Lilly, has a credo that is woven into the very fabric of that holy green patch when it comes to having a good time: "Do it now!" They did. And they still do.

When that cat flew out of the bag, the popularized fear was that he was bent on shredding and hunting prey. In reality that fast, sleek animal was just living up to his reputation for curiosity and playful prowling. For wanting to sniff out every aspect of life. Eat, drink, fool around, chase an occasional mouse, cough up a hairball or two after a tad too much consumption, and, in general, just enjoy the heck out of living.

"Every original Boozefighter I've met," club historian Jim "JQ" Quattlebaum says, "—Wino, J. D. and Jim Cameron, Red Dog, Jim Hunter, Ernie and Johnny Roccio, Les, Gil, Lilly, and Vern Autrey—all exhibit signs that they are made of common threads: Spirited and daring character, challenging competitiveness, strong bonding friendship, a caring and giving nature, the love of motorcycling, and brotherhood with bikers. They're honest and law-abiding citizens, but not beyond the embellishment of a good story." Even in their old age they've stayed active. No rocking chairs for them! Still riding motorcycles as long as their health and bodies would allow.

"Yeah, they let off a lot of steam, partied hearty, got jailed for getting drunk, got a lot of speeding tickets, and occasionally duked it out with redneck bar patrons that hassled them . . . and sometimes they fought with each other. Then they'd sit down together and laugh about it over a beer.

"But no original ever got put in jail for a serious crime like murder or drugs. They got along with all other MC clubs, sponsored races, baseball games, and different events with other clubs. They never considered themselves *outlaws* the way that term is used today. This was a term that the

AMA applied to riders and clubs who didn't follow the structured AMA racing rules back in the 1940s.

"And the originals didn't discriminate toward any ethnic, religious, or political group. Wino said, 'We fought side by side for *all* Americans to have freedom of choice.'

"That freedom also extended to the members' choice of bikes to ride, as long as they could keep up! Indians and Harleys were the most available, so they were the most used. However, many old BFers started acquiring the Triumph because of its improved racing speed. Hendersons and other pre–World War II bikes were used, too. When the BSA was introduced in the 1950s, it became the bike of choice for the still-racing BFers, like Jim Hunter, Jim Cameron, Ernie and Johnny Roccio.

"Present-day BFMC requires members to ride an American or World War II–allied brand of bike. But some exceptions are made in some chapters for special consideration. 'Brooklyn' is allowed to ride a touring Moto Guzzi in honor of his grandfather, who fought with the Italian underground resistance against the Germans.

"The present-day Boozefighters revere our originals and the club's founders for their intent, purpose, and priorities: Family, job, and club brotherhood. We're family men, engaged in legitimate businesses and careers, enjoying getting together as a social group for parties, rides, and special events. We're into this thing strictly for having harmless, *good clean fun*. We couldn't care less about 'territory' and things like that.

"We don't push religion on anyone, but we do have a national chaplain, 'Irish Ed' Mahan, who, in a nondenominational way, conducts Bible study class every Tuesday night, performs legal marriages and funerals, and visits members that request special counseling or have illness issues. He also conducts Easter sunrise services at our clubhouse every year. It's attended by a lot of friendly clubs.

"And we're involved in giving back to society through fundraising, toy runs, March of Dimes, Wish With Wings and such. We have a blood bank for members. We're active in motorcycle rights organizations, and many of us are state delegates to our respective political parties.

"We believe in peaceful coexistence with all clubs, but we don't wear support patches for any other organization. And we don't believe in displaying any antisociety or anti-American items."

Apparently some of the original members' priorities and the club's eventual evolution based on those principles were neglected just a bit in *The Wild One*. But, with another shrug of the shoulders, that, too, is OK. The Boozefighters are comfortable with who they are. And who they were. They're very proud of their founders. And they're happy with the continuance of the all-important "fun" tradition.

They're content with their personalities being somewhere in between Brando's "Johnny," Marvin's "Chino," and the brilliant 1940s/1950s abandon of, oh maybe, a Red Skelton or a Jackie Gleason.

In a letter dated September 18, 1946, the San Francisco Boozefighter prez, Benny "Kokomo" McKell, wrote to the L.A. chapter to order four club sweaters for his newest members. They had just passed the rigorous series of seven tests required of a "prospect":

1. Get drunk at a race meet or cycle dance.
2. Throw lemon pie in each other's faces.
3. Bring out a douche bag where it would embarrass all the women (then drink wine from it, etc.).
4. Get down and lay on the dance floor.
5. Wash your socks in a coffee urn.
6. Eat live goldfish.
7. Then, when blind drunk, trust me ("Kokomo") to shoot beer bottles off of your heads with my .22.

Would Johnny or Chino do all that?
No.
Would Skelton or Gleason?
Probably.
Would the Boozefighters?
Just ask 'em.
So, are all of the tales and legends in this book the sworn gospel?
JQ answers that (more or less) in an interesting discussion about memory and motorcycle lore:
"If you ask me today what I did last night, I'd be hard pressed to remember all the details precisely right. I know I started off with 65 or 70 dollars in my pocket and got home with about 7. For the life of me I can't remember what I spent the money on. But to get the story

*Lee Klancher*

more accurate, that doesn't count that $100 bill I had stashed away for an emergency. Man, I hope I didn't blow that, too . . .

"Ask the original wild ones what happened fifty years ago and they, too, are hard pressed to remember the *precise* facts. Once, sitting with three such old-timers, I witnessed a heated—but friendly—debate about what club one of them raced for during the Hollister melee. They finally all agreed on one thing; whether it was the 13 Rebs, Yellow Jackets, or Boozefighters, they all had one heck of a good time, excluding the jail time for rowdiness, of course.

"I had a good time last night, too. (That is, unless I can't find my $100 bill.)

"But anyway, if Patrick Henry had said, 'If I don't get my rear end outta here, I'm gonna get it shot off,' and some historical writer quoted him as actually saying, 'Give me liberty or give me death,' then what kind of respect would you have for that writer? As historian, I've had to dig deep into the facts about the Boozefighters, and there are times I wished I hadn't found out that some stories just weren't so. But then again, the more I dug, the more I found out that there are great stories that were *never* told.

"They *need* to be told, so we'll tell them. Some are fantastic, but I'll let the listener or reader sort out what they want to believe. Most importantly, though, the telling of these stories will be geared to the essence of truth as the old-timers wanted to remember it."

And the heart of that truth—those stories—beats with the same wide-eyed wonder that drives the fertile imagination of that inquisitive five-year-old.

Is there milk in that bottle, some 90-proof hooch, or a genie that will pop out and take us directly into a unique and exotic land, a growling jungle that members of the button-down, mainstream, overly protected, boy-in-the-bubble society fear, envy, and would give their eye teeth to journey into?

Maybe it's all three.

# Evel Knievel

## By James Stevenson

*First published in The New Yorker*

July 24, 1971

*Some of the vital questions begging answers are: Why is art needed? How and for what purposes is it used in a particular society? What is needed and what is made?*

—Introduction to *Tradition and Creativity in Tribal Art*, edited by Daniel Biebuyck

EVEL KNIEVEL IS a thirty-two-year-old native of Butte, Montana, who makes his living by riding a motorcycle at high speed up a wood-and-steel ramp, off the top, and into the air, with the intention of landing it on another ramp some distance away. Automobiles are usually parked side by side on the ground between the two ramps, and early this year, in Ontario, California, Knievel went over nineteen of them in one jump. Nobody else in the world has ever done that, or is willing to try. Knievel has almost killed himself nine times—a lot of things can go wrong—but Americans will pay good money to see him jump (make it or not make it), and next year, on Labor Day, Knievel hopes to attract several million customers to Twin Falls, Idaho, where he intends to make a mile-long leap over the Snake River canyon, using a jet-powered motorcycle. The week before last, in New York, wearing his red-white-and-blue-decorated white leather jump-suit, he made four jumps in Madison Square Garden at the Auto Thrill Show, clearing ten cars—the maximum he could fit into the available space.

Knievel is a lean, handsome man with curly hair, a hard-looking exterior, a quick temper, and a good deal of humor, perception, and charm. From the choppy years of his youth he has retained the wary eyes of a cardsharp, a thief's nerve, the combativeness of a brawler, the aplomb of a professional athlete, the flamboyant instincts of a promoter, and the glibness of a con man. There are trace elements of Robert Mitchum,

*Ralph Crane/Time & Life Pictures/Getty Images*

Elvis Presley, Captain Ahab, and an astronaut. When he's taking himself most seriously, delivering a solemn set of opinions, ad-lib homilies, and ponderous generalizations, he will abruptly stop and say, with a grin, "You can't con a con man." His vanity and temperament are considered unusual even by show-business standards, and he will give anybody bloody hell on a moment's notice. His courage speaks for itself. A writer once described Knievel as "the last great gladiator," and Knievel liked that well enough to have it inscribed in several places on the sides of a hundred-and-forty-thousand-dollar tractor-trailer in which he travels around the country. "They never saw anything like what I do," Knievel says flatly, "and they'll never see it again."

At 11 p.m. a few weeks ago, Knievel was having a late dinner with his family and some old friends in a restaurant in his hotel, near Madison Square Garden. They had just attended a screening of a new movie, *Evel Knievel,*" in which the hero is played by George Hamilton. Knievel's wife, a very pretty, serene, and gentle woman named Linda, and their three children—Kelly, ten; Robbie, nine; and Tracy, seven—were eating quietly while Knievel reminisced, gave opinions, asked questions, and joked.

*Ralph Crane/Time & Life Pictures/Getty Images*

"How'd you like the movie?" he inquired around the table—like a dealer asking "How many cards?"—and fixed his eye on each speaker, reading all he could from the replies. Knievel was amused by the portrayal in the movie of some of his old Butte friends, who appeared in a barroom sequence. "Remember that old guy in the bar who mentions the Conoco station? I was a security guard for a while, supposed to guard that place, and I robbed the owner about thirty times. Later on, I went back to Butte and gave him eight hundred bucks. I've paid back about sixty percent of the people I robbed—all the ones who weren't insured."

He turned to the children. "How'd you like the movie?"

The children shrugged, grinned, and continued to eat their dinner. Knievel had finished his.

"Hey, Tracy," he said to the little girl, "give me some of your pork chop." Tracy shook her head.

"Please, Tracy," said Knievel.

He continued to implore her, and finally Robbie reached over and cut a slice from the chop and passed it to his father.

Knievel thanked Tracy.

"How many ducks can Daddy kill with four shots?" he asked the children.

They answered almost simultaneously, "Five ducks."

Knievel beamed. "I got two with one shot one time," he explained to his guests. "I bet I've fished and hunted more than any son of a bitch in Montana. I got three shotguns in my truck. If anybody gives me trouble, I'll come out blazing." He paused. "And my kids know how to reload." He grinned.

The children smiled, dinner was over, and Knievel hailed the waiter. "Put everything on my bill," he told the waiter, "and give it to that man over there"—gesturing vaguely into the distance.

A couple of weeks later, two days before the opening at the Garden, Knievel was having a midmorning glass of grapefruit juice in the same restaurant. "We were in the Poconos over the weekend, and my back got so sunburned I can't sleep," he said. "I've broken every bone in my body— except my neck—at least once, but right now this sunburn is killing me." (Knievel still limps because of a severe wipeout in Las Vegas three years ago, when he jumped the fountains at Caesars Palace.) He looked through some Polaroid pictures of his sons riding and making small jumps on their motorcycle in the Poconos. "I started the boys when they were about five, riding a minibike in Montana. I'd put them in an irrigation ditch with a rope tied to the end of the minibike so they couldn't go too fast or get out of control; I'd run down the ditch after them, holding on to the rope."

The talk turned to his hometown of Butte. "Anaconda came in and tore up half of Butte—open-pit mining—and the whole town is undermined. Everybody in Montana depends on Anaconda. They've done a tremendous job, they're making a lot of money, and that's what life is all about. A lot of my friends were killed in the mines—by gas, by falling down shafts, by getting crushed. One was a skip tender, and a rock caught up with him. I worked underground in the copper mines when I was sixteen, seventeen, as a diamond-drill-hole operator—you drill a hundred feet with a brace and bit by hand, to lower the water level and keep the passages clear. Butte was a wide-open town. When I was a kid, the main activity was to go up and throw rocks at the whores, bang on the doors, and have the pimps chase us down the street. I was raised by my grandparents; my parents were divorced. My grandparents tried extra hard, but they couldn't understand me—you can't bridge that distance. My dad came back for a while when I was six, but we were too far apart by then. I was always a short, skinny little kid—I was eighteen before I really started to grow—but I could always do things other kids couldn't do. When I was eight, I saw Joey Chitwood's Auto Daredevils at Clark Park, in Butte. A guy jumped a motorcycle over one car, and I remember them saying, 'The last guy who tried that got killed.' I thought that was pretty wild. That night, I stole a motorcycle from a neighbor, ran it three blocks, then put it back in the guy's garage. Pretty soon, I was jumping my bicycle. I'd make a pile of dry baby's-breath, light it, and jump over it.

"I went through high school, but I didn't graduate. I was a very good pole-vaulter and hockey player, and I was Rocky Mountain ski-jump champion two years. First time I was arrested, I was sixteen. I fell in with these kids—you're broke one day, you don't know what life's all about—and we started stealing. I kept on until I was about twenty-five, and I never really got caught. I spent maybe a total of two weeks in jail. I was in a lot of barroom brawls, and I won thousands cheating at cards. I'd run a game with an old Indian friend of mine named Yellowbird. He's blackballed all over now—can't even go into the state of Nevada. He was unbelievable. He was so fast he'd change my cards for me and I wouldn't even know it. The town was full of pimps, hayseeds, and cross-roaders. [A cross-roader is a man who doesn't follow the roads; he goes across them.] One time, I was the steerer and found a hayseed, and we took all his money, then went and got his TV and all his clothes. A cross-roader might watch the game, and if he'd see the juice on the cards, maybe he'd stroke his nose or his chin, and that meant he wasn't going to butt in. If a man came in and we thought he was an F.B.I. or police, Yellowbird and I would call each other Tom or George—that would be the warning. When I was stealing, I'd go into a store and ask if they had fire-and-theft, pretend I was selling insurance. (I was selling insurance for a while—I sold a hundred and ten policies in one day in an insane asylum in Warm Springs.) If the man in the store said he already had insurance, and if his attitude was bad—if he told me to get the hell out—then I'd go back that night and rob him. I never carried a gun, never hurt anybody except the insurance companies, and they're bastardly thieves anyway. I'd climb up on the roof—cops never look on the roof; they're too goddam lazy, or too busy chasing goofballs and homosexuals—and I'd rip up the tarpaper, make some holes with a brace and bit, then pry up the section with a big screwdriver, tie a rope to the air conditioner, and drop down. I can open any safe—Diebold, Mosler, Star, anything—but don't let anybody tell you you can pick a safe. There's only two ways to open a safe—you can beat the son of a bitch open, or you can blow it. You can knock the dial off and peel the door, but I'm not going to tell you exactly how. Then you take the guy's stepladder and get out the way you came in. I drilled so many holes in so many roofs all over Washington and Oregon. It was a challenge, and I got a kick out of it.

"I had a terrible breakdown when I was about twenty-five. The police chased me across four states—I was in a Pontiac Bonneville, going a hundred and twenty miles an hour—and after that I just couldn't stand the pressure. I started changing my life, and I got back up. But my friends who stayed in got on drugs, and they're still doing it. Last night, I was on the phone four hours to Yakima, trying to get a friend of mine out of jail and into a mental home. His brain is scrambled by narcotics. I turned him down a couple of months ago, and maybe I made a bad decision; I didn't know how bad off he was. I like to help kids, work with kids in detention homes. Don't tell a kid what's right and wrong. He knows what's right and wrong. Find out what his attitude and his aptitude are, try to help him where he wants to go. I've been everywhere talking to kids, working with them. This city is terrible for kids. I'm trying to arrange to take five kids out of here to Montana with me."

*Michael Ochs Archives/Getty Images*

*Heinz Kluetmeier/Sports Illustrated/Getty Images*

Knievel served a year and a half in the army ("I hated it, bugged out as much as I could"); played pro hockey in Seattle; coached, managed, and played on his own hockey team in Butte; raced motorcycles professionally in California; had a Honda dealership in the state of Washington; and started Evel Knievel's Motorcycle Daredevils. "We had a traveling show. I'd do five or six stunts—ride through fire walls, jump over boxes of live rattlesnakes and land between chained mountain lions, get towed down a dragstrip at two hundred miles an hour holding on to a parachute. We slept in flophouses or in little hotels with signs that said 'Welcome Pensioners. Black-and-White TV. Free Coffee.' Now I've got a dollar in my pocket, and I travel in a hundred-and-forty-thousand-dollar trailer. Last year, I had two Rolls-Royces and two Lincoln Mark IIIs. Sometimes I keep a car for only a week or two. I like the newest and the flashiest. I've got an Eldorado right now." He said he has had only three ambitions in his life; one was to jump out of an airplane (which he did), another was to race at Indianapolis (which he hopes to do), and the third had something to do with Elizabeth Taylor.

He talked about the jump at Madison Square Garden. "I'll be riding a Harley-Davidson XR 750—a factory-produced racing machine. It uses ethyl gas. The ramps are wooden—four-by-twelves—seven feet wide, with steel supports, set at a thirty-degree angle. Before the jump, I concentrate on what to do—I'm worrying about the sparkplugs, the chain, throttle, tires, the r.p.m. at the takeoff point. I've missed nine times, but I don't have a death wish. Life to me is a bore, really, and jumping has replaced card games, ski-jumping, stealing. How some of the other people survive, I don't know. If it weren't for me, they'd have nothing to do—and if it weren't for them, I couldn't make a living. If I'm right with the man in the glass [mirror], that's all that matters. It's a challenge, like a ski jump. Everything is waiting, and then you've done it, and that's what your life is. I live to beat that challenge."

At one o'clock the next morning—the morning of the day before the opening—Knievel was momentarily alone in the arena of Madison Square Garden. Since 10 p.m., he had been supervising the unloading of his ramps from his tractor-trailer, which was parked just outside the arena, on the fifth floor of Madison Square Garden. It is a huge red vehicle, in two sections. The rear is a van, containing the ramps, Knievel's Harleys, a Baja motorcycle that his sons use, and a white golf cart. The van is decorated outside with white drawings of Knievel jumping his Harley, the words "Evel Knievel Enterprises, Butte, Montana," an endorsement of Olympia Beer, and a drawing of a coiled snake with the promise "Snake River Canyon Jump, Labor Day 1972." The front section is designed for driving, dressing, and office use, and is decorated inside in Las Vegas Executive—black leather chairs, red wall-to-wall, wood paneling. A small plaque bears a quotation from Robert Frost:

"The people I want to hear about are the people who take risks."

During the earlier part of the evening, Knievel had angrily cursed an obdurate worker; yelled at others ("Don't step on the chrome!"); chewed out a moviemaker who had asked him to reenact something; shared hot dogs and soft drinks with his family, his promoter, his personal representative, three Harley mechanics from Brooklyn, and anybody else who wanted food or drink; insulted the promoter and the representative in lavish terms (both seemed accustomed to this and appeared to enjoy it); delivered rambling indictments of the American Motorcycle Association, insurance companies, manufacturers, promoters, filmmakers, and assorted other individuals; told amusing stories of his recent activities; and conferred with the mechanics ("Someday that carburetor's going to cost me my neck").

Now he was alone in the arena. High overhead were the futuristic concentric circles of the Garden ceiling; all around were the rows and rows of empty seats—bland motel pastels. It was vast, desolate, and barren, and the air was full of flies. (The rodeo had just left.) The ramps, faded red, white, and blue, were lying in the middle of the arena; between the end of the takeoff ramp and the beginning of the landing was seventy-five feet of bare gray concrete. Knievel's plan for the jump was to start his motorcycle in the wings, gun it to seventy miles an hour, go up the ramp, take off, land on the far ramp, go out into the wings on that side of the arena, and somehow come to a stop before he hit the concrete sidewall of the Garden. "It can't be done," one of the men had remarked, out of Knievel's hearing. "He may be able to make the jump, but he can't stop." Knievel limped along down the middle of the arena, past the ramps—a somber figure, his face set and grim. Suddenly, lilting music began to play over the loudspeakers.

Around four in the morning of the day of the opening, Knievel made his first trial jump, landed, zoomed into the wings, and smashed into the wall, injuring himself (one of the handlebars went into his groin; his legs were bruised) and wrecking the front end of his motorcycle. There was talk of canceling the show, but Knievel decided against it. The motorcycle was repaired, and thin strips of corrugated rubber were taped to the floor of the Garden; these, it was hoped, would slow him down so that he could stop a few feet short of the wall.

Evening: The crowd watching the Auto Thrill Show in the Garden has been worked up to a point of high tension, apprehension, and excitement—the announcer has filled the air with lurid warnings, ominous pronouncements—and now Knievel, having raced his motorcycle back and forth on one wheel a few times, has gone into the wings. The ice-cream hawkers and the guards stand in the exits, watching. The audience moves to the edge of its seats. Knievel's Harley can be heard, and then suddenly he is tearing out of the wings—a flash of white suit and gleaming white helmet—and up the ramp, and he is free; he is in the air, standing over his motorcycle, flying in a graceful arc over the ten automobiles; and he lands smoothly, halfway down the far ramp, and is almost instantly out of sight again in the wings. The crowd roars, screams, cheers, applauds, and then Knievel rides back into the arena, one arm raised to receive the wild adulation of the crowd. The challenge has been met one more time.

# The TD1
# Sugar Daddy

By Joe Scalzo

*City of Speed*

Motorbooks, March 2007

J ANUARY, THE COLD WINTER OF 1964: Outdoors, Los Angeles is storming and raining. Indoors, my road-racing Honda Super Hawk and I are domiciled together in a grubby grotto, whose props consist of a telephone, a wind-up Victrola for listening to jazz, a stack of Dunlop Green Spot rubber, a case of Castrol R lubricant, an oil drip pan for the Honda, and an unmade bed to lay on top of as I recover from my latest assault-and-battery job.

This lovely little bungalow, the Tarantula Arms (actually named the Bella Vista Terrace), is located due east of Pasadena at the mouth of a firetrap canyon on the lower flanks of the often-fiery San Gabriel Mountains. Once an Irving Gill classic, now it is in such total ruin that when I offer to pay money to live here, the guy who manages the Bella Vista Terrace is overcome with gratitude. He even meets my request to quarter the Super Hawk inside.

Various things consume me: becoming a motorbike champion as quickly as possible; remembering to change the dressing on my leaking elbow; smashing out of the plaster of Paris cast trapping my broken foot; and, crucially, locating a crazy sugar daddy to go to Yamaha International and buy me a model TD-1, one of the hot little two-strokes that have rendered my Honda obsolete.

Chettie Baker is coming out of the gramophone, his voice assuring me, "It could happen to you." I don't believe him.

Whereupon it does happen to me. The phone rings, and it is my old pal Neil "Peachtree" Keen, a prominent member of the two-wheel danger gang running the curves without brakes at Ascot Park. Peach's instructions are that I make myself and my sore body parts present-able by drying out the elbow, taking a chainsaw to the cast, and in the morning gassing it across Antelope Valley to the Tehachapi crucible of

Willow Springs, nine corners and 2.5 miles. Yamaha International is itself playing sugar daddy and holding auditions for players for the season's TD-1 blacktop squad.

I am ashamed of myself for forgetting that this is Los Angeles, where wonderful sugar daddies who commit seemingly irrational acts of largesse for the village's racers—whether two wheels or four—are always around.

In fact, during the prior decade, Willow was already serving as Tony Parravano's private auditioning grounds, back when Tony was playing L.A. sugar daddy filling positions on his mysterious million-dollar scuderia. A shadowy building contractor and secretive businessman, Tony, before he abruptly disappeared, had the true Italian passion for racing: exotic red toys he passed around, included something like 13 Maserati sports cars and Formula 1s and 14 Ferraris—one of which bearing the designation 4.9, the hottest Ferrari numbers going in those times.

During the go-go-go Parravano days, you'd see everybody from Indy 500 winners to sports car champions trying out, hoping to claim a ride. Well, at Willow for the Yamaha International workouts, matters were standing-room-only also.

All sorts of lively personalities were parachuting in. These guys weren't clowns. Eddie Wirth, a future sprint car champion of the California Racing Association, was bending his 6-foot frame around a TD-1; Dickybird Newall, later to draw slammer time, was lapping very fast; as was Prince Albert Gunter; and of course Peachtree.

Under the desert sun was a whole fleet of TD-1s, maybe two dozen of them, white streamlinings and blood red gas tanks gleaming. I got aboard one, took it down Willow's hammerhead downhill, cruised in and out of tightening turn nine, and was captivated. What an ax! Nobody at Yamaha International seemed to know or care what was happening to all its TD-1s, so I steered mine off the racetrack straight to my red panel truck, an old Chevrolet, where I ramped it into the back. And before anybody could begin shouting, I then boogied out of there with my new TD-1.

Nine months later, when I returned it to Yamaha International with thanks, the TD-1 and I had gotten the company ink at all the local

L.A. meets, plus up north at Vacaville and Cotati, as well as in Florida, Ohio, Illinois, Iowa, Kansas, and even Tecate, Mexico. For eight glorious months I led the freewheeling life of the itinerant motorcycle racer. The binge had fed the rat, and now I was wrapping up my racing. Later I felt terrible when I discovered that the sugar daddy executive responsible for the Yamaha auditions had gotten fired. But so it goes with sugar daddies.

# Mozambique and Tanzania

By Dan Walsh

*Endless Horizon*

Motorbooks, 2009

"**E**XCUSE ME," husked the Portuguese girl, arching a Brooke Shields eyebrow and cocking a salsa-sharp hip. "Is that your beeg motorcycle?" Gosh. Lazy Sunday afternoon in Maputo, Mozambique, and I'm about to get grifted. The open-air Café Mimo's easing its way out of Saturday's hangovers to the tune of espresso-machine hisses and welcoming air kisses. Mwah, mwah, mwah. There're a couple of tables of middle-class Mozambicans sipping South African whites' wine and flirting into mobiles. There's a happy Indian family chuckling at each other's spaghetti-stained chins. There's a table of Scottish aid workers getting student-union giddy on over-strength African beer. And there's me, a stray dog with a wagging tail and "I've not spoken to anyone in days and I'm a sucker for a pretty face" shining out of my eyes.

"Can I sit down?" Every word is perfect, loaded and suggestive. "Didn't I meet you at the UN building?" Respectable, charitable. "I'm sorry to be so rude, but I have to have lost my lift." Polite, vulnerable. "Would it be possible to take me home?" Take. Me. Home. "I live in the suburbs with my sister." Family-orientated, a hint of quiet nights lounging around in underwear painting each other's toenails. "We moved here when my mother died." Look after me. "Also, she has all my money and I've eaten." Here we go. "Could you lend me the money till we get back?" Hook, line, sinker. "I'm just sitting around the corner." Hooked, blinded, blinkered. I hand over 20 bucks. "I suppose there's a 50-50 chance you'll come back," I half laugh. She smiles and disappears.

Outside a man with his feet on backwards wearing a "Will Work for Sex" T-shirt is holding up traffic, ranting like Mussolini. Two street kids in baggy granddad shirts are swinging off a lamp post. I eat a plate of prawns fried in chili and ginger. I drink another cup of scalp-tighteningly strong coffee. I know straight away, but it takes an hour before I burst out laughing and admit it. "You've been grifted."

■ ■ ■

Maputo, baby. A place to fall in love, a place to fall in love with. The Portuguese certainly know how to build—beautiful not beautified avenues lined with red flame trees and long cool shadows, full of faded colonial elegance and modern stainless chic. It feels like a mythical revolutionary dream, the streets read like a fantasy leftist dinner party—Avenida Karl Marx next to Patrice Lumumba next to Ho Chi Minh.

It's an easy city where every day is like Sunday. No one's ever in a hurry. No hassles, no hint of violence. But not stuck in a time warp—there's Visa ATMs and internet cafes. They just don't work very often.

I run into Werner, a German Jeremy Hardy lookalike on a DR650. You have a scrambler, I have a scrambler, let's be friends. We go for a drink. He's living in Cape Town, ridden up here to sell his bike. I produce a map. I've got a vague plan about heading straight up the coast to Dar es Salaam. Most overlanders go west via Malawi 'cause the roads are so bad. "What roads?" he laughs. He's ridden it before. "It's passable—just." He reckons it will take three weeks to cover the 2,000 miles. He's bang on.

■ ■ ■

Three weeks, 2,000 miles. Werner rides with me as far as Vilanculos. He speaks Portuguese. That's helpful. He's quicker than me. That's not. We pit-stop in Maxixe (rhymes with hashish) and have lunch with a family of German Methodist missionaries. I just can't help myself, "So you're a missionary? That's a great position to be in." They stare blankly as I shudder uncontrollably and splutter soup out of my nose.

During the civil war, this was the first front line. For three days we ride past broken bridges, torn-up railway lines, burned buildings, and bullet-scarred ghost towns. And mines. There's an estimated million still lying around, waiting. It's a shock to find the rope cordons and death heads so close to live villages full of curious kids, horny teenagers, and blind old folk. The war's been over since 1994, but no one's told the mines. According to the UN, every time one goes off it kills 1.47 people. How do you kill 0.47 of a person? Ask the double amputee begging at the side of the road.

In Vilanculos we're stopped at a roadblock. It's just outside a bar. A convoy of Save the Children Land Cruisers zips past. Who's that then? "Princess Anne," says Josef the bar owner. I wave. She doesn't wave back— mustn't have seen me. "God shave the Queen," shouts Werner. We laugh and go for a drink.

■ ■ ■

Three weeks, 2,000 miles. And an awful lot of luck. I met a Chinese guy who pointed out that a belief in luck is the same as a belief in fate. I pointed out that "Fatalistic" Luciano doesn't have the same ring. Just outside of Beira, just after dark, I'm waved down at a sentry box.

"Jabber jabber," says the grim-faced cop, stabbing at me with his trigger finger. "Jabber jabber." Driving license? Head shake. I'm stumped. A geezer in a Newcastle shirt intervenes. "Oakleys." What? "Oakleys," stabbing at my goggles. Yes, Oakleys, what of it? "The officer says he prefers Ray-Bans."

I smile and get back on the bike. I should have kissed him. He'd just saved my life.

Two klicks down the road there's a level-crossing sign. I dunno whether it's live or dead. I slow, the van behind impatiently overtakes, hurries onto the level crossing, and gets hit by a very dark, very solid train.

The next bit doesn't make any sense. My eyes aren't expecting to see what they see, my brain doesn't know how to process it. I get off the bike and walk to the ticking, twitching van. The bike light shadows as much as it shows. "You'll be all right, amigo, I'll get help." The driver's right arm's missing. "Can you hear me, amigo?" The driver's right leg's missing. "Wait here, I'll get an ambulance." The right side of his head is missing. "Are you all right, amigo?" He's very dead.

A Land Cruiser stops. We look at each other. I'm waiting for an adult to turn up and tell us what to do. The train driver's walking around in circles, mumbling. We coax him back into the cab, and he moves the train. We attach a rope to the wreck and drag it into a field. Then we spot the passenger. Motionless, apparently unhurt, staring straight ahead, deep shock. Smart suit, clean shirt, and neat tie, trying to ignore the fact that his mate's brains are all over his shoulders. We turn our lights off.

We can't open the passenger-side door. The chassis is too twisted. More cars stop. It's been maybe 15 minutes. I get back on the bike and return to the police post. There's another cop now, and he speaks English.

"Quickly, sir, a train has hit a car."

"Ah, you are from England. London?"

"Er, no Manchester, but that's not important. Sir, there are dead people, we go now?"

"Manchester? Manchester United? My team is Sporting Lisbon."

"Right. Er, there are dead people. Is there an ambulance?"

He shrugs and walks away. It's not apathy, it's resignation. There is no ambulance. He is not a doctor. A minute or two will make no difference to a man with half a head. He gets on his bicycle. I get on my bike. When I pass the level crossing I don't stop. There's blood on the tracks.

By the time I get to Beira, baby, I've decided that I'm dead. *I* hit the train. That's why the passenger couldn't see me. That's why the cop ignored me. I'm dead and Beira is the City of the Dead. The streets don't match the map. Screeching faces lurch out of the darkness. I can't get my bearings. A drunk takes a swipe at my tankbag. I can't find the sea. The dead man's wife will be here, somewhere, waiting for him. I know. She doesn't. A car pulls up—no bonnet, no windscreen, driver wearing a balaclava and welder's goggles. It's the Devil. "Hey Dan, are you lost?" It's a taxi. "Follow us." In the bar are George and Margot, Belgians I met in Vilanculos. Next thing I'm in Biques bar listening to pint pots clunk and stir-fries sizzle and pool balls rattle.

"I thought I was dead, George."

"No, Dan, you're not dead." He smiles. "You just smell like it."

■ ■ ■

Three weeks, 2,000 miles, about half of it off-road. The worst of it is from Beira to Inhaminga. Slowest damn piste I have ever ridden, a narrow squeeze that's a river in the wet season and a bitch in the dry, a steeply cambered, granny-knuckled finger covered with slippery sand and jaw-clunking rocks. The day is lived through blistered feet on jarring footpegs, through aching wrists on slapping bars, through not-quite-numb-enough bum that's on and off that bucking seating. The bike winces "eeesh" as if it's banged its knee on a coffee table as we clip a pothole and ding the rim.

I suspect the rear shock's burst. I know my kidneys have. Every time we hit a bump, I groan and the bike creaks. We sound like Steptoe doing star jumps. This is not sexy off-roading.

And then it rains. Proper tropical wet rain. I'm bone-dry and sweaty. I count to seven. I'm soggy-wet and shivering. It's like riding through a car wash. The sand turns to muddy clay. I spend an hour sitting in a puddle the size of whales, smoking soggy cigarettes, stuck behind a stick-in-the-mud truck.

Suddenly it's dark, I'm a wreck, there's still at least an hour to go, and the track's getting worse. Get off the bike. Relax. Eat toothpaste. Try to conjure up an appropriate deity. Papa Legba, Lord Shiva, or St. Jude? I settle for the Ghost of Future Dan—picture myself up the road with a belly full of food, mouth full of beer, ears full of soap. It works. An old man wobbles past on a bicycle burdened with palm oil. If he can make it, I can. An hour later I shuffle into Inhaminga's oil lamp–lit sandy streets. I find a pensao. The cook's just about to go home. She says she's not killing a chicken at this time of night. The chicken looks relieved and clucks off. Two hours later she returns with a plate of undercooked chips and a bottle of beer that stinks of mutton. I eat and collapse. Kid next door's playing with his radio. Just as I'm about to bang on the wall, he finds "King of the Road." I drift off. Ain't got no cigarettes.

■ ■ ■

Three weeks, 2,000 miles and a lot of good people. I couldn't have made it without them. I have always depended on the kindness of strangers. Two hours out of Inhaminga, heading for the Rio Zambezi (Zambezi, zam), it occurs to me I haven't seen another soul all day. No one knows I've left, no one's expecting me. If I bin it and break something out here, I'm in serious trouble. Just as I'm about to start crying, a bus pulls up. The driver asks if I'd like to ride with them. Says he'll look out for me. He didn't have to do that. It completely changes the day. Suddenly I've got a guardian angel and everything's all right. The piste levels out. The view opens up. I get a chance to look around and see the helicopter shot, little blue bike on a swooping red track bouncing through a palm-green jungle vastness under a sky so big it makes me dizzy and so blue it seems to stain the distant mountains. I can see for miles.

I stop for a perfect picnic. Boiled eggs and custard creams. I'm teased by a circus of cheeky monkeys. "The only reason we don't speak is so we're not obliged to work," says one. "Shush, here comes the farmer," warns another. "If he hears us chatting he'll make us pay for all those bananas."

I wave goodbye to the bus when we reach the Zambezi (Zambezi, zam). There's a queue of trucks a mile long. "What time's the ferry due?" I ask a driver. "About two o'clock." It's midday. "On Friday." It's Tuesday. Arse. A couple kids stroll up. They'll take me across in a canoe. No problem. But I can't get the bike in on my own. Half a dozen drivers jump up and help out.

They didn't have to do that.

It's an awfully big river, and this is an awful little boat. And it's leaking an awful lot of water. But it feels awfully good to hand over responsibility to someone else—even if it's a grinning teenager in an "I heart Lady Diana" T-shirt. Between the banks, this is his world. I feel decidedly feminine. Lie back and think of England. Wonder what I was doing this time last year? Que sera. I can swim, and if the bike ends up at the bottom of the Zambezi, would that really be so bad? I ask him if his name's Charon. He says no, Nelson. I pay the ferryman and get off.

Just outside Nampula I stop for a smoke. A pickup stops, and a smile hops out. "Hi. That looks hard work. Fancy a cold Coke?" He didn't have to do that. His name's Shari, and he works for Coca-Cola. He's been on the road investigating cooler abuse. "If we catch those boys selling anything but Coke out of our coolers they are in big trouble!" He insists that I follow him to a hotel. He insists on taking me home to meet his mother and wife. Before finally insisting that he take me to dinner and introduce me to his friends in his favorite bar. I'm ashamed to say that I'm looking for an angle. I'm happily humbled when there isn't one. Why, man? "Hospitality to travelers is an important part of Muslim culture," he winks, sinking a large Johnnie Walker.

■ ■ ■

Three weeks, 2,000 miles. A lot of sanctuary. The rougher the day, the softer the relief when it's finally over. Unload the bags, take off my boots, retch, relax. Tension and release. Really can't beat a hard day's night. A dusty mouth makes any beer taste wetter. A hungry stomach makes food taste hotter. And an aching body makes any bed seem comfier. Night is part of day.

"Let me guess—a cold beer, a hot shower, and some warm tucker. In what order?"

After another 12-hour day I hit Pemba beach campsite. Aussie Russell greets me with a real smile and a big handshake. There's a coconut-mat bar swaying with English, French, and Uruguyan overlanders, in from Zambia, Zimbabwe, and Malawi. There's a barbecue licking tandoori chicken and garlic squid. Sky Sports on the telly, Massive Attack on the stereo, all muffled by the roar of the Indian Ocean. And paradise is now.

■ ■ ■

Three weeks, 2,000 miles. And one big off. Why do they always happen like this? A stretch of cement-powder-fine sand, get on the gas, repeat the mantra "I have never fallen off in sand when going too fast, only when going too slow." Next thing I'm slip-sliding away, still holding the bars, lost in a cloud of dust. Eventually, we stop. I hear a voice murmuring, "You're OK, Dan, you're OK, kidda," while my shadow groans, "Get off me, you fat bastard, I can't breathe."

Odd moments. Lying there in the dust, moving my parts. Yep, all there. The kit did its job. Get up. Check the bike. No damage. The only thing that's broken is my bottle. Suddenly I'm terrified. A truck stops. The driver asks me if I want to put the bike on the back. He didn't have to do that. I almost say yes. A woman walks past with a 50-kilogram sack on her head. If she can do it, so can I. The truck drives away. I instantly regret my bravado and want to cry. I ride off with both feet down. I get overtaken by a Land Rover full of nuns. This is both humiliating and odd. Nuns shouldn't drive butch Land Rovers with Tonka-toy chunky tires and jacked-up leaf springs down adventurous pistes. They should ride bicycles. Down cobbled streets.

The sisters herald a miracle. The map says 50 miles to Kilwa, the next town. That's about three hours at this speed, and it's getting dark. Ten minutes later I reach a magic roundabout, incongruous tarred traffic circle fed by sandy tracks. A sign says, "Kilwa 15 km." But? Another ten minutes and I'm plotted up in a truck stop eating fish heads out of a tin tray and watching *Kids Say the Darndest Things*. Thanks, sisters.

■ ■ ■

Three weeks, 2,000 miles. Just outside Dar es Salaam, just after dark, I stop for a smoke. Burning hayfields set the night on fire. I'm alive. And I'm happy. Properly alive and properly happy. Somewhere out there, between the sandpits and the potholes, the monkeys and the leopards, the ship-wrecks and the train wrecks, the shredded tires and campfires, the death heads and the fish heads, somewhere between the Beira Devil and Pemba's deep blue sea, I kinda found what I was looking for. A self-contained, self-fulfilling journey. A great escape.

I ride into town and find the seedy Hotel Shirin. There's an English kid in the lobby. He asks me where I've come from. I tell him. Says he's just ridden the same route. I ask him what on. He points to the push-bike locked up outside. We laugh. We go for a drink. In the bar I'm approached by a camp Somalian waiter. "Excuse me, sir," he simpers. "Has anyone ever mentioned that you look like Elton John?"

■ ■ ■

It doesn't last. It never does. I wish there was a way of holding onto that sense of auto-achievement, that feeling of self-generated self-worth, but I always fail. Maybe that's the secret of success. I try to put it in my pocket but it curdles quick as milk in the midday sun. Takes just two weeks to turn dusty Dar's wide-open circle delights into just another drunk's triangle—flophouse for a cry and a wank, internet café for long-range abuse, bar to get bed-wetting drunk on a school night with the usual crowd of lost expats and ambitious hookers. And Mozambique's deep wilderness magic drowns in the smell of fighting and onions.

Email home:

Wake up. Cold shower in a brown trickle that doesn't even disturb the mosquitoes. Flip flop downstairs, pay the surly concierge and walk out into the chicken market. It smells. Walk round past the mechanics to the internet. Drink a coke, have a smoke, message you.

Today I went across the city. Sometimes it all looks very familiar. Today I saw it again.

This is a city where most people live on less than a dollar a day. Imagine that in England. I woke up and walked past a chicken market where the entrail-stained, white-coated chicken-chokers sit in car seats. Imagine that in England. I saw a cop with an AK giving his mate a backie on a pushbike. Imagine that in England. I was held up by a man who earns his living walking around selling nail varnish, dreaming of a stall in the market ("one day . . ."). Imagine that in England. I skipped past dungareed mechanics welding an exhaust on a crowded pavement. Imagine that in England. I ate spaghetti Bolognese in an open air café while a Casio synth churned out pre-programmed sub-Kenny G with a shop dummy sat behind the keyboard. Imagine that in England. I avoided a crippled woman walking on her flip-flop-ed hands, dragging her wasted legs underneath her, carrying her shopping on her head. Imagine that in England? You can't. It can't be done.

Sometimes I think Africa is the same. Other times I think it's very different. Tonight I'll get drunk with the imported Indian belly dancers in Bombay Knights. Gods make it easy on me.

The trip's starting to unravel. I see the signs but hide my face. I don't want to climb back into that crusty cocoon, deluded that only the devil or a dick would try to turn this fragile butterfly back into a maggot. But in less than a month I'll be back on my way home, ambushed by bosses, kidnappers, and a best friend's funeral.

First, I get fired. Decommissioned. "Message from the boss—we're not taking anymore Africa stories. Where next?" I have no real clue, but I go through the motions, pack up and head north with a vague idea of shopping, chasing a "worked my passage from Mombasa to Bombay" punchline. I ride out through a riot. Muslim youth protesting about police brutality are burning tires and smashing mouths. A kid in a headscarf stops the bike. "I have a sister in Leicester." So have I.

The teargas keeps me crying all the way to Tanga. I spend the evening with a Kiwi nurse and hit the Kenyan border. Plot up in Diani Beach, watch the Twin Towers burn and wait for another fall.

Lou flies in. We lie on white sand so soft it squeaks, play in the blue-green ocean, eat crab claws the size of sweet pigs' trotters, laugh at the palm trees full of cheeky monkeys, fuck on this 15-mile paradise beach that's been empty of tourists since the Nairobi embassy bombing warnings, and tear each other to shreds. What secrets silent, stony sit in the dark palaces of our hearts?

Bad moon rising. The sun sets on the Indian Ocean, coloring the moon Welsh gold then Sterling silver and painting the palm trees inky black silhouettes. I sit on a typhoon-downed casherina tree, watching a fire-imp born on the road dance round a crackling charcoal pit, watching my ex-best girl fly a kite, chatting knuckleheads with a German Harley mechanic, arguing politics with a shifty Rhodesian, talking designs with a South African tattooist, and wonder how the fuck it went so wretchedly wrong. A distant affair turned this paradise into hell. "It's better to dwell in the wilderness alone than with a contentious and angry woman." It's time to make a split.

Real life intervenes. While we're at the beach, the room gets cleaned and I get cleaned out—passport, palmtop, credit cards, camera. The thief used a key to open the door—clever. Then used a key to lock the door behind them—stupid. It had to be an inside job.

I complain. Nothing happens. I go to the cops. Nothing happens. I waited a patient week, then went back to the cops. "So, have you caught the thieves?" Er, aren't I supposed to say that, not you? I went back to the hotel. I lost my temper. I overturned tables. Someone in here stole my stuff. Who was it? Was it you? Was it you?

They rush me—manager, bouncer, couple of beach boys. Drag me and Lou upstairs, talking all kinds of Mau Mau shit. It's violent and tense. "Get out of this hotel now!" It's 2 a.m. Fine. But when we try to leave, they've locked the security cage that surrounds the stairs. We're locked in.

It's a zoo. Drunken painters, hustlers, and hookers from the bar start rattling the cage, running machetes along the bars, spitting through it, throwing beer through it, cursing through it. Open the fucking door. "Yes, open the door, let us at him. He calls us thieves." Lou tries to call the embassy. We're being held by force. That's kidnap, isn't it? She gets the ansaphone.

A night of this shrieking shit. Then the cops turn up—that's good. They arrive in a manager's Merc—that's bad. "You're under arrest." You're kidding. He's not and there's nothing funny about Kenyan cop shops. Unless you're tickled by cockroaches and bloodstained floors. Pay compensation to the hotel for disrupting business, or you and the girl spend some time here. He winks and rubs his crotch. I pay. We move hotels. Lou leaves. And for some reason, I don't.

Email from home:

Hi Dan,

Sorry mate but Mo asked me to get in touch. It's some really shit news. Will died on Sunday. A heart attack in Police custody. He'd been on it all weekend and got nicked on his bike. Died while being restrained. Really sorry the first time I've been in touch and it's such shit news. The funeral is next Wed' in Wales.

Take care dude, see ya soon, Neil.

Keep drifting.

# Chapter 4
# Journeys

"We looked through the bushes down the valley. At the point where what had been the farm gave way to what still was bush, there was a lone **alder tree.** It was old and gnarled, and in the bracken at its foot was George **Orwell's motorbike.**"

—Jock Mackneish, The Search for George Orwell's Motorbike

# *The Road*

## By T. E. Lawrence

*The Mint*

Jonathan Cape London (1955)

THE EXTRAVAGANCE in which my surplus emotion expressed itself lay on the road. So long as roads were tarred blue and straight; not hedged; and empty and dry, so long I was rich. Nightly I'd run up from the hangar, upon the last stroke of work, spurring my tired feet to be nimble. The very movement refreshed them, after the day-long restraint of service. In five minutes my bed would be down, ready for the night: in four more I was in breeches and puttees, pulling on my gauntlets as I walked over to my bike, which lived in a garage-hut, opposite. Its tyres never wanted air, its engine had a habit of starting at second kick: a good habit, for only by frantic plunges upon the starting pedal could my puny weight force the engine over the seven atmospheres of its compression.

Boanerges' first glad roar at being alive again nightly jarred the huts of Cadet College into life. 'There he goes, the noisy bugger,' someone would say enviously in every flight. It is part of an airman's profession to be knowing with engines: and a thoroughbred engine is our undying satisfaction. The camp wore the virtue of my Brough like a flower in its cap. Tonight Tug and Dusty came to the step of our hut to see me off. 'Running down to Smoke, perhaps?' jeered Dusty; hitting at my regular game of London and back for tea on fine Wednesday afternoons.

Boa is a top-gear machine, as sweet in that as most single-cylinders in middle. I chug lordly past the guard-room and through the speed limit at no more than sixteen. Round the bend, past the farm, and the way straightens. Now for it. The engine's final development is fifty-two horse-power. A miracle that all this docile strength waits behind one tiny lever for the pleasure of my hand.

Another bend: and I have the honour of one of England's straightest and fastest roads. The burble of my exhaust unwound like a long cord behind me. Soon my speed snapped it, and I heard only the cry of the wind which my battering head split and fended aside. The cry rose with my speed to a shriek: while the air's coldness streamed like two jets of iced water into my dissolving eyes. I screwed them to slits, and focused my sight two hundred yards ahead of me on the empty mosaic of the tar's gravelled undulations.

Like arrows the tiny flies pricked my cheeks: and sometimes a heavier body, some house-fly or beetle, would crash into face or lips like a spent bullet. A glance at the speedometer: seventy-eight. Boanerges is warming up. I pull the throttle right open, on the top of the slope, and we swoop flying across the dip, and up-down up-down the switchback beyond: the weighty machine launching itself like a projectile with a whirr of wheels into the air at the take-off of each rise, to land lurchingly with such a snatch of the driving chain as jerks my spine like a rictus.

Once we so fled across the evening light, with the yellow sun on my left, when a huge shadow roared just overhead. A Bristol Fighter, from Whitewash Villas, our neighbour aerodrome, was banking sharply round. I checked speed an instant to wave: and the slip-stream of my impetus snapped my arm and elbow astern, like a raised flail. The pilot pointed down the road towards Lincoln. I sat hard in the saddle, folded back my ears and went away after him, like a dog after a hare. Quickly we drew abreast, as the impulse of his dive to my level exhausted itself.

The next mile of road was rough. I braced my feet into the rests, thrust with my arms, and clenched my knees on the tank till its rubber grips goggled under my thighs. Over the first pot-hole Boanerges screamed in surprise, its mud-guard bottoming with a yawp upon the tyre. Through the plunges of the next ten seconds I clung on, wedging my gloved hand in the throttle lever so that no bump should close it and spoil our speed. Then the bicycle wrenched sideways into three long ruts: it swayed dizzily, wagging its tail for thirty awful yards. Out came the clutch, the engine raced freely: Boa checked and straightened his head with a shake, as a Brough should.

The bad ground was passed and on the new road our flight became birdlike. My head was blown out with air so that my ears had failed and we seemed to whirl soundlessly between the sun-gilt stubble fields. I dared, on a rise, to slow imperceptibly and glance sideways into the sky. There the Bif was, two hundred yards and more back. Play with the fellow? Why not?

duty to do nothing but wait hour after hour in the warm
g out southward.

utterly content to speak, drugged with an absorption
than physical contentment. Just we lay there spread-
of bodies, pillowed on one another and sighing in happy
ion. The sunlight poured from the sky and melted into
n the turf below our moist backs there came up a sister-
d us to it. Our bones dissolved to become a part of this
lgent earth, whose mysterious pulse throbbed in every
dies. The scents of the thousand-acre drome mixed with
breath of our hangar, nature with art: while the pale sea
bed in little waves before the wind raising a green surf
d flowed by the slats of our heat-lidded eyes.

ts of absorption resolve the mail and plate of our person-
e carbo-hydrate elements of being. They come to service
because of our light surrender to the good or evil of the

no possessions, few ties, little daily care. For me, duty
the brightness of these five buttons down my front.
are cared for as little as they care. Their simple eyes, out-
tural living; the penurious imaginations which neither
their lowlands of mind: all these expose them, like fallows,
of air. In the summer we are easily the sun's. In winter
efended along the roadway, and the rain and wind chivy
are wind and rain. We race over in the first dawn to the
cent swimming pool, and dive into the elastic water which
losely as a skin: and we belong to that too. Everywhere a
loneliness any more.

Finis' to this book, while I am
I hope, sometimes,
ver write it.

I slowed to ninety: signalled with my hand for him to overtake. Slowed ten more: sat up. Over he rattled. His passenger, a helmeted and goggled grin, hung out of the cock-pit to pass me the 'Up yer' RAF randy greeting.

They were hoping I was a flash in the pan, giving them best. Open went my throttle again. Boa crept level, fifty feet below: held them: sailed ahead into the clean and lonely country. An approaching car pulled nearly into its ditch at the sight of our race. The Bif was zooming among the trees and telegraph poles, with my scurrying spot only eighty yards ahead. I gained though, gained steadily: was perhaps five miles an hour the faster. Down went my left hand to give the engine two extra dollops of oil, for fear that something was running hot: but an overhead Jap twin, super-tuned like this one, would carry on to the moon and back, unfaltering.

We drew near the settlement. A long mile before the first houses I closed down and coasted to the cross-roads by the hospital. Bif caught up, banked, climbed and turned for home, waving to me as long as he was in sight. Fourteen miles from camp, we are, here: and fifteen minutes since I left Tug and Dusty at the hut door.

I let in the clutch again, and eased Boanerges down the hill along the tram-lines through the dirty streets and up-hill to the aloof cathedral, where it stood in frigid perfection above the cowering close. No message of mercy in Lincoln. Our God is a jealous God: and man's very best offering will fall disdainfully short of worthiness, in the sight of Saint Hugh and his angels.

Remigius, earthy old Remigius, looks with more charity on Boanerges. I stabled the steel magnificence of strength and speed at his west door and went in: to find the organist practising something slow and rhythmical, like a multiplication table in notes on the organ. The fretted, unsatisfying and unsatisfied lace-work of choir screen and spandrels drank in the main sound. Its surplus spilled thoughtfully into my ears.

By then my belly had forgotten its lunch, my eyes smarted and streamed. Out again, to sluice my head under the White Hart's yard-pump. A cup of real chocolate and a muffin at the teashop: and Boa and I took the Newark road for the last hour of daylight. He ambles at forty-five and when roaring his utmost, surpasses the hundred. A skittish motor-bike with a touch of blood in it is better than all the riding animals on earth, because of its logical extension of our faculties, and the hint, the provocation, to excess conferred by its honeyed untiring smoothness. Because Boa loves me, he gives me five more miles of speed than a stranger would get from him.

At Nottingham I added sausages from my wholesaler to the bacon which I'd bought at Lincoln: bacon so nicely sliced that each rasher meant a penny. The solid pannier-bags behind the saddle took all this and at my next stop a (farm) took also a felt-hammocked box of fifteen eggs. Home by Sleaford, our squalid, purse-proud, local village. Its butcher had six penn'orth of dripping ready for me. For months have I been making my evening round a marketing, twice a week, riding a hundred miles for the joy of it and picking up the best food cheapest, over half the country side.

## A Thursday Night

The fire is a cooking fire, red between the stove-bars, all its flame and smoke burned off. Half-past eight. The other ten fellows are yarning in a blue haze of tobacco, two on the chairs, eight on the forms, waiting my return. After the clean night air their cigarette smoke gave me a coughing fit. Also the speed of my last whirling miles by lamplight (the severest test of riding) had unsteadied my legs, so that I staggered a little. 'Wo-ups, dearie' chortled Dusty. 'More split-arse work tonight?' It pleases them to imagine me wild on the road. To feed this flight-vanity I gladden them with details of my scrap against the Bif.

'Bring any grub?' at length enquires Nigger, whose pocket is too low, always, for canteen. I knew there was something lacking. The excitement of the final dash and my oncoming weariness had chased from my memory the stuffed panniers of the Brough. Out into the night again, steering across the black garage to the corner in which he is stabled by the fume of hot iron rising from his sturdy cylinders. Click, click, the bags are detached; and I pour out their contents before Dusty, the hut pantry-man. Tug brings out the frying pan, and has precedency. The fire is just right for it. A sizzle and a filling smell. I get ready my usual two slices of buttered toast.

Nigger turns over the possibilities. 'What are eggs?' he asks. I do a lightning calculation: penny ha'penny. Right: he chooses one egg. Rashers are a penny. Two of them and two dogs, at tuppence. He rolls me his sixpence along the table. 'Keep the odd 'un for fat,' he murmurs.

The others choose and pay. S
this supper scandal among o
dearer, though not dear; and
own fetching and cooking. /
minutes, to be pertly served.

Paddy, the last cooker of
wiping out its dripping on a hu
see him put this bread to belly
ingly. Meanwhile the gramoph
My brain is too dishevelled af
dope of a wet evening. For to
finds us all willing for sleep. T

## Interlude

Service life in this way teache
to a big thing, which will exis
tions of standard airmen, like
and type remind us of that. A
clusters of us widen out beyon
beyond Depot, over hundreds
'belonging to something or ot
of many things.

As we gain attachment, so
spiritual importance of such t
ourselves for work, like robots
or particularity, and careless, c
pay are fetters to him, unless h
dress provided us by the RAF
put it on, oil, water, mud, pai
our friends.

A spell of warm weather
to quit this bleak north. The
a calm crescent of tarmac an
sun-trap. Through the aftern
which had gone away south, a

to have it for ou
sunshine, looki

We were to
fathoms deepe
eagled in a mes
excess of relaxa
our tissues. Fro
heat which join
underlying ind
tremor of our b
the familiar oil
of the grass bo
which hissed ar

Such mome
ality back into t
men very often,
moment.

Airmen hav
now orders only

And airmen
turned; their n
harrow nor reap
to the processe
we struggle und
us, till soon we
College's translu
fits our bodies
relationship: no

I can't write
still serving,
that I will n

# The Heart of Africa

## A casual adventure in South Africa
## becomes a full-blown love affair

### By Jamie Elvidge

*Motorcycle Escape*

October/November 2006

I T IS POSSIBLE to fall in love with a country the same way we fall in love with another human being. The texture of its landscape can make your heart race, the sound of its name send shivers. You can be sure of this fate when you understand a country more inside your chest than with your mind. When you look into the eyes of its people and their smiles leave you breathless.

This was South Africa to me. A love affair.

Of course, it would have been even better without the butt rash, but that's life. The Nothing's Perfect clause. Early in the adventure I'd rather unwisely forgotten moto-traveler's rule No. 157: "After impromptu dips in the ocean, always change out of your wet suit before riding away, taking care to dry your bum completely." A folly, indeed, and one exaggerated by the cruel stock seat of my rental BMW R1200GS. I love this bike almost as much as South Africa, but I must admit I fantasize about slashing its seat to the beat of a tribal drum.

Despite such physical malady, motorcycle touring in South Africa is a powerful elixir, and one made especially potent when administered via an Edelweiss experience. The tour I joined was a 14-day trek running from Cape Town northeast to Johannesburg. This particular affair was a "scouting" tour, which means you could have the happy option to explore a little uncharted territory. Edelweiss runs its South Africa tours in two one-way segments back and forth between the two major cities twice each year during the warm, South African summer.

BMW motorcycles are the mode du journey on almost all Edelweiss tours, and in South Africa we were able to choose an F650GS, R1200GS, R1150RT, or R1150R. In my opinion, the big GS is the only way to go on a trip like this because it allows you to chase horizons in absolutely any direction. You can conquer the trickiest dirt road, be comfortable on the longest highway, and, once you're used to it, pass your sportbike friends in the tightest corner—waving see ya with one hand. Our route involved very few dirt roads, and those were hard-packed and easy for everyone. However, when there were options to explore more unruly dirt, it was a blessing to be on a big GS, and the four riders who did have these machines (and the experience to utilize their capabilities) were able to enjoy a supplementary trek or two, which would turn out to be the icing on the adventure.

## West Meets West

I arrived in Cape Town after a two-day transit that included a 5-hour red-eye and a 19-hour nonstop from Atlanta, feeling more like an eggplant than an eager tourist. Markus Hellrigl, an Edelweiss lead guide with whom I'd already had the pleasure of traveling on an Alps tour, met me at the gate with such enthusiasm for our pending adventure that I couldn't help but feel a spark of excitement. After all, Hellrigl's passion was the reason I was here. It was his charged account of South Africa, first heard over rounds of hearty German beer, that originally piqued my interest. Meeting Christian Preining, our second tour guide, would complete the transfusion. Preining is so intensely humorous and immediately charming I knew I was going to spend much of the next 14 days enduring fits of laughter.

I enjoyed our group immediately. Twelve guests, as different as could be: From 34 to 69, married to single, rich to struggling, Austrian, German, and American. Somehow we jelled immediately and stayed cohesive the entire two weeks. No subgroups, no splintering. Before leaving the city we would also meet Edelweiss clients who had just come in from the route we would be taking. They were so animated—like kids just getting off a roller coaster and running down the ramp shouting, "Let's do it again!" And so tan, these moms and pops, telling tales about carefree ocean swims and whoop-ridden dirt roads.

We all found Cape Town an easy place to be, especially for Westerners. The official language in South Africa is English, after all, so we Americans didn't even need to apologize for our notoriously lazy attempts at linguistics. The city is bright and lively, sided by the Atlantic and swept clean by its sea-charged air. Though thoroughly cosmopolitan at its core, Cape Town is encircled by shantytowns, a reminder of this country's ongoing disparity. And though we never felt it, we heard that the dark shadows cast by apartheid linger here in the city. Not surprising, knowing it was only 10 short years ago the country was still in turmoil. Robben Island and the prison that held Nelson Mandela captive for 18 years sits only seven miles off Cape Town's shore. Such reminders make it all feel too fresh to be history, and too shameful to possibly be so fresh.

We were able to visit many local treasures on our first riding day, including the Cape of Good Hope, but most of us will remember it as the day we spent weirded out trying to ride on the left side of the road while dodging baboons and wild ostrich. You get used to such oddities as you spend more time here. Each day would bring entirely new experiences as we rode farther from the gleaming port city and closer to the real South Africa—the heart of this country.

## Immersion

Isn't it crazy how we understand on an intellectual level that unrealistic expectations are at the root of nearly all human dissatisfaction? Yet we conjure expectations relentlessly, and usually without even realizing it. I had ideas about what I'd find in South Africa, though I cannot trace them to any particular research or reasoning. I thought it would be dangerous, less than clean, and maybe even dripping with villainous bacteria. My imagined South Africa would be rough—plagued with poverty and therefore filled with unhappy, resentful people. And, of course, the black culture there would feel a special animosity toward whites for the cruel injustice of apartheid.

Sometimes what we think we know about a situation turns out to be so utterly different, so conflicting, that we have nothing left to do but clear our minds entirely. To be washed clean.

One rider described this phenomenon as having all the dirt—all the sediment—he'd been carrying in his existing life shaken off so that he felt reborn. It's true the effect may have been exaggerated by his riding an R-bike over way too much washboard, or he might have felt extra squeaky because of our near-daily romps in the Indian Ocean. But truth be told, South Africa was a journey of enlightenment for all of us. From the simple adjustment of having drivers treat you with respect, for example, by pulling toward the emergency lane to let you pass every single time, to having men and women and children absolutely beam at you from the side of the road, waving and clapping and literally dancing at the sight of our motorcycle caravan.

And the sights? How could one not be entertained by such diverse geography? From the immense cliffs cradling the cool blue Indian Ocean, we'd stare down in awe at empty white beaches that went on for miles. In and out of mountainscapes we'd ride, where layers of the earth's crust—ribbons of reds and grays and lichen greens—would tilt and twist enough to make you dizzy. Coast, mountain, prairie, bush, it was all brand new and familiar at once. One day could remind you of the Cascades, the next, southern New Mexico, the next, Thailand. "What about the riding?" my go-fast friends ask. Man. The riding in South Africa is phenomenal. The roads are mostly well kept and quite empty, too. Of course, it helped that our guides knew where to find the twistiest action, and almost every day one of the two optional routes was laced with such tangles, along with bouts of hugely fast and rhythmic sweepers.

## Best of the Best

I believe it's impossible to shove a story so grand into a "today we had scrumptious gruel in Hanover" format, so perhaps the best I can do is encapsulate the highest of the high points. Those on the tour with me will undoubtedly shout, "What about the waterfalls pouring thousands of feet down the Langeberg Mountains!" and, "What about the World's Highest Bungee Jump!" and probably even, "What about the time Roger stuck that lady's corn cob in his ear and had to pay for it?" Sadly, there just isn't room to report all the amazing and crazy things we saw and did.

One of our most giddy highs was an optional early evening run with Hellrigl over a dirt pass called Swartberg just outside of Oudtshoorn. We'd already had several days of alarmingly beautiful vistas, so we were really in it for the promise of an off-road adrenaline rush. And sure enough, our teeth were coffee brown by the time we got to the summit, since we'd been unable to stop laughing during the dusty ascent. Top of the world? Pretty close. It was certainly as high as we could get without drugs.

Yummy babootie. Sounds kinda sexy, I know, but it is really just good South African–style chili, and my favorite thing we ate on the trip.

On the afternoon of the sixth day, Preining offered those interested a little scouting opportunity that would take us into the tribal lands of the Transkei region, near Umtata, where Nelson Mandela was born. We'd attempt to close a loop to a bay called Qora Mouth, which we could tell on the map would offer a completely remote beach experience, maybe even time for another dry-your-bum dip in the ocean. What we found was vastly more refreshing. The tribal villages of the Tembu, only one of several indigenous cultures we encountered between Cape Town and Johannesburg, are made up of whitewashed mud-and-thatch huts scattered among the rolling green hills like so many flower petals after a summer wind. Even though it required a strong hand to negotiate the winding, rutted dirt roads, we still made the effort to wave back to the kids who came running across the fields to greet us.

Everywhere we went in South Africa people would gather around our bikes, and the same was true out here in the Transkei. There came a moment, though, when the magnetism of those smiling faces suddenly became much more important than our destination. So we stopped. And we let ourselves be totally embraced by these kids with their magical sense of simplicity and joyful curiosity. At one point I was taking digital pictures of them and then showing them the screen. And they were so floored. I was so floored. I'd shoot and then they'd dogpile me. We took them for rides on the bikes; they asked us our names and we tried to pronounce theirs. I don't know how long we stayed, but we never made it near the beach, and when we finally did ride away we'd all been moved to the point of feeling shaken. These people had an inexplicable feeling of happiness surrounding them, yet they were very poor, their futures so limited. It was a kind of happiness that was new to us. Haunting, almost, because the purity of it seemed unobtainable.

This experience wouldn't have been available from the seat of a car or a tour bus, of course. When you are on a motorcycle you are infinitely more connected to your surroundings. There's no ignoring the smells, the temperatures, the hands outstretched in greeting. All day we would wave back to people, even to the drivers of oncoming cars and trucks who would flash their lights in greeting. We were surprised at how even this fleeting bit of contact seemed to make them so happy. You can imagine the cumulative effect it had on us. Our souls grew fat and jolly.

After we'd seen South Africa so close up, it was impossible not to be infected by its generosity of spirit. I know our last gourmet roadside picnic (an original Edelweiss tradition) at Torgaat Beach was not only a favorite moment of the guests, but also of the guides, simply because of the people we shared it with. We had extra food, so Hellrigl and Preining invited everyone around us to join in. The warm feeling made it easier to say goodbye to the crazy-blue Indian Ocean, which we'd turn away from that eighth day so we could make our way inland toward Zulu territory and finally Kruger National Park for a bit of the real, real Africa. The one involving lions, rhinos, zebras, and giraffes . . . and a food chain that doesn't include brie cheese.

Our time among the Zulu was priceless. We stayed in huts on the location set of the 1986 miniseries *Shaka Zulu* that follows Africa's most famous tribal king's life and his people's struggle during the height of British invasion. The sets are now used as dioramas, and the locals dress in somewhat authentic fashion and reenact period lifestyle. This was colorful and fun, if a bit hokey. The coolest thing was talking to the Zulu about how modern tribal life stays surprisingly true to ancient structure and ritual. If you have enough cows, for example, you can buy as many wives as you can handle.

Doing a "game drive" at Kruger is kinda like a quickie safari. You spend a half-day hunting Africa's Big Five: elephant, leopard, lion, rhino, and water buffalo, only with cameras instead of guns. From our two hired Rovers (you'd get eaten on a bike) we saw three out of five (no leopard or rhino), plus about 100 other animals that amazed us, many of which we'd never heard of. No Africa Safari U.S.A., this government-protected reserve shelters more than 50 million acres. The animal viewing was definitely a highlight, but perhaps more unforgettable were the two nights spent at the Protea Hotel at Kruger Gate. Edelweiss accommodations are always high-quality and memorable, but this place was enchanting, and it wasn't just the amazing food or the wild monkeys hanging about the elevated, open-terrace lobby either. The nights at Kruger Gate were so special because we'd gotten to know each other so well. We'd shared so much by that point.

South Africa had become a part of us, and in that sense, we'd become a part of each other.

## Farewell to Transcendence

Leaving the wilds of Kruger, I didn't expect more than a trudge to Johannesburg, where I knew my euphoria would be spoiled by another 24-hour plane ride (and a lifetime of not being in South Africa), but the route from the park to Waterval Boven turned out to be rather exceptional. First we wound our way up onto the Drakensberg plateau to gaze down into Blyde River Canyon. I'd heard it referred to as South Africa's Grand Canyon, which I thought an insult because this shocking geologic wonder is far too distinct to be compared to anything else on the planet. The next stop was God's Window. Surely some of you remember the cult film *The Gods Must Be Crazy*. Well, this is the exact spot the little bushman, Xi, throws the troublesome Coke bottle over the "end of the earth." Having no evil of my own to expel, I was left to consider whether this was a window looking into heaven or a window looking out.

Butt rash and all, this particular Edelweiss trip has become my favorite experience in 20 years of riding. Totally unexpected. Also unexpected was the difficulty I had saying goodbye to the people I'd shared it with. Sooner than any of us wanted, we were toasting farewell and catching planes in different directions.

When I finally got home I was still waving, though hardly anyone waved back. Weeks later, I'm still smiling at people I pass on the street, still throwing out animated hellos and good mornings. Trying, anyway. It's inevitable, I suppose, that the elixir of Good Hope begins to fade. In the absence of reciprocation I may become a little sullen myself, yet this unrequited joy has a certain positive: It only deepens my appreciation for all the wonderful things I found in South Africa. For what you will find, too, should you choose to journey there.

To this day, as I tell people about riding motorcycles in South Africa, my hand unconsciously rises to cover my chest. Perhaps I fear my heart will simply leap out and disappear.

And I'll have to take another 24-hour plane ride to retrieve it.

# Ghost Town

## By Elena Filatova

*www.kiddofspeed.com*

MY NAME IS ELENA. I run this website, and I don't have anything to sell. What I do have is my motorbike and the absolute freedom to ride it wherever curiosity and the speed demon take me.

I have ridden all my life, and over the years I have owned several different motorbikes. I ended my search for a perfect bike with big Ninja, a bike that boasts a mature 147 horsepower, some serious bark. It is fast as a bullet and comfortable for long trips.

I travel a lot, and one of my favorite destinations leads north from Kiev, toward the Chernobyl Dead Zone, which is 130 kilometers from my home. Why is this my favorite? Because one can take long rides there on empty roads.

The people all left, and nature is blooming. There are beautiful woods and lakes.

The roads that have not been traveled by trucks or army vehicles are in the same condition they were 20 years ago—except for an occasional blade of grass or some tree that discovered a crack to spring through. Time does not ruin roads, so they may stay this way until they can be opened to normal traffic again . . . a few centuries from now.

To begin our journey, we must learn a little something about radiation. It is really very simple, and the device we use for measuring radiation levels is called a geiger counter. If you flick it on in Kiev, it will measure about 12–16 microroentgen per hour. In a typical city of Russia and America, it will read 10–12 microroentgen per hour. In the center of many European cities the reading will be 20 microentgen per hour, the radioactivity of the stone.

A reading of 1,000 microentgens equal one milliroentgen and 1,000 milliroentgens equal 1 roentgen. So one roentgen is 100,000 times the average radiation of a typical city. A dose of 500 roentgens within 5 hours is fatal to humans. Interestingly, it takes about 2 1/2 times that dosage to kill a chicken and over 100 times that to kill a cockroach.

This sort of radiation level cannot be found in Chernobyl now. In the first days after explosion, some places around the reactor were emitting 3,000–30,000 roentgens per hour. The firemen who were sent to put out the reactor fire were fried on the spot by gamma radiation. The remains of the reactor were entombed within an enormous steel and concrete sarcophagus, so it is now relatively safe to travel to the area—as long as one do not step off of the roadway and does not stick around in the wrong places.

The map shows our journey through the dead zone. Radiation went into the soil and now appears in apples and mushrooms. It is not retained by asphalt, however, which makes rides through this area possible.

I have never had problems with the dosimeter guys who man the checkpoints. They are experts, and if they find radiation on your vehicle, they give it a chemical shower. I don't count those couple of times when "experts" tried to invent an excuse to give me a shower, because those had a lot more to do with physical biology than biological physics.

On the Friday evening of April 25, 1986, the reactor crew at Chernobyl-4 prepared to run a test the next day to see how long the turbines would keep spinning and producing power if the electrical power supply went offline. This was a dangerous test, but it had been done before. As a part of the preparation, they disabled some critical control systems—including the automatic shutdown safety mechanisms.

Shortly after 1:00 a.m. on April 26, the flow of coolant water dropped, and the power began to increase.

At 1:23 a.m., the operator moved to shut down the reactor in its low-power mode, and a domino effect of previous errors caused a sharp power surge, triggering a tremendous steam explosion that blew the 1,000-ton cap on the nuclear containment vessel and raised it in the air.

Some of the 211 control rods melted, and then a second explosion, whose cause is still the subject of disagreement among experts, threw out fragments of the burning radioactive fuel core and allowed air to rush in—igniting several tons of graphite insulating blocks.

Once graphite starts to burn, it's almost impossible to extinguish. It took nine days and 5,000 tons of sand, boron, dolomite, clay, and lead

*Elena Filatova*

dropped from helicopters to put it out. The radiation was so intense that many of those brave pilots died.

It was this graphite fire that released most of the radiation into the atmosphere, and troubling spikes in atmospheric radiation were measured as far as thousands of miles away.

These were inexcusable errors of design.

The causes of the accident are described as a fateful combination of human error and imperfect technology. Andrei Sakharov said that the Chernobyl accident demonstrates that our system cannot manage modern technology.

In keeping with a long tradition of Soviet justice, they imprisoned several people who worked on that shift—regardless of their guilt. Twenty-five people working the shift died.

Radiation will stay in the Chernobyl area for tens of thousands of years, but humans may begin repopulating the area in about 600 years—give or take three centuries. The experts predict that, by then, the most dangerous elements will have disappeared—or have been sufficiently diluted into the rest of the world's air, soil, and water. If our government can somehow

*Elena Filatova*

find the money and political will power to finance the necessary scientific research, perhaps a way will be discovered to neutralize or clean up the contamination sooner. Otherwise, our distant descendents will have to wait until the radiation diminishes to a tolerable level. If we use the lowest scientific estimate, that will be 300 years from now . . . some scientists say it may be as long as 900 years.

I think it will be 300, but people often accuse me of being an optimist.

In the Ukrainian language (where we don't like to say "the") Chernobyl is the name of a grass, wormwood (absinth). This word scares the holy bejesus out of people here. Maybe part of the reason for that among religious people is because the Bible mentions wormwood in the book of the Revelation—which foretells the end of the world.

Revelation 8:10: And the third angel sounded, and there fell a great star from heaven, burning as it were a lamp, and it fell upon the third part of the rivers, and upon the fountains of waters;

Revelation 8:11: And the name of the star is called Wormwood: and the third part of the waters became wormwood; and many men died of the waters, because they were made bitter.

*Elena Filatova*

Also, in our language, if you break the name up, "chorno" means "black" and "byl" means "pain." If I tell someone that I am heading to Chernie . . . the best response is, "Are you nuts?"

My dad used to say that people are afraid of any deadly thing they cannot see, cannot feel, and cannot smell. Maybe that is because those words are a good description of death itself.

Dad is a nuclear physicist, and he has educated me about many things. He is much more worried about the speed my bike travels than about the direction I point it.

My trips to Chernobyl are not like a walk in the park, but the risk can be managed. Sometimes I go for rides alone, sometimes with a pillion passenger, but never in company with any other vehicle because I do not want anyone to raise dust in front of me.

I was a schoolgirl back in 1986, and as soon as the radiation level began to rise in Kiev, Dad put all of us on the train to grandma's house. Granny lives 800 kilometers from here, and Dad wasn't sure if it was far enough away to keep us out of reach of the big bad wolf of a nuclear meltdown.

The communist government that was in power then kept silent about this accident. In Kiev, they forced people to take part in their preciously stupid

*Elena Filatova*

Labor Day parade, and it was then that ordinary people began hearing the news of the accident from foreign radio stations and relatives of those who died. The real panic began 7–10 days after the accident. Those who were exposed to the exceedingly high levels of nuclear radiation in those first 10 days when it was still a state secret, including unsuspecting visitors to the area, either died or have serious health problems.

Time to go for a ride. This is our road. There won't be many cars on those roads. This place has ill fame, and people try not to settle here. The farther we go, the cheaper the land, the less the people, and the more beautiful nature, quite the reverse of everywhere else in the world—and a forecast of things to come.

As we pass the 86th kilometer, we encounter a giant egg—which marks the point where civilization as we know it ends—and the Chernobyl ride begins.

Someone brought the egg from Germany. It represents life breaking through the hard shell of the unknown. I am not sure if this symbolism is encouraging or not. Either way, it makes people think, and for us this is our last chance to stock up on edible food, drinkable water, and uncontaminated fuel. Our journey from here is a gradually darkening picture of deserted towns, empty villages, and dead farms.

*Elena Filatova*

Radiation from the reactor's explosion was disbursed unevenly by the winds, as if in a chessboard fashion, leaving some places alive and others dead. It's hard to say where the fairyland begins.

To me it begins behind a bridge in a dead village that is located some 60 kilometers west of the reactor.

Each time I pass into the zone, I feel that I have entered an unreal world. In the dead zone, the silence of the villages, roads, and woods seem to say something to me . . . something that I strain to hear . . . something that attracts and repels me both at the same time. It is divinely eerie—like stepping into that Salvador Dali painting with the dripping clocks.

How many people died of radiation? No one knows—not even approximately. The official casualty reports range from 30 to 300,000, and many unofficial sources put the toll over 400,000.

The final toll will not be known in our lifetime, and maybe not our children's either.

It is easier to calculate material losses. It was a crippling economic catastrophe for the region—from which it may never recover.

This hellish inferno became a sort of paradise for wild animals—at least on the surface. They thrive with no humans to prey upon them, but nobody fully

*Elena Filatova*

understands how the nuclear poisons have altered their genetic makeup, the extent of their migration, or their interactions with the adjacent "safe" areas. Grotesque mutations have been reported, but zoologists deny that.

Populations of wolves and wild boars grow rapidly. They occupy the abandoned houses and sheds. They are curiously not aggressive here. Maybe that has something to do with the food supply, which is plentiful for all species except man but contaminated. It's not unusual to see a wolf, a fox, a wild boar, or a wild deer casually crossing the road.

Roads that lead into places where no one lives are blocked.

The roads are blocked for cars, but not for motorcycles. Good girls go to heaven. Bad ones go to hell. And girls on fast bikes go anywhere they want.

# The Racer As Tourist

## By Kevin Cameron

*Cycle World*

March 1980

RACING WILL MAKE OF YOU an international Philistine if it can. You get a start money offer at a foreign circuit, pack madly, grab your passport, and fly. You arrive out of breath and short on sleep, force your way through the language barrier, buy your way to the circuit, race, and finally get out, thankfully, win or lose. Back on the airliner you can remember in fitful torpor that you have completely ignored an entire different people, culture, and history. Wasn't I within 50 miles of where Caesar crossed the Rubicon? But there's never time. Crankshaft in, crankshaft out, weld that crack, tote that crate.

After the AGV Cup at Imola, Italy, in the fall of 1978, it was different. The race came at the season's very end. With nothing else to do, we could stay out the full 14 days of our economy flights, a full week to spend after the races. We rented (or did we buy it?) a tiny car and set off to start a second career as tourists.

My first trip to Italy had been in 1972, and it was a classic, a trans-Europe mad hustle in a 24-horsepower van of no known make. Refused at one German border point for lacking the green insurance card, we tried another, less businesslike frontier and sped on. Practice was a nightmare of hurry and anxiety. Even dinner at the hotel was a fright. We tried to order, searching desperately for cognate words the waiter would understand. Aha! Spaghetti! The tired man was using a kind of passive resistance towards our ignorant babble. They want spaghetti! I'll give them spaghetti. Here it came, a big steaming plate of plain, tasteless, boiled spaghetti. Sauce? Meat? Incomprehension. Salad? Maybe. Much gesturing. Here he came back again with a plateful of plain lettuce. We eat this. This is our dinner.

The 1978 trip was a revelation. We stayed in an excellent provincial hotel far from the track and staffed by friendly people. Much of the time we had an Italian-speaking guide who liked to eat and drink, and saw to it that we all did too. Every meal was a leisurely and civilizing affair of several courses, each of which was brought around in advance for our inspection. Yes, please, I'd like some of these and some of that and a little of those. Wine and water bottles lined every table. There was time to talk over the day and digest its events, to relax completely. Each course followed imperceptibly and was often unusual as well as very good. These were not the war horse favorites made familiar by U.S. dining Italian restaurants. Afterwards, if we liked, an evening in the sitting room, sipping something agreeable from the bar.

All the little details of life were rewardingly different. Really, it was a matter of sparing the energy required to open my eyes and look at things. Wonderfully worked wood was everywhere. Windows were fastened with graceful and effective cast bronze fittings. A remarkable variety of ceramic tile and rock surfaces promised to last forever. The ordinary parts of things seemed to have commanded respect in the making. The well-cared-for land showed the same attention, miles of neat grape arbors lining all the roads.

After the racing, our itinerary called out a trip to the Moto Guzzi museum near Lake Como in the northwest, then a visit to Minarelli in industrial Bologna, where the great racing engineer Jörg Möller is engaged in a 125 Grand Prix program. Then we would run down to the Adriatic coast and see the Morbidelli factory where Grand Prix machines for all classes are in preparation.

We already had plenty of *autostrada* experience from the many trips to Milan airports in search of missing bikes and tools. Each of these 600-kilometer round trips had cost us $96 in truck rental, fuel, and tolls, carried out at a steady, governed 107 kilometers per hour. The extremely noisy open-chamber Fiat diesel had given us an amazing 20 miles per gallon at near-70-mile-per-hour speeds, pulling this very large vehicle. I wish I had one now.

Our little rented Opel hummed along marvelously on the flat but detected the slightest hill by slowing depressingly. I curled up in the back among the piled luggage to enjoy my post-race headache. Richard Schlachter drove while Jeff Cowan, Wes Cooley's mechanic, puzzled over the pleated pieces of paper that we had been told were maps.

Giant, unfamiliar-looking Saab-Scania and Fiat trucks with strange wheel arrangements rule these roads, and the usual German and Swiss businessmen bear past at 80 and 100 miles per hour. The service plazas offer gasoline at nearly two dollars a gallon, together with faster-paced and less tasty versions of the meals we had enjoyed at the hotel. Our *lire* left us quickly wherever we went. Onward to the bank!

An early start got us up to Lake Como in the morning. The lake's three arms lie among the feet of the Alps, where great fractured masses of limestone cliff towered up in the electric morning sunlight. The rock itself was creamy and glowing in the light, but here and there streaked with dark gray, as though years of dingy smoke had been imperfectly washed away by rain. My headache made it all a bit unreal—the rock walls didn't seem to me hard surfaces that I might climb so much as interesting apparitions of light.

The shore road passes through tunnels, some cut through solid stone with no inner facing of masonry and no lights. Others had crude windows blasted through to the light, making us inhabitants of an ancient fortress, armed in imagination with terrible bronze bombards. People have been doing clever things in these parts for a long time. Other tunnels are really roofed roadways with rows of heavy columns supporting the earth above, providing a shaded secret view of the lake from within.

Here in the new sun were the grand closed-up summer places and the former estates, perhaps staffed until just recently by servants able to remember more opulent times. Architecture ascends the hillside on one side of the road, and a solid row of matching formal boathouses fronts the lake on the other. Each boathouse has a sundeck caged in wrought ironwork to keep out less fortunate citizens. Various neglected boats are still in the water. In one place a heavy stone breakwater many feet high shelters an ancient cabin cruiser beyond repair. Its owners are interested in other things now.

The destination is Mandello del Lario, the home of Moto Guzzi on the eastern leg of the lake. In the boom years of the 1950s Italians were eager for cheap motorized transport, and Guzzi turned out just what was needed. To nourish the imaginations of moped owners there was road racing. A great era of racing flourished, with the many makers pushing technology forward quickly in rapid developmental strides. From Guzzi there came a remarkable series of machines, concentrating at first on a single exquisitely simple theme, then spreading out into wide innovation.

*Lee Klancher*

The pre-war machines had been horizontal singles; the new Grand Prix racers were developments from them. The center of gravity of these powerplants was actually below the axle centerlines, contrasting strongly with recent multi-cylinder engines whose crank centers are 15 to 18 inches off the ground.

These Guzzi singles were remarkably efficient for a variety of interesting reasons. Their cylinder heads faced straight forward, so direct cooling air had a straight shot at the hot, troublesome area between the valves. This excellent cooling allowed engineer Carcano to narrow the angle between the valves for better entry to the cylinder and reduced short-circuiting of charge from intake to exhaust during overlap. The horizontal cylinder also allowed complete freedom in locating the intake tract. On the contemporary Norton Manx and Matchless G50 singles, the intake angle could not be raised too far without interference between carburetor and fuel tank or seat. On these Guzzis, a steep downdraft angle contributed to good breathing, putting the carburetor bell just below the lower steering race. There was room for everything, and Carcano exploited every means to make the result handy and light. Power was never staggering, but the good torque spread and extreme light weight made a potent package on all but the fastest circuits.

By concentrating on this simple design, Guzzi was able to win and defend its championships for a long time. Eventually, despite the 210-pound weight of the 250 and 350 Guzzis, the horsepower of multi-cylinder competition from Gilera, MV Agusta, and others was beginning to tell. After sporadic adventures with V-Twins, inline threes and fore-and-aft fours (looking for all the world like miniature Offys), Carcano decided to go straight to the heart of the matter. If cylinder multiplication was the technology required, he would master it. The new Moto Guzzi would be a watercooled V-8. Transverse fours and sixes were too wide. Air-cooling could not scoop out the heat from the many recesses of such a complex engine. So it was done.

Two questions remained: really high rpm was still a mystery, and there were troubles with crank and rod bearings. Handling had been worked out a long time before for the remarkable singles, but with eight times the cylinders there was no place for the weight to go but up, both in pounds and in height off the ground. Traditional geometry and the tires of those times put engine and rider at the extreme rear of the frame, and the frames themselves were none too strong. Suspension was just emerging from the friction-damper era. There were too many problems to solve all at once, though the eight was moderately successful. After much development and a rising tide of expense, Guzzi was ready to withdraw from racing. It would be left to the growing Japanese company, Honda, to continue the struggle with the problems first defined by Carcano's design, and even they would need lots of help.

The Guzzi offices turned out to be cool, humid, and nearly empty. There was in their dark corridors the atmosphere of a severely run school, or even of a convent. The floors were of the inevitable stone. An austere graph on the wall lectured the visitor about reduced stopping distances with integral braking, a modern Guzzi feature. There was a woman under glass in a kind of office. My tentative questions about the *museo* provoked a telephone call. Moments later another woman, clad in a seminary uniform and thick, rope-soled sandals, arrived to assess our request. She, in turn, summoned yet another level of judgment, a thick-lipped young man in a white, turtle-necked sweater. He looked very like the men in the scooter ads of the late 1950s: foppish, sleek, and self-conscious. Please come back at three. The "please" was not his goodwill, but his training. He should be happy if we came back on Doomsday. Apparently the museum is not a walk-in, but only to be seen by appointment. We have no appointment, but perhaps . . .

All right then. We can drive down to the lake and look around. I would like to find a quiet place to leave my headache. Good fortune showed us the way to a fine little park. I walked down to the water's edge and looked out to the far shore. Maybe that's what's so nice about the ocean—it has no far shore. Yet this lake was extremely pleasant, misty, and blue in the distance. Somewhere behind the trees a harsh mechanical chattering came from a gravel separator. This was strange because the area is so obviously populated by the rich, their private hoardings all protected and fenced. Here is noisy work invading every preserve.

An empty gravel streamed led down to the water nearby, crossed by a caged and padlocked bridge. This dry run must thunder and shoot in the springtime because it is pointed right at the mountains above, already topped with new snow.

I couldn't cross the bridge, so I walked along the park road where a wounded bronze soldier was subsiding pitifully on a stone plinth. Dead men are listed there, officers first.

Here came a Guzzi three-wheel truck, right out of the 1940s, its single-cylinder 500 engine thudding so heavily I fancied I could almost feel the combustion shock reverberating through the connecting rod at each power stroke. It was massively loaded down with gravel.

Back at the factory, we rousted out the young fashion plate, who listlessly led us through the offices and out into the unusual courtyard of the factory complex. This could easily be a small provincial town, for the buildings are tile-roofed and of a relaxed and almost residential character—unlike any factory I have seen. Big open wooden doors revealed high-piled steel baskets of fresh castings, and dark shapes moving within the rooms beyond suggested people at work. We entered another building and came to yet another metal cage, this one enclosing a stairway. It was like the rare-book section of a library. The man unlocked the wire door and we made our way up a stair, which by now had the character of a luxury private apartment—modern banister, genteel stone steps, steep but

*Lee Klancher*

definitely not industrial. At the top, another door, another key. He entered and switched on some lights. We were there.

I sized up the room as the fluorescents blinked. It was a long hall with racing machines to the left. On the right were the many commercial products that had paid for them.

I turned to the left and thought no more about my headache. Here were the legendary singles, not on paper in a book, but right in my face. The cylinders were enormous! The finning of the 250 must be 8 inches across, and that of the 300 perhaps 10. How did they get those machines down to 210 pounds? These engines look very solid. The early ones carried magnetos on their backs, and the later ones are evidently coil and battery. That must be the influence of the V-8—since no one could conceive a compact magneto to fire so many cylinders, they were forced to use coil and battery, just as Maserati did with their V-12 at nearly the same time.

Here is the inline four. There are the ponderous-looking transverse triples. Most of these machines have short leading-link front ends, the ones I used to see in the pictures. Friction dampers! Here are two of the venerable and successful 120-degree V-Twin 500 racers with their exposed hairpin valve springs.

I noticed considerable wear on the footpegs, the seats, and the handlebar grips. All these motorcycles had done thousands of miles of hard racing all over Europe on a busy, vital schedule 25 years ago. Under a long bench were more engines, looking as though they had been pulled from their frames after their last races and just never made it to the rebuild shop before their programs were cancelled. Here were two more, black with oil. These things are all frozen bits of a departed life.

And here was the V-8. There were several of them, complete machines and engine units. Here were the eight tiny Dell'Orto carburetors, inter-locked like the fingers of two hands. The sweater man wasn't looking, so I took the throttle linkage in my hands and made the phalanx of throttles rise and fall. Years before I had read the hero-worshipping accounts of the eight and of Dickie Dale, Ken Kavanagh, and Bill Lomas. The machine that was greater than anything that could be conceived. Staggering complexity, incredible engineering. Well, I was glad enough to be here looking at it now. Back then they needed that much machinery to get 75 bhp from a 500, and it is a nice piece of work.

On a table was a scale model of the Guzzi *galleria del vento*, the special wind tunnel that tamed all the little eddies and turbulences into the improbable but effective bird-beak fairings used then. To my question, the guide answered that the tunnel is still active today.

The only racing equipment of recent construction to be seen was all based on the transverse V-twin Le Mans, long-distance speed record versions. Though they look a bit like masquerading police bikes, each one has its neatly lettered little card proclaiming the records set. No more exotica. That's all over with. The company's business is limited and well defined now—no more wildly expanding post-war market, no more vast sales to justify the cost of racing. This isn't 1953, and these are prosperous people whose currency is rising against our own. These Europeans are buying cars, and fancy ones at that. Their motorcycle boom is over, it was over way back in 1957 when the big Italian companies signed the secret protocol that ended factory racing. The costs had become too great and the returns, in a world that wanted cars now, had become too small. Only the maverick upstart, MV Agusta, continued to race, establishing a great reputation against scanty opposition. The great machines are put away now in places like this museum, and they have been for a long time. The great riders of that era are paunchy and balding if they are with us at all.

But think of it—the 1950s, the many companies, some very large and some little more than garages full of tools, all producing scores of designs filled with ideas. Fabio Cesare Taglioni and his springless valve gear, Giulio Carcano and his subtle singles, all the incredible Morinis, Mondials, Gileras, Benellis.

That particular set of conditions is over, its hopes have been hoped, flags have fallen, tracks have closed. Genial older men, former racers, builders, and designers, still come to the events to see the Japanese machines perform the latest steps. We had seen the hills around Imola solid with people the previous Sunday. Big-time factory racing has simply moved to other places, where it flourishes.

The guide was obviously getting restless. Time to go. We all thanked him and filed out down the stairs. Outside, Mandello del Lario was still a lovely place of trees and reposed buildings on a lakeshore. In Italy can anything truly be over with entirely?

We had a long drive back to Bologna and stayed again at our race-week hotel, where the staff greeted us with surprise and pleasure. The next day a short drive and some good directions got us to Minarelli, quite near the Ducati factory. Via Melozzzo da Forli is a dead-end residential street. Just up the way, exclusive shops rub shoulders with an aluminum foundry, and old men in flat caps totter past with their groceries in their arms. It would be unthinkable to find an engine factory in such a neighborhood in the U.S. But here is Minarelli. Through this arched brick gate pass thousands of sturdy, unexciting cyclomotor engines, power for a dozen or a score of little-known moped brands. These engines look like smooth aluminum eggs, each with a finned cylinder projecting from one side. Here is steady, if minor, industry, supplying transport for those who cannot or will not afford cars: students, pensioners, people with other uses for their money.

Because of that strange spark that glows here and there, Minarelli has sought speed records from time to time. Italians, it seems, can convince themselves that racing makes sense; to hear that records have been set

*Lee Klancher*

by a Minarelli means to this public that the company is healthy and the management is still interested in something. Under the heading of reminding the public of this, and no doubt because it pleased him, Sr. Minarelli contracted with Jörg Möller to design a 125 twin for Grand Prix road racing. This machine came a whisker's distance from the World Championship in its first year, running off from the reigning Morbidellis (Möller was previously with Morbidelli) with comparative ease when all was well.

Here was the door to the race shop. The secretary was opening it, and we were meeting the man Möller. He was a fit, stylishly dressed figure in his mid-30s with a large face. The shop resembled a small railroad terminal in the grand style with its broad arched roof and clerestory windows that offered a light, spacious work area. Here was the big Mercedes diesel transporter emblazoned, MINARELLI REPARTO CORSE. And a big solid new lathe. Lots of cylinder detailing equipment. There was a row of small offices, then a gap, and at the end, the test-house. Running along the wall above, a row of drying, curling victory wreaths. Motorcycles, unique hand-built factory racers on work stands, tiny and purposeful.

We introduced ourselves as well as language permitted. Möller's English, he explained, was 14 years old and unimproved by time. It was not, he continued, technical English. We must excuse any difficulty on that account.

His small office was largely bare. A drawing board stood up at a bold angle bearing a print of a new frame. He has found that frames are too important to be left to the "experts," those well-publicized frame salons we hear so much about.

I felt badly to have invaded his operation on such short notice. I had fed nearly a pound of telephone tokens into the instrument at the hotel, trying to make this appointment. May an American journalist and two racers come by for a few minutes of your time? It is possible. Come tomorrow at two.

Here was a clean desk with nothing on it but two magnesium center-float Dell'Orto carburetors and a hand-held calculator. He must, I thought, do a lot of work at home.

As our fitful conversation staggered along, a terrible noise assaulted us; an engine test! Unable to talk, we went out into the shop. The test technician, with ear protectors clamped to his head, was slowly and rhythmically revving the tiny twin against the dyno load in warm-up, the torque meter needle of the Borghi & Saveri eddy-current brake swinging sharply up and back as the frightful noise advanced and died away. The engine spoke a single mindless syllable each time, "OUANGGN! OUANGGN!" and the room vibrated with the three or four very loud pure tones from the exhaust pipes, dissonant in the extreme, and multiplied by the hard walls of the room. It was a very unusual sound. Just what I had come for.

The technician was waiting for water temperature. The moment he had it, he snapped the throttle open, and the engine spun up quickly to near maximum rpm, the heavy load of the dyno slowing the rise near the top, the insistent resonance drilling into and permeating everyone and everything. Möller walked over to the open test house door and leaned there watching the torque scale as the engine sang its hideous huge notes unrestrained for a full 75 seconds. Just try a 75-second full-throttle run with your production racer engine sometime. I was impressed.

The test over, the throttle sides closed, and the notes tapered steeply away to a popping idle, a sound from the familiar world. Then another

*Lee Klancher*

run and another. There was a white flash from beneath the engine, bright and sudden like a magnesium fire. The technician and Möller paid it no attention whatever. Fuel or oil apparently was dropping off the engine onto the very hot pipes.

I had approached the door myself and could see that the test was probably concerned with efforts to broaden the powerband. The pipes on the test motor had two-stage baffle cones, and it appeared that this unit might be equipped with extra-large intake disc valves. The bigger the disc, the shorter the time taken to open and close the port. Suzuki and Morbidelli are also testing engines with this feature. There was another set of the special magnesium Dell'Ortos here, but these had enormous intake bells.

Later, in the office again, Möller showed us one of the pistons, very thin, light, insignificant things with the narrowest ring grooves I have ever seen. There was little to ask Möller not already covered in the European motoring press. Did he have interests in engineering outside racing? Yes, and in perhaps five years he would turn to them for his livelihood, but for now, well . . .

We had expected to see something like a silver-gray Mercedes somewhere in the compound, his personal car. Where was it? No Mercedes, he answered smiling. A Ferrari. The smile became a bit sly. I think this man is having a very good time. He is doing distinguished engineering work, verifying the results in international racing, and is always in demand. The rumor of a tie with Honda for future projects? No, but certainly a major company.

Technical questions were harder. Did he think there was any present barrier to two-stroke brake mean effective pressure? (Four-stroke bmep has been as high as 200 psi, while that of two-strokes has been limited to some 135 psi.) Now Möller and others have pushed it beyond 165 psi. No, he did not see any limit thus far, except that there appears to be some critical crank speed for each cylinder size, placing a ceiling on delivery from case to cylinder. Yes, perhaps bmep might rise as high as that of four-strokes. Hopes for four-stroke engines in FP racing? Where there is money there can be hope, and four-stroke power requires only money, not ideas.

Machines for sale soon? No plans. The horsepower of the present machine—42 to 43. What about the 48 predicted last year? Not necessary just now. How many ports? Enough. A smile. Thank you very much.

He was visibly restive towards the end of our conversation. Are these people staying forever? I, however, could not keep myself from smiling just to be there, and I told him so. We left.

An interesting man. He had been affable and interested in his guests but within limits. He was sure of himself and of his results—no need to say much. Better to just get the power up and let the engine do the talking.

The next day we discovered the Morbidelli factory in an industrial section of Pesaro, near the Adriatic. We were given a factory tour by a deputy in the absence of Sr. Morbidelli and saw a large assembly floor covered with automatic furniture panel positioning and drilling equipment. All this impressive activity was the result of the founder's determination as an apprentice craftsman years ago to eliminate meaningless repetitive work.

After touring the public side of the factory, we were taken to lunch at a local hotel. This is the sea coast, we were told, and there are many seafood specialties; perhaps you would like to sample some of them? Yes, we would. Course after course of fish, clams, mussels, and more was brought, all wonderful and impossible to refuse. All the while the talk was racing, a small window with a big view of the European scene.

Vastly full, we drove down to the sea. On this warm and sunny afternoon the perfect Adriatic beach was almost empty. Europe takes its vacation in August—no other time, so all these many resort hotels were now closed. Impossible to get a room. All that beautiful beach was ours.

Later we were led around behind the main Morbidelli operation to a connected series of small shops—the racing department. In the first a patternmaker was at work, using a special chisel to refine a wood pattern for the upper case casting of the new 500 square four. Dark green against the walls was the expected row of wreaths, victories memorialized in the manner of the Caesars. A second room was full of 250 activity, two technicians fitting components to a prototype chassis. Morbi has had endless trouble with 250 and 350 handling. The combination of massive power and conservative geometry has been as hard for Morbi as it was for MV Agusta before them.

Two dynamometers were bolted to cement and steel mounts in the next shop, and on one of them was the latest 250 prototype engine, said to give nearly 75 bhp. Though designed originally by Möller during his stay here, this one is now the personal project of Sr. Morbidelli himself.

The last room had been Möller's office and contained evidence of the recent occupant. A dark and cheerless place from which to plan World Championships, I thought. Rather like an army installation—regulation gray filing cabinet, regulation drafting board, regulation potted plant, one small window high up on the wall. Never mind. Results! There have been lots of small offices like this one, especially in Italy. Small operations like this, directed by one man, have their strengths. There is more than one way to build fine racing machines. One man who truly knows his business can concentrate the work on the real problems according to a flexible plan that quickly changes to take account of field conditions. He doesn't try to cover every useless case, such as by testing two-stroke exhaust pipes that are fat on the ends and skinny in the middle (would they work?), or by trying hopeless aluminum shift forks in the gearbox. His experience can be worth more than entire graduating classes of Magna Cum Laudes. He can leave the nonsense for the time-serving general-purpose engineers in the giant companies, whose drawings must first be initialed by J, then approved by

B, revised by M, and then filed for study. Those men can go home at night to dinner and forget the whole thing.

Not Möller. Not Taglioni, not Kaaden. You can be sure that as they work on the daily problems of this year's machine they already have most of the features of next year's effort well in mind. These brains are pregnant all the time with ideas, not just when they have been inseminated with corporate money, not just when the time clock is running. Because they are genuinely engaged by the problems and are living that life. The victory wreaths are more important perhaps even than the coveted key to the executive washroom.

Not that the big budget approach of the giant factories isn't supremely productive. Guzzi had been a giant in its time and scale, and it had the results. A mature factory with an experienced and well-financed racing department is the most powerful possible force in racing. Their three shifts of engineering task groups will ultimately solve any problem, develop any necessary technology. It's just that for their results they are inefficient and wasteful compared with the one-man operations. Very few companies can afford it for long. When they get tired and go home, the one-man shops continue; the Möllers, the Villas, the Bossaglias find ways to stay at it.

Only economic necessity can muster up the real money. Only when the image of a big company needs freshening do the lights stay on all night and weekends in the race shops. That is reality, however much we like to remember the wonderful accomplishments of Guzzi, Gilera, BMW, or Norton in the years of their greatness. The money simply isn't there for them now. It has moved on to the Japanese industrial giants who dominate world markets today.

The Guzzi *museo* was full of thought-provoking mementos of a long-gone era of factory racing. At Morbidelli and Minarelli I had seen two important proofs that racing doesn't die when the giants get out, that important and original work still gets done because there are always people who like to do it, who find ways. And fresh from the knuckle-cracking and wide-eyed running of the Grand Prix wars, it was comforting for us racers as tourists to know that long after the Castrol clouds and cheering crowds are gone, something of racing still remains.

# Rockin' and Rollin'... Rollin' ... Rollin'

## By Brian Catterson

*Cycle World*

February 2003

I T'S SEVEN MINUTES 'til sound check at Salt Lake City's Delta Center Arena, and Neil Peart is on the phone with Ride West BMW in Seattle scheduling a service appointment for his R1150GS. Liam Birt, the rock band Rush's long-suffering tour manager, had poked his head through the tour bus door a few moments ago to make sure the band's drummer was "coming along," but the service manager just transferred Peart to the parts department, and now he's on hold pending word on whether the taller windscreen and driving lights he desires are in stock. Meanwhile, across the aisle, the band's security manager, Michael Mosbach, is seated at a computer calculating mileage for the following day's ride from Salt Lake City to Denver.

Such is life on the road with rock music's most acclaimed percussionist.

I'm here because I had contacted Jack David of ECW Press about getting a review copy of Peart's new book, *Ghost Rider*. An act wherein I disclosed the fact that I'm a lifelong Rush fan, having first seen the band perform live in 1978. This led to a phone call from Rush's publicist, Shelley Nott, who informed me that Peart is a devout *CW* (*Cycle World*) reader and had asked her to invite me to accompany him as he rode from one concert to another on the (Vapor Trails) tour.

"How does next week look?" I replied, doing my best to contain my enthusiasm. Noting that the band had a night off between Albuquerque and Salt Lake City shows, I suggested we meet there.

Agreeing, Shelley gave me Michael's cell phone number, and we arranged to meet in Gallup, New Mexico, one week later.

In his book, Peart admits that he's always perceived concert touring as a "combination of crushing tedium, constant exhaustion and circus-like insanity." While he enjoys the planning and rehearsing in

203

preparation for a tour, and the early shows as the band and crew strive for the perfect performance, once they've achieved that, the thrill is gone.

Motorcycling has made touring palatable again. "The good parts are lots of riding, and I can eat anything I want because I drum for three hours every night," Peart says.

After which, most nights, it's a mad dash to the tour bus, where Neil and Michael snooze as bus driver Dave Burnett navigates through the darkness. In the morning they pull over, unload the bikes from the enclosed trailer in tow, and Neil and Michael ride to the next show, arriving early before the throngs, as we did this afternoon.

A late bloomer in motorcycling terms, Peart didn't take up the sport until the age of 41, when his wife Jackie bought him a BMW R1100RS for Christmas 1993. An avid bicyclist, he always suspected he'd enjoy motor-cycling, but once the bug bit, Peart was infected and quickly made up for lost time. He and his best friend Brutus rode all over Canada and shipped their bikes to Mexico and Europe for extended moto-vacations. And then, during the 1997 Test for Echo tour, the pair rode from concert to concert, clocking tens of thousands of miles as they visited 47 of the 48 contiguous United States.

Life was good: In addition to the new album, which Peart considered his masterwork as a drummer, he'd just completed his second Buddy Rich tribute album and an instructional video. Though always something of a cult band, Rush had by this point sold upwards of 35 million records, won a score of Canadian Juno Awards, and been nominated for a Grammy three times. Perhaps most impressively, the three band members had been awarded the Order of Canada, the commonwealth equivalent of being knighted by the queen.

And then, the music stopped.

On August 10, 1997, Peart's 19-year-old daughter, Selena, was killed in a car accident en route to beginning her freshman year of college. His wife Jackie never recovered from that emotional blow, and just 10 months later, she passed away, too. "The doctors called it cancer, but of course it was a broken heart," Peart later wrote.

Suddenly alone and stricken with grief at the loss of his loved ones, Peart told his bandmates to consider him retired and set out on an epic 14-month, 55,000-mile motorcycle journey. A journey that ended happily when he met and ultimately married Carrie Nuttall, a fine-art photographer whose work, "Rhythm and Light" (www.carrienuttall.com), captures her husband back at work in the studio. Peart chronicled his adventures in *Ghost Rider* and in a song by the same name on Rush's long-awaited new album, *Vapor Trails.*

That album is a milestone in that it marks the return of the man who *Modern Drummer* magazine voted "Best Rock Drummer" so many times he was finally retired to his own personal Hall of Fame. And the man who, during his self-imposed "exile," didn't touch the drums for two years.

Equally significantly, it marked the return of rock music's most thought-provoking lyricist, because while it's bassist Geddy Lee's voice that you hear, it's Peart's words; with rare exceptions, he's written every lyric since joining the band for their second album, *Fly By Night*, in 1975.

Taking his penchant for the written word to the next level, Peart in 1996 penned *The Masked Rider*, about a bicycle journey through West Africa. Though an entertaining read, with colorful imagery and no shortage of the author's thoughts and observations, that effort was rather impersonal—his family and bandmates barely rated a mention.

In *Ghost Rider*, however, Peart bares his soul, candidly detailing his progress on what he calls "The Healing Road." A heady read destined to rank alongside *Zen and the Art of Motorcycle Maintenance*, the book works on three levels, appealing to Rush fans, to motorcycle tourers, and, perhaps most importantly, to anyone who's ever suffered the loss of a loved one. Motorcycling, as many of us have come to know, is therapeutic.

How therapeutic, I'm in the process of finding out. We'd rendez-voused the previous morning at a truck stop off I-40 in Gallup. By this point, I'd been in touch with Peart's publisher, publicist, and security manager, but I'd not actually spoken to the man himself. And as I approached the tour bus door, there was only one Rush lyric on my mind. It was from a song called "Limelight" on the 1981 *Moving Pictures* album about the harsh reality of fame: "Living in a fisheye lens, Caught in the Camera eye, I have no heart to lie, I can't pretend a stranger is a long-awaited friend."

And so it was with apprehension that I knocked. An anxious few moments passed, and then Neil himself threw open the door and greeted me with a warm handshake and a smile. He quickly proved to be an educated *CW* reader, a fan of Kevin Cameron and well aware of *Off-Road* editor Jimmy Lewis' exploits in the Dakar Rally and my reputation as the staff Italophile—never mind that I was aboard a BMW F650GS for this outing. Neil himself had owned a Ducati 916, which he kept parked in the living room of his lakefront home in Quebec, but had traded it in along with a K1200RS to purchase his current mount. He kept the original Christmas-present RS for sentimental reasons, and the R1100GS he rode during the making of *Ghost Rider* now serves as a backup bike, parked alongside his and Michael's newer R1150GSs in the trailer.

Not surprisingly, the TV in the bus was tuned to the Weather Channel. Looking at the forecast, I noted that it read "Ceiling Unlimited"—title to one of the songs on *Vapor Trails*.

"Yes, that's where that came from," Neil said, smiling. "You're the first person to make that connection."

"So, what's the plan?" I asked.

"Well, I've never been to Canyon de Chelly, so I'd like to go there first," he replied.

I actually figured we'd be going there, since Neil wrote in his book that he'd been turned away by bad weather during a previous attempt.

We saddled up, then headed north and west, back across the Arizona border (for me) and up into the barren grasslands of the Navajo Nation. We paused at a couple of canyon overlooks, then departed to the northeast, taking the dirt turnoff for Route 13—a number that we should have regarded with the customary suspicion.

A mile or so up the road, we encountered a construction crew that was preparing to pave the road. A series of large highway markers stood in a row, and the three of us began slaloming between them. The party ended abruptly when the dirt turned to slippery mud, a water truck having just done its thing. We pressed on—carefully—and eventually returned to pavement, where we marveled at the fact that we would probably be the last motorcyclists to ride that road in "unimproved" form.

We continued in the dirt on Route 63, only to have the main road dead-end, symbolically, at a cemetery. So we turned back and took the path less traveled, which quickly deteriorated from graded dirt road, to two-track jeep road, to single-track. It then merged with a sand wash, whereupon Michael's rear wheel promptly sank up to the axle.

I snapped the obligatory humiliating photo with my new digital camera, and then we headed back the way we came, turning the other way at a fork. The day before, my younger brother Paul had said to me, "Whatever you do, don't hurt Neil. I have tickets for the Madison Square Garden show." Those words reverberated through my head as I watched Neil's BMW slither sideways climbing a rise and then fall over, pitching him over the top and back down the hill!

Fortunately, the desert sand broke his fall, and Neil emerged unscathed. And not the least bit embarrassed because he encouraged me to snap another photo before righting his bike.

"Do you guys always ride like this?" I asked.

"No, the only time I've ever ridden off-road in the desert was in Baja, and when Brutus and I tried to cross the Sahara," Neil replied.

Forging on, we arrived at a rocky ledge, from where we spied a graded dirt road leading to a highway on the horizon. And so we eventually made our way back to "civilization."

By now it was late afternoon, and we still had a couple of hundred miles to go to Moab, Utah, our evening's destination.

"If there were a show tonight, we'd be calling in a chopper right about now," remarked Michael. He carries a satellite phone for just such emergencies, but so far, the worst the pair has suffered is a ruptured oil line.

With Neil leading we high-tailed it to Moab, covering the distance in little more than two hours.

"You said your 650 cruised comfortably at 95," he told me later, "so I took you literally."

"Actually, I think I said 85," I replied, "but I stand corrected."

Our accommodations for that evening were at the Gonzo Inn (expensive—and worth it), where we were booked under the aliases Wayland Smithers and Nelson Muntz, *Simpsons* characters. Security is a never-ending concern for musicians of Peart's stature—especially when they're as intrinsically private as he is.

"Neil wants to be known for his hands, not his face," offered Michael.

And privacy is more important than ever in the wake of Peart's recent "sabbatical." To avoid having to re-live past events over and over, he currently isn't doing any "meet and greets" with fans, or granting any interviews. As Shelley told me, "*Cycle World* and *Modern Drummer* are it."

Neil gave me a copy of the September 2002, issue of *Modern Drummer* with him on the cover, and I read it at my first opportunity. According to the author, William F. Miller, Peart is a changed man.

"In my many get-togethers with him in the past, there was never any sense of weakness or vulnerability. The old Neil was driven, self-assured, strong, brilliant and at times a tad aloof. He's different now. Brilliant? No doubt. Confident and strong. Perhaps. Aloof? No way. There's a greater sensitivity in him today, a look of compassion behind the eyes. Neil Peart has emerged from tragedy an even greater human being."

Strong words, and ones for which I have no basis for comparison. But in my two days of palling around with Neil, he struck me as a happy-go-lucky guy—polar opposite of the nerdy intellectual I'd envisioned while listening to previous radio interviews. Not to mention a gracious host: He and Michael picked up my hotel room, meals, gas . . . my money was no good, they said. "You're our guest." And so in one evening, I recouped all the money I'd ever spent buying Rush records—first on vinyl, then on CD. The concert ticket score would be settled by the "All Areas" laminated pass that Michael had given me that morning, with the words, "You must be special, because NOBODY gets one of these."

I certainly felt special. We had dinner at a restaurant that Neil had discovered during a previous visit, predictably talking about music and motorcycles, each obviously curious about the other's "gig." At one point, I noted that Neil had been into cars, cycling, and now motorcycling.

"What's next?" I asked.

"Nothing," he replied. "Motorcycling is it."

A "serious" journalist, if afforded this opportunity, would no doubt have asked The Big Question, something to do with the unfortunate turns that Neil's life had taken. But I couldn't do it. Reading his book, I got the sense that he'd had enough sorrow to last two lifetimes; he didn't need me to bring him down.

And maybe it was the wine, but as we talked about past albums and concerts I could feel myself regressing, the inquisitive journalist replaced by the teenage Rush fan I used to be. A teenage Rush fan sitting across the dinner table from Neil friggin' Peart.

It was a memorable evening. After dinner, we walked down Moab's main drag, ducking into the Back of Beyond Bookstore, where on Neil's recommendation I purchased a copy of *Desert Solitaire*, a superb novel about author Edward Abbey's experiences as a park ranger in the nearby Canyonlands National Monument. Or "Money-mint," as he called it.

We then retreated to Neil's suite for a nightcap of the Macallan, poured from the flask made famous (or infamous) in *Ghost Rider*. Noting our upscale surroundings, Michael remarked that because the other two members of Rush travel in private jets that cost 10 times as much as Neil's bus, the management company lets him splurge on hotels.

The next morning, we had a lazy breakfast at a converted jailhouse, then took the scenic route to Salt Lake City over to Route 191. It was my turn to lead now, and not having ridden many twisty roads the previous day, I took it easy at first, unsure of my companions' skills. But I needn't have worried because both turned out to be very capable.

This stands in marked contrast to the story Peart tells in his book. The spring after Jackie gave him the R1100RS, he and Rush guitarist Alex Lifeson (who had just bought a Harley) enrolled in a new-rider course, and Neil failed on his first two attempts. Despite being one of the world's preeminent drummers, Peart insists he's actually quite unco-ordinated and has convinced himself that drumming is really more "dis-coordination." This struck me as humorous, considering that my brother Paul had just taken an MSF course and told me that the instructor had stated that riding a motorcycle is "a lot like playing the drums." Yeah, says who?

In Price, bus driver Dave joined us on Neil's old R1100GS and led us on the final leg of our journey into Salt Lake City. We arrived at the Delta Center early that afternoon, and Neil and Michael got straight to work—changing their oil!

"Ah, the life of a rock star," I remarked as I watched. "If ever there were a term that I despise, that's it," Neil shot back. He prefers the unadorned title, "musician."

Oil change completed, Neil escorted me inside, introducing me to Alex, Geddy, manager Ray Daniels, and the various members of the 50-member crew. He took me up on stage, where I snapped a photo of him wearing a *CW* cap behind his drum kit, then invited me to have a seat on the stool. I declined on the grounds that it was "his" place—and besides, I'm a bass player, not a drummer. I didn't tell him that, though, figuring that telling

Neil Peart you played an instrument would be like telling Valentino Rossi you rode a motorcycle.

We then went backstage to the dressing room.

"Make yourself at home," Neil said. "Sound check is at 5:30. If you need anything, I'll be in the bus."

I showered, changed into my street clothes, then headed back to the bus, where Neil was on the phone and Michael on the computer. Neil finished inscribing a copy of his book for me, and then we hurried inside for sound check, where I grabbed one of the 15,000 empty seats in the arena and watched, an audience of one. We then adjourned for dinner in the dressing room—just Neil, Alex, Geddy, and me. I felt like the fifth Beatle, the talent-less one.

Grabbing my digital camera, I showed the photos of the previous day's "desert crossing" to Alex and Geddy, remarking that if they knew what Neil was really doing on his bike, they'd make him ride in the bus.

Geddy smiled and said, "We couldn't stop him anyway."

Time came for the show, and with Neil planning to depart immediately after the final cymbal crash, he invited me to come backstage during intermission to say our goodbyes, which I did. We shook hands, he encouraged me to keep in touch via e-mail, and then, out of the blue, said, "Aw, give old Neil a hug." So much for that whole "stranger" thing. . . .

At the end of his book, the Ghost Rider symbolically rides off the end of the Santa Monica Pier, never to be seen again. Peart, though, is still riding. Truth be told, he's been riding with me for years—seldom have I traveled without a Rush CD in my case. But it was nice to finally get a chance to ride with him.

# *The Search for George Orwell's Motorbike*

### By Jock Mackneish

*(George Orwell, renowned author of* Animal Farm *and* 1984, *lived and worked for some time on Jura, off the coast of Scotland. Jock Mackneish went looking for his motorbike.)*

**D**ID YOU KNOW that George Orwell was a biker? Do you know that his bike is supposed to be just where he left it, in a clump of bushes on the Scottish island of Jura? Would you like to go and track it down?

I had returned to Scotland to visit the Clan Macneish, and my two motorcycling brothers Donald and Iain were keen to show me around. A cartoonist can get overly attached to his drawing board, and the chance of a bike tour with a "Quest-for-the-Holy-Motorbike" was too good to miss.

Orwell had left London to live on Jura in 1945. He retreated to an abandoned farmhouse called Barnhill to write *1984*. He would have had few interruptions. Barnhill is a remote and isolated building, 10 kilometres from the nearest neighbour and 40 kilometres from Craighouse, the one village on the island. Orwell's only transport was his bike, and I can assure you he was some rider. Just getting there was an epic trip.

We set off from Clan headquarters, Lamlash on the Isle of Arran, my brothers on Don's rare Honda 650 Four and myself astride something even rarer, a borrowed, brand-new K755. Who, you may well ask, lends anyone a brand-new BMW? My brother-in-law, the remarkable J. Stanley Anderson, that's who. May the world take note and pay homage to such Highland generosity.

The first leg of the trip was a ferry crossing from Lochranza to Claonaig. It was rough.

I was torn between spectacular scenery, seasickness, and worrying about the bike falling over. I huddled beside the bike and watched it rocking gently on its forks. We both survived.

The short ride to Kennacraig and the next ferry trip to Port Askaig on the island of Islay were smooth. Too smooth. The ferry's steel plate floor, soaked in diesel oil and sprinkled with salt water, makes an extremely smooth surface for the motorcycle tyre. The extra weight of all that camping gear on the back of the bike was all that saved me.

We stayed that night on Islay, near a beach. I encouraged damp driftwood into a campfire using motor spirit while Don and Iain encouraged each other with the distilled variety. There was a lot of laughter. We visited the pub at Port Charlotte for fresh supplies. On the wall was a map of the island, its coast decorated with the last hundred or so shipwrecks, showing the year of impact and the number of lives lost. It made the roads seem suddenly a healthier place to be.

Riding back to the campsite, glowing with inner warmth, I came across an unhealthy phenomenon in the middle of the road. Grass. Yes, grass. The green stuff, quite common really. It's just that I wasn't expecting it to be growing in the middle of the bitumen. It did terrible things to the front wheel when my thoughts and my bike went drifting out on a sweeping curve.

I took longer than normal to fall asleep that night.

The morning brought the final ferry trip, from Islay across to Jura, and I started to get that "this is the place" feeling. We alighted on Jura at a place with no name. Just a pier and a road. It's a place with no place.

Just a road. The road is not easy to recognise. The black-faced sheep certainly don't recognise it as a road. They stand there, watching the approaching motorbike with hesitant curiosity, but the idea of moving out of the way is slow to dawn. When the penny finally drops they are apt to suddenly change their minds about which way to run. Left? Right? Left again?

Tense.

We made it to Craighouse and stopped for petrol. "Aye, we sell petrol," they said in the only shop. "Go away up the road a wee bit(!) turn left, and there's a pump in the bushes. I'll be there in a wee while"(!). He was; and then it's back to the shop. "And I'll be there in a wee while te tak yer money(!)"

From Craighouse, the road gets rapidly worse. The weedy grass bit in the middle of the bitumen gets wider and wider till the whole road is weedy grass bit. Then it turns into stony creek bed with lumps of moss and finally, peat bog with occasional boulders. About three quarters of it is now under water.

I wondered how Orwell had coped. He had learnt to ride with the British police force in Burma where he gained quite a reputation astride his huge American motorbike. (Henderson? Indian? Harley?) With his mate Roger Beadon, Orwell scandalised the colonials by going tiger hunting on the bike, armed with a Luger Parabellum pistol. There is a questionable story about one of Orwell's more spectacular step-offs outside the gates of Fort Dufferin, but he could certainly handle the rough going. He was renowned for riding along tracks that the locals claimed were "unfit for bullock-carts."

However, writing from Barnhill in 1965, Orwell described the road on Jura as "Hell."

Hell is what it was. I loved it. Yet out on that lonely road there was also a feeling of desolation. In the eighteenth century there were 100,000 people living on Jura. When Orwell went there, there were only 300. Today, maybe less than half that. When we arrived at the crest overlooking Barnhill, it was a long time before any of us felt like speaking.

The house sits at the head of a narrow valley, leading down to wild and windswept Jura Sound. To the north, one of the largest whirlpools in the world, to the south, the full power of the North Atlantic. A place that puts politics into perspective. A place for writing *1984*.

"If you had a bike and it wouldn't go, where would you bump it to before giving up?"

We looked through the bushes down the valley. At the point where what had been the farm gave way to what still was the bush, there was a lone alder tree. It was old and gnarled, and in the bracken at its foot was George Orwell's motorbike.

The man of words would have said something fitting. We could only manage gestures, nods, and an overwhelming sense of occasion. I knew: "This is the place."

Of the bike there was not much left. Forty years of exposure to the salt air had left only the engine, frame, and forks. A major restoration project for the devoted. Our devotion was perhaps more reverent.

We left it where it lay.

It was a 499cc Rudge Whitworth four-valve single, built sometime in the 1930s. There are probably quite a few still going. The lack of rear suspension would have made for hard going on that road. I don't expect the handling was all that wonderful either. It was what we would now call "agricultural." In the 1930s it was an elegant street machine. At no time would it have been easy, but I bet it was fun.

We took photos, paid our respects, replaced the vegetation, and left. The long road back to the ferry offered spectacular glimpses of the island's huge herd of wild deer, its three stately mountains, and its windswept valleys. But our minds were back in Barnhill, back in 1948, and back with George Orwell and his faithful Rudge.

In the cramped comfort of the hotel bar back in Port Askaig, we joked about my being the eldest, Donald the strongest, and Iain the tallest. Who should be Big Brother?

On the mainland, the heavens, which had been kind, decided that the party was over, and we arrived home cold, tired, soaking wet, and very happy.

Did you know that George Orwell was a biker?

Do you know that his bike is still just where he left it? Wouldn't you like to go and see it too?

# Open for Business

### Touring Louisiana Post-Katrina
### By Lee Klancher

*Motorcycle Escape*

October–November 2006

*You can't drown an attitude. You can't blow away jazz. You can't swamp the bayou-born love of visiting and eating that New Orleanians will bring back to their city when the all-clear finally blows.*

—Steve Hendrix, *Washington Post*

"THREE POUNDS of crawfish for ten bucks is about the best deal you'll find," the server told me as I eyed the menu at a smokey Cajun bar and grill in LaPlace, Louisiana, "At least after Katrina."

I gave in and ordered, and she brought out a plate of the bright red crustaceans steamed in butter, garlic, and red pepper sauce.

"The right way to eat them," she told us as she served them, "is to suck the juice out of the heads."

My buddy Mark Frederick—a meat and potatoes man who won't eat any fish, much less those served with legs and antennaes attached—winced as I cracked and ate a plate of about 50 crawdads. And, yes, just to get in the spirit of things, I sucked a few crawdad heads.

"Dude," he said, "That's gross."

The spicy meal, along with three cups of strong coffee, chased away the chill of a morning cruise on the backroads north of New Orleans in damp, 40-degree weather.

Frederick and I were there to tour the area post-Katrina, to see if it was back open for business. We found the elegant city and its vibrant people alive and well despite the disaster, and sampled a bit of the bittersweet 2006 Mardi Gras.

My first view of the city came from the car of Al Gomez, the owner of EagleRider tours in New Orleans. EagleRider was flooded and shut down by Katrina, but Al had a couple of bikes in his garage to loan us for the story. He picked me up at the airport and appointed himself an unofficial tour guide for the trip.

During the ride from the airport to my hotel, Gomez explained that New Orleanians post-Katrina refer to the high ground that survived the storm relatively intact as the "Island" and the parts flooded by the broken levees as the "Dead Zone."

Our trip from the airport started by going through the Island. Wind damage is still visible, with homes being rebuilt, the occasional stoplight out of commission, and piles of rubble here and there on the street. But these areas are up and running, filled with businesses with shoe polish script in the windows advertising, "NOW OPEN."

The Dead Zone is another story. Gomez took us for a tour of some of the Dead Zone, the areas that were flooded by the broken levees, and seeing it was a shock to the system. Shopping malls with wind-twisted signs and boarded-up windows were backed up by neighborhoods full of crumbling homes and the skeletal remains of apartment complexes. Driving through was like visiting the set of a post-apocalyptic science fiction film.

"Home Depot was the first thing to reopen," Gomez told us as we passed it. The parking lot for the home improvement store was an oasis of normality in the surreally abandoned area, with the lot choked with contractors' trucks and minivans loaded down with lumber, paint, and other building supplies.

At Gomez's neighborhood in Slidell, a cluster of nice homes on the coast of Lake Pontchartrain, rebuilding is going ahead full force. Driveways are filled with dumpsters and contractors' pickups, and the sounds of table saws and nail guns echo down the street.

As we passed a three-story condominium, Gomez pointed to a 45-foot-long splintered gash on the roof.

"A sailboat was sitting up there during the storm," he said. "And I don't mean just a little boat—I'm talking about a 60-foot *yacht*."

An equally large barge sat in the front yard of the condo, resting sadly in a debris-filled sea of ravaged grass.

Gomez showed us his house, where four feet of muddy ocean water had washed through. The house smelled of new lumber and sheetrock dust. He was living on the second floor while the first was refinished. Others on his block were not so fortunate and were living out of white

*Lee Klancher*

travel trailers parked in their front yards. The trailers were provided by FEMA and could be seen parked all over Louisiana and Mississippi.

When I was 11, I spent a long summer traveling in a pop-up trailer with my family. Considering that experience, I believe six months of family life in a FEMA trailer would rank somewhere between unpleasant and one of those rooms in hell designed for child molesters and politicians.

That afternoon, we began our trip with a run north to find some backroads to explore and see how far off the coast Katrina had crept. North of New Orleans, you pass through a mix of rolling countryside and sprawling strip-mall towns. A bit off the main highways, you'll find tight little two-lane roads worthy of exploration.

Like the Island portion of New Orleans, the area is definitely open for business, but you can find plenty of wind-damaged roofs protected only by the distinctive blue tarps provided by FEMA. Winds of nearly 100 miles per hour were recorded as far north as Jackson, Mississippi, and nearly everyone you talk to has a story about weeks without power or water, and rebuilding.

*Lee Klancher*

Restaurants, gas stations, and roads are all open, however. About the only drawback of traveling the areas away from the coast was finding hotel rooms. In February 2006, the hotels were still full of workers in town clearing rubble and rebuilding the city, and displaced people waiting for their homes to be ready.

After our ride, we came back to New Orleans and visited the French Quarter for a taste of Mardi Gras. With Katrina's impact six months in the past, the people of New Orleans needed Mardi Gras for financial, promotional, and emotional reasons. The 2006 version attracted a lot of press attention, so much so that the New Orleans Convention and Visitors Bureau hosted daily press conferences for visiting journalists where people key to Mardi Gras spoke about what the event meant to them and to the city.

"We need the rest of the world to know we're not under water," said Arthur Hardy, the publisher of *Arthur Hardy's Mardi Gras Guide*. The annual economic impact of Mardi Gras is estimated at $600 million, and even a greatly reduced event would bring $200 million to a city desperately in need of resources.

Down on Bourbon Street, the crowds for Mardi Gras were reduced but hardly demure. The smoky street was packed with throngs of beer-lubricated people draped in beads, feathered masks, and glittery paint. The street is lined with clubs, most of them hosting cover bands with good-looking singers that belted out reliable rock anthems—Van Halen, AC/DC, Guns N' Roses and Ozzy Osbourne were alive and well on Bourbon Street. I think I heard "Highway to Hell" five times in three hours on the street.

The purient interest is also well-served on that beer-soaked stretch of Bourbon Street, with plenty of strip clubs and the expected bevy of young women earning their beads from the throngs of people packing the second-floor balconies above the street. At the Mardi Gras press conference, Blaine Kern told us that Mardi Gras is about more than bare breasts, but you'd never know that down on Bourbon Street.

The impact of Katrina on the Bourbon Street scene was, according to those who had been there before, mainly positive for visitors. The crowds were down, and lines to buy a beer, get into a club, or go to the bathroom were nearly nonexistent. I won't be going back to that scene anytime soon, but if a college frat party is your idea of a perfect evening, by all means get down to Bourbon Street.

For residents, Mardi Gras is not to be found on Bourbon Street. The celebration is citywide and involves nearly two weeks of parties with family and friends as well as a nonstop stream of parades. It's the party of the year in a town whose people love to party, a celebration of a celebrated life.

"Mardi Gras is a way of life. It's sewn into the very fabric of who we are," said Blaine Kern, the owner of Mardi Gras World.

Last year's Mardi Gras included 34 parades in the New Orleans parish (Louisiana-speak for a county), and the 2006 version had 28. These parades feature themes that range from African culture to dogs, and vast quantities of trinkets ranging from beads and medals to stuffed animals and Frisbees are thrown from the floats to the throngs of people gathered on the streets. Families have spent the afternoon or evening on the same street corner for years, visiting with neighbors, drinking beer, and grilling out while the parades go by.

These community-based celebrations were something that the people of New Orleans welcomed in 2006. In a town where having a good time is a way of life, the six months after Katrina had been consumed by rubble hauling, insurance settlements, and rebuilding damaged homes and businesses.

"You cannot put a price tag on doing something that is normal again," said Kim Priez of the New Orleans Convention and Visitors Bureau. "If you cancel Mardi Gras, my family is still going to be on that street corner."

We attended one of the parades and easily found space on a corner between a family grilling brats and hot dogs and another settled into lawn chairs while their kids played Frisbee in the grass median.

The parade featured a stream of floats loaded with people throwing trinkets, street vendors, high school bands, and even a colorfully costumed blues band. People clamored for goodies, and the crowd was nearly as decked out in feathers, beads, and masks as the people on the floats.

After the parade, we loaded up the Harleys and headed south down the coast for a ride. We intended to ride the coast between Gulfport and Biloxi, which is a favored route with bikers in the area. It also was one of the areas hardest hit by Katrina.

Riding the coast near Gulfport proved to be the most sobering part of the trip. As soon as we exited off Interstate 10, the ravages of the storm were evident. The coast roads looked like the aftermath of a nuclear blast. Rubble was everywhere, and many of the homes had been reduced to flattened piles of bricks, shingles, and siding. Some relatively intact homes sat off-kilter or teetered on the edge of falling, remains of a torrent of water that turned a thriving coastal community into a wasteland. Houses were picked up and dropped on the house next door, and others were stripped of all but bare studs and a ravaged roof. Boats were scattered around the area at random, picked up and deposited inland by Katrina. One boat perched forlornly in the trees was spray-painted with a phone number and a message pleading, "CALL BEFORE YOU MOVE MY BOAT."

Among the rubble, we saw a few clusters of tent communities. The thought of living for six months among this wreckage in a nylon tent was simply unfathomable. At the remains of what appeared to be a large coastal home, an elderly man wandered around the lot, picking up the occasional useful item from the rubble that remained of his home.

The devastation hit us at gut level, a visceral reminder that our world is a fragile place. One minute a house on the coast, the next a nylon tent blown over in the wind.

*Lee Klancher*

The ride back to New Orleans was the longest 100-mile ride I can remember. The damp, 40-degree February air cutting through my riding jacket was as chilling as the images of devastation on my mind.

We took a tour through the Garden District on the way back to the hotel, happy for the comfort of the arching oaks over the boulevards and the graceful homes lining them. New Orleans has the rumpled elegance of a deposed dignitary, with elegantly detailed architectural details on stunning homes in various states of repair. Cruising the broad boulevards, the signs on lawns reading "We're Home" reassured me that parts of the city were still alive and well.

On a stretch of Magazine Street packed with battered shotguns (duplexes), tattoo parlors, and music shops, a sign for live music and hot food drew us into Le Bon Temps Roulé. A small crowd filled the bar, with a guy in pajama bottoms with shorts over the top playing pool with a bandana-wearing 50-something. The kind of place where two guys disheveled from a day of riding fit right in.

We met some of the regulars over the course of the night, ranging from a guy who told us he could build us a chopper, but it would have to be on the sly because his business wasn't totally legal, to Julie, a vocalist pursuing a solo career and Amanda, an art photographer from Santa Fe.

The thump of a drum set drew us back to a small stage and dance floor in the back of the bar, where we found a band playing a catchy mix of folk rock and the small room packed with people dancing.

In between sets, Julie and Amanda introduced us to some of their friends, all of whom had a story. JR was a pitcher for the Oakland As farm club, taking a break from a summer job painting a fence in Texas with his pro football buddy to catch the band. Michael Hornsby was a local musician who was the son of musician Paul Hornsby. Lucky was, well, a small man with a quick wit who avoided straight answers. He did say that vampires turned him on and that he thought Mark's Harley leathers were a bit too "Village People" for his taste. We could only speculate about his life. Was he a comic? An actor? Maybe a small-time coke dealer? Everyone in New Orleans has a story, or so it seemed that night.

As the band pounded out tracks, the local bike builder periodically appeared at my shoulder to shout random snippets of advice about the town in my ear. "The Maple Leaf. Best fucking music in town. You *gotta* go," he'd yell, and then he'd vanish into a dank corner of the bar.

The next day, we rode north of New Orleans and out toward Breaux Bridge, a place near Lafayette known as the crawdad capital of the world that had an afternoon zydeco show we wanted to catch. The day was cold and rainy, and our choice of roads was poor—it took us most of the day to get about 50 miles north of New Orleans. The day was saved by a curvy stretch of Hwy. 61 and the plate full of crawfish mentioned previously, but we didn't make it to Breaux Bridge.

That night, Julie and Amanda made themselves our unofficial tour guides for the night and took us to two of the Uptown area's signature places. We had dinner at Jacquimo's, a long, narrow little restaurant with a cozy bar out front. We ordered a bottle of wine and sat at the bar while we waited for dinner.

As the wine flowed freely, I chatted with Amanda. We agreed that Sebastiao Salgado is a great photographer but too pretentious and that Diane Arbus is a genius. She also told me that she loved New Orleans, that it was one of the few truly interesting cities in America. I heard that

*Lee Klancher*

*Lee Klancher*

line from most of the people who live there. Like San Francisco, the town's character and complexity earn it a dedicated following

Our table ready, we made our way to the warm dining area in the back with colorfully painted window frames set in bright walls. The food was outstanding, from the shrimp and sausage cheesecake and fried oysters to the barbeque shrimp and stuffed redfish.

I mentioned that between our foray to Bourbon Street, the night at Le Bon Temps Roulé, and long days of riding and taking photographs, I was getting a bit worn out.

"Sleep deprivation is a way of life in New Orleans," Julie said, laughing. "*Especially* during Mardi Gras. And we still have to see the Maple Leaf."

So our sleep-deprived selves went next door to the Maple Leaf to catch a funk band. Another old New Orleans venue, this place had gold-leaf ceilings and a band packed with talent. The guitarist was the star of the group, a 40-something Asian with a face that carried lines beyond his years. When he played, he lit up the room with powerful riffs and a joyful smile that made him look 15 years younger.

We made our way to the dance floor, which was packed with a young, energetic crowd of people shaking their bodies to the booming funk. Among this gyrating throng was a 70-year-old man impeccably decked out in a black topcoat over a grey vest and black-and-white-striped tie, nodding his head to the music and taking in a Saturday night in Uptown.

During a break between sets, Amanda turned to me and said, "Austin."

"What?" I said.

"I'm thinking of moving to Austin."

I asked her why, and she just raised her eyebrows, shot me the look of a person who spent half a lifetime with an interesting but difficult lover, and went back to her drink.

We later moved from the dance floor to the bar, and I found myself sitting next to the man in the black topcoat. He told me that he owned a local automotive repair shop and had been coming to the Maple Leaf for more than 30 years to see bands. He also said he had his business open shortly after the storm, since he hired a crew to fix the damage. Business stayed steady enough for him to still find time to slip away for a weekend or so each month to his place in Mississippi, where he raised hogs and enjoyed the peace and quiet.

He looked around as we sat there, and I commented that, at least in this little club, the people of New Orleans seemed to be dealing with the aftermath with surprising life and energy.

He smiled at that and said, "New Orleans loves to party."

My flight left the next day. I sat in a window seat, and the city slipped out of sight under the cover of a bank of low-lying clouds. The town's long-awaited week of sleep deprivation was just getting started, but it was time for me to go home.

# Chapter 5
# Turning Points

"**So speed addled** was I when we crested Banner Summit that I kept edging past 80— not a good idea on a bike whose **harmonic balancer** disappeared decades ago due to **endemic** self-destruction."

—Jack Lewis, Riding Home

# The Empty Road

## By Robert Pirsig

*Zen and the Art of*

*Motorcycle Maintenance*

Bantam, 1974

'M AFRAID THESE OTHER CHARACTERS will sleep all day if I let them. The sky outside is sparkling and clear. It's a shame to let them go to waste like this.

I go over finally and give Chris a shake. His eyes pop open, then he sits bolt upright, uncomprehending.

"Shower time," I say.

I go outside. The air is invigorating. In fact—Christ!—it is *cold* out. I pound on the Sutherlands' door.

"Yahp," comes John's sleepy voice through the door. "Umhmmmm. Yahp."

It feels like *autumn*. The cycles are wet with dew. No rain today. But *cold*! It must be in the forties.

While waiting I check the engine oil level and tires, and bolts, and chain tension. A little slack there, and I get out the tool kit and tighten it up. I'm really getting anxious to get going.

I see that Chris dresses warmly, and we are packed and on the road, and it is definitely cold. Within minutes all the heat of the warm clothing is drained out by the wind and I am shivering with big shivers. Bracing.

It ought to warm up as soon as the sun gets higher in the sky. About half an hour of this and we'll be in Ellendale for breakfast. We should cover a lot of miles today on these straight roads.

If it weren't so damn cold this would be just gorgeous riding. Low-angled dawn sun striking what looks almost like frost covering those fields, but I guess it's just dew, sparkling and kind of misty. Dawn shadows everywhere make it look less flat than yesterday. All to ourselves. Nobody's even up yet, it looks like. My watch says 6:30. The old glove above it looks like it's got frost on it, but I guess it's just

231

*Lee Klancher*

residues from the soaking last night. Good old beat-up gloves. They are so stiff now from the cold I can hardly straighten my hand out.

I talked yesterday about caring, I *care* about these moldy old riding gloves. I smile at them flying through the breeze beside me because they have been there for so many years and are so old and tired and so rotten there is something kind of humorous about them. They have become filled with oil and sweat and spattered bugs, and now when I set them down flat on a table, even when they are not cold, they won't stay flat. They've got a memory of their own. They cost only three dollars and have been restitched so many times it is getting impossible to repair them, yet I take a lot of time and pains to do it anyway because I can't imagine any new pair taking their place. That is impractical, but practicality isn't the whole thing with gloves or anything else.

The machine itself receives some of the same feelings. With over 27,000 on it, it's getting to be something of a high-miler, an old-timer, although there are plenty of older ones running. But over the miles, and I think most cyclists will agree with this, you pick up certain feelings about an individual machine that are unique for that one individual machine and no other. A friend who owns a cycle of the same make, model, and even the same year brought it over for repair, and when I test rode it afterward it was hard to believe it had come from the same factory years ago. You could see that long ago it had settled into its own kind of feel and ride and sound, completely different from mine. No worse, but different.

I suppose you could call that a personality. Each machine *has* its own, unique personality which probably could be defined as the intuitive sum total of everything you know and feel about it. This personality constantly changes, usually for the worse but sometimes, surprisingly, for the better, and it is this personality that is the real object of motorcycle maintenance. The new ones start out as good-looking strangers and, depending on how they are treated, degenerate rapidly into bad-acting grouches or even cripples, or else turn into healthy, good-natured, long-lasting friends. This one, despite the murderous treatment it got at the hands of those alleged mechanics, seems to have recovered and has been requiring fewer and fewer repairs as time goes on.

There it is! Ellendale!

A water tower, groves of trees, and buildings among them in the morning sunlight. I've just given in to the shivering that has been almost continuous on the whole trip. The watch says seven-fifteen.

A few minutes later we park by some old brick buildings. I turn to John and Sylvia, who have pulled up behind us. "That was *cold!*" I say.

They just stare at me fish-eyed.

"Bracing, what?" I say. No answer.

I wait until they are completely off, then see that John is trying to untie all the luggage. He is having trouble with the knot. He gives up, and we all move toward the restaurant.

I try again. I'm walking backward in front of them toward the restaurant, feeling a little manic from the ride, wringing my hands and laughing, "Sylvia! Speak to me!" Not a smile.

I guess they were really *cold*.

They order breakfast without looking up.

Breakfast ends, and I say finally, "What next?"

John says slowly and deliberately, "We're not leaving here until it warms up." He has a sheriff-at-sundown tone in his voice, which I suppose makes it final.

So John and Sylvia and Chris sit and stay warm in the lobby of the hotel adjoining the restaurant, while I go out for a walk.

I guess they're kind of mad at me for getting them up so early to ride through that kind of stuff. When you're stuck together like this, I figure small differences in temperament are bound to show up. I remember, now that I think of it, I've never been cycling with them before one or two o'clock in the afternoon, although for me dawn and early morning is always the greatest time for riding.

The town is clean and fresh and unlike the one we woke up in this morning. Some people are on the street and are opening stores and saying, "Good morning," and talking and commenting about how cold it is. Two thermometers on the shady side of the street read 42 and 46 degrees. One in the sun reads 65 degrees.

After a few blocks the main street goes onto two hard, muddy tracks into a field, past a quonset hut full of farm machinery and repair tools, and then ends in a field. A man standing in the field is looking at me suspiciously, wondering what I am doing probably, as I look into the quonset hut. I return down the street, find a chilly bench, and stare at the motorcycle. Nothing to do.

It was cold all right, but not *that* cold. How do John and Sylvia ever get through Minnesota winters? I wonder. There's kind of a glaring inconsistency here that's almost too obvious to dwell on. If they can't stand physical discomfort and they can't stand technology, they've got a little compromising to do. They depend on technology and condemn it at the same time. I'm sure they know that and that just contributes to their dislike of the whole situation. They're not presenting a logical thesis, they're just reporting how it is. But three farmers are coming into town now, rounding the corner in that brand-new pickup truck. I'll bet with them it's just the other way around. They're going to show off that truck and their tractor and that new washing machine, and they'll have tools to fix them if they go wrong, and know how to use the tools. They *value* technology. And they're the ones who need it the *least*. If all technology stopped tomorrow, these people would know how to make out. It would be rough, but they'd survive. John and Sylvia and Chris and I would be dead in a week. This condemnation of technology is ingratitude, that's what it is.

Blind alley, though. If someone's ungrateful and you tell him he's ungrateful, okay, you've called him a name. You haven't solved anything.

A half hour later the thermometer by the hotel door reads 53 degrees. Inside the empty main dining room of the hotel I find them, looking restless. They seem, by their expressions, to be in a better mood, though, and John says optimistically, "I'm going to put on everything I own, and then we'll make it alright."

He goes out to the cycles, and when he comes back says, "I sure hate to unpack all that stuff, but I don't want another ride like that last one." He says it is freezing in the men's room, and since there is no one else in the dining room, he crosses behind a table back from where we are sitting, and I am sitting at the table, talking to Sylvia, and then I look over and there is John, all decked out in a full-length set of pale-blue long underwear. He is smirking from ear to ear at how silly he looks. I stare at his glasses lying on the table for a moment and then say to Sylvia:

"You know, just a moment ago we were sitting here talking to Clark Kent . . . see, there's his glasses . . . and now all of a sudden . . . Lois, do you suppose? . . . "

John howls, "CHICKENMAN!"

He glides over the varnished lobby floor like a skater, does a handspring, then glides back. He raises one arm over his head and then crouches as if starting for the sky. "I'm ready, here I go." He shakes his head sadly. "Jeez, I hate to bust through that nice ceiling, but my X-ray vision tells me somebody is in trouble." Chris is giggling.

"We'll all be in trouble if you don't get some clothes on," Sylvia says.

John laughs. "An exposer, hey? 'The Ellendale revealer!' " He struts around some more, then begins to put his clothes on over the underwear. He says, "Oh no, oh no, they wouldn't do that. Chickenman and the police have an understanding. They know who is on the side of law and order and justice and decency and fair play for everyone."

When we hit the highway again it is still chilly but not like it was. We pass through a number of towns, and gradually, almost imperceptibly, the sun warms us up, and my feelings warm up with it. The tired feeling wears off completely, and the wind and sun feel good now, making it real. It's happening, just from the warming of the sun, the road and green prairie farmland and buffeting wind coming together. And soon it is nothing but beautiful warmth and wind and speed and sun down the empty road. The last chills of the morning are thawed by the warm air. Wind and more sun and more smooth road.

So green, this summer, and so fresh.

There are white and gold daisies among the grass in front of an old wire fence, a meadow with some cows, and far in the distance a low star rising off of the land with something golden on it. Hard to know what it is. No need to know.

Where there is a slight rise in the road, that drone of the motor becomes heavier. We top the rise, see a new spread of land before us, the road descends, and the drone of the engine falls away again. Prairie. Tranquil and detached.

Later, when we stop, Sylvia has tears in her eyes from the wind, and she stretches out her arms and says, "It's so beautiful. It's so empty."

I show Chris how to spread his jacket on the ground and use an extra shirt for a pillow. He is not at all sleepy, but I tell him to lie down anyway, he'll need the rest. I open up my own jacket and soak up more heat. John gets his camera out.

After a while he says, "This is the hardest stuff in the world to photograph. You need a 360-degree lens or something. You see it, and then you look down in the ground glass and it's just nothing. As soon as you put a border on it, it's gone."

I say, "That's what you don't see in a car, I suppose."

Sylvia says, "Once when I was about 10 we stopped like this by the road, and I used a half a roll of film taking pictures. And when the pictures came back I cried. There wasn't anything there."

"When are we going to get going?" Chris asked.

"What's your hurry?" I ask.

"I just want to get going."

"There's nothing up ahead that's any better than it is right here."

He looks down silently with a frown. "Are we going to go camping tonight?" he asks. The Sutherlands look at me apprehensively.

"Are we?" he repeats.

"We'll see later," I say.

"Why later?"

"Because I don't know now."

"Why don't you know now?"

"Well, I just don't know now why I just don't know."

John shrugs that it's okay.

"This isn't the best camping country," I say. "There's no cover and no water." But suddenly I add, "All right, tonight we'll camp out." We had talked about it before.

So we move down the empty road. I don't want to own these prairies, or photograph them, or change them, or even stop or even keep going. We are just moving down the empty road.

# *Riding Home*

## *An Iraq War Veteran*
## *Comes Back from the Front*
## By Jack Lewis

*Motorcyclist*
August 2007

T WAS SUNNY and warm when I stepped off Amtrak's #507 Cascades line in Portland, Oregon. Bill was waiting on the station's oak pew; he stood and I gave him a hug with my free arm.

"One-arm hug, huh?" he grinned. Mucho macho, we are.

My heavy, black goatskin Langlitz jacket, still squeaky-new, smelled like bad folks wearing good leathers. I got measured in Portland while on R&R,[1] then picked up my custom-cut masterpiece after I redeployed. It has a gun pocket built in. People moved away, trying to be subtle. It's hard to care about scaring the home folks. I'll get used to them as they get used to me.

Twenty miles south, my black beauty lay waiting. We drove straight to the storage unit and pulled boxes off her. Unearthed after 12 years, she had two flat tires and gray layers of dusty crud, but otherwise looked about the way I remembered. It's not always that way, is it?

We aired up the tires with her onboard squeeze pump and I pushed her half a mile in the sun to Bill and Mom's house, sweating happily. Then we worked her over for a day and a half.

As a mechanic, I make a pretty good wheel chock. But Bill, Jedi warrior of the garage, makes parts that he can't find, and he's pretty well memorized every last bolt on vintage BMWs.[2] So I immersed myself in his short induction to the mysteries of de-varnishing Bing carburetors and lubricating ignition flyweight arms. We put in a new, vintage-look battery he had stashed: six volts of thundering fury! Ah, well, the magneto will spark even when the thing is dead as a doornail. We adjusted the idle, replaced

---

1 Rest and Recuperation—mid-tour vacation that is intended to prevent you from going bats.

2 *Bayerische Motoren Werke,* possibly the greatest motorcycles in all the world. They also manufacture cars for snotty attorneys and social-scrabbling Realtors™.

*Lee Klancher*

the right side carb slide when it wouldn't quit sticking (an old habit of this bike), replaced the balding Magura throttle grip (after disassembling the original Hella bar-end winker), adjusted the idle again, checked the timing (slightly retarded to run on crappy, 91-octane "premium"), adjusted the idle some more. We stepped back and looked at her: still dirty, but chuffing away with industrial purpose. Beautiful.

"Some of that dust is probably from Steen's Mountain," Bill said, referring to a good, long trip we took with passengers and tents, fifteen years, two college degrees, a wife-and-a-half ago.

Then he rolled out his workhorse R90/6, and we went for a shakedown ride, south over the road to the shop of a guy who does boutique restos —i.e., no dust! That guy comped me a petcock liner so I could run in the "AUF"[3] position without running out of gas every two blocks. He's good people.

---

3  German for "on."

Our second stop was at the house of Bill's friend, Ben.

Ben's a nice guy, practicing engineer and wood technologist. He lives in an octagonal house carefully handmade from recycled and exotic woods, overlooking a pond, with a stream running through and under the place. Once upon a time in Vietnam, Ben was a scout/sniper. We checked out his house, enjoyed the details, took note of the guard tower, scoped rifles at the doors, and the armory and reloading center that are not shown on the plans. He took note of my stained desert boots.

"I used to walk my perimeter with a weapon every night," he said as we were adjusting the idle once more in his driveway. "I don't do that anymore."

"So long, my brother. Be well."

So long. I tightened down the left side mixture adjustment nut, shook his hand, clunked her into gear, rolled around the barn and back up to the road.

"He's kind of, uh . . . stuck, isn't he?" I asked afterward, through a mouthful of roadhouse Reuben.

"Yes. Ben's good for three or four hours a day, then that's it."

"I don't want to get stuck like that."

Bill smiled his slight smile, dry but warm. "That's what motorcycles are good for."

That night, I bungeed a big CFP-90 rucksack[4] onto the bike, got some last minute tips from its long-term owner, and gave Bill a hug. With both arms.

Then I rolled out my summer bag in his pickup bed, pulled it up against mosquitoes, and slept my series of one-hour periods, startling up to check my water-proof, impact-resistant, scratch-defying, gas-illuminated watch five or six times before finally sitting up and pulling on my boots in the purple predawn, listening for movement, checking for roaming packs of feral dogs.

Hollow, agitated feeling. Got to move. So quiet with no prayer call. Need to go before the neighbors get up and wonder. Familiar heavy feeling of gear and helmet, but no weapon. Just Honey and me, bag and baggage.

---

4 Oversized backpack, designed to carry more than you should. Now obsolete, it has been replaced by the MOLLE ruck, which holds even more. You can easily get 120 lbs into a CFP-90, close to 150 lbs in the new gear.

This bike and I are old friends reunited. She's an R69-S,[5] the U.S.-market model with telescopic forks (Euro bikers of the Sixties got the sidecar-friendly Earles fork arrangement) and wide American-style "comfort" seat. I call her "Honey" by default, because it suits the way I talk to her: "Let's go, honey," or, "Ah, come on, honey!" when she's recalcitrant or mysterious.

Her seat's a little wider and softer than I remembered, but isn't that always the way with an old flame? Memories are fickle. A little morning tickle to her Bing buttons, then she started on the second kick and we were off into the fire-born dawn.

Bye, Mom.

En route to Estacada, I stopped for gas, mostly to dry the stinging tears with which the sun was punishing me for riding east at dawn. I bought a Power Bar inside, walked up to the side of the bike and kicked down the start lever, which simultaneously started Honey and snapped off her sidestand bolt flush at the frame lug. I wrestled the foundered, sputtering motorcycle back onto her wheels and took inventory: one sprained ankle (my four times-broken left leg, which sprains in a high wind), one busted toe and a dangling sidestand spring, calling for its mother.

Great start.

The attendant goggled through the glass, but didn't say a word. Scary biker man, I guess, or just good entertainment.

Shut down the bike, sat on the curb, taped up my toe with electrical tape from the tool compartment in the tank, ate the Power Bar. Got warmer. Thought of roads sweeping through the Cascade range. Good to be home. Good to be alive. Good to have a center stand. "Hmm.

"Bet I can still start that bike . . ."

Yup.

Highway 224 runs two sweet lanes southeast from Estacada through the Mt. Hood National Forest, flowing sinuously along the Clackamas River. I missed my planned turn east at the Oak Grove Fork due to throes of extreme road ecstasy, and ended up 40 miles south in Detroit, Oregon, in time for a nice breakfast and a tankful of premium.

---

5  600cc super-sports model. High compression, hot cam and a harmonic balancer for extended high-speed running. Made 42 bhp when it was brand-new, about what small dirt bikes make now.

A Beemer-mounted couple (R1100RS[6] and F650GS[7]) greeted me as we swapped nozzles at the busy gas station pumps.

"Where're you coming from?" the man asked. Now there's a poser. I settled for where our house is. "Seattle."

"Is there a good spot for breakfast?"

"The place across the highway has great food, but we waited 90 minutes for a table. They said they're putting on another cook, if they can find him."

The place across the highway was surrounded three cars deep. I passed it by, only to find a log roadhouse three blocks further on. It was attended by seven or eight prominently posed Harley-Davidsons, looking new and shiny. I parked off to the side under a shade tree.

Inside, the menu face had a note: "We speak . . ." followed by a little graphic of a motorcycle. The owner was dressed in a black shirt with stitched-on flames. He held court behind the counter, making eggs and conversation. Allowed as to how he liked old Beemers pretty well, even if they're not Harleys.

My waitress was a blonde girl of maybe nineteen with a sunny side up disposition and a startling lack of focus. She shorted the couple ahead of me ten bucks at the till, then overcompensated by handing them a twenty. Then she forgot to hand back my credit card, offering a giggle and a dazzling smile as her apology when I pointed it out.

"You know, I've just been like this all *day*." Longer than that, I imagine, but the eggs were good and the coffee had flowed.

That day was filled with rivers, forests, and roads to make you weep for their beauty. We touched the Mt. Hood, Willamette, Deschutes, Ochoco, and Malheur National Forests, crossed or tracked along the Clackamas River, Oak Grove Fork, Santiam River, Breitenbush River, White Water Creek, Metolius River, Squaw Creek, Deschutes River, Murderer's Creek, Crooked River and John Day River—to name a few. Honey and I straightened many a bent road on our fantastically inefficient one-day jaunt to John Day, Oregon.

---

6  A great, big sport-touring road burner, descended from Honey and her ilk.

7  A dual-sport bike with one piston and dirt bike styling, plus saddlebags.

244 THE DEVIL CAN RIDE

These roads were fresh to me, but not the region. Growing up in the Pacific Northwest, I always itched to leave for some less boring place. Now, wherever I go in the world, I always know I'm coming home to here. Polite people living among stunning natural beauty are not easy to appreciate until you've un-spoiled yourself with grimy Third World exotica. Musical accompaniment this day included the constant murmur and splash of clean, fast water; rush of wind through the trees; hum of tires older than my teenage daughter (!) and the balanced drone of aircraft-quality, vintage German engineering.

Known in her day as the Gentleman's Express, BMW's dreamboat R69-S easily nabbed the U.S. coast-to-coast speed record in the mid-Sixties. Smooth, powerful, durable, well-featured and classy, this was the bike for chomping big bites of highway with swift ease.

"Gentleman's Express" or not, a 1969 time capsule is nobody's hyperbike today. This was the last of the Slash Two BMWs, produced the same year Honda shocked the world with the first "superbike," its CB 750 with four buttery little pistons and a hydraulic disk brake. Suddenly, BMWs were considered more premium for their prices than for their engineering—even if they weighed in a hundred pounds less than the big-chested Honda.

Unlike my late-lamented rubber-band Ducati, since passed along to a steadier lover, you don't chainsaw up the road on an R69-S, dodging gnats and hula-hipping the rear with tight throttle grabs. You don't stand her on her nose at a corner entry, nor paw at the air in the lower gears. Honey offers a balanced palette of subtler colorations.

Too mature for slam-dancing, she asks for more of a graceful waltz. Even with a fresh shot of 7w Bel-Ray,[8] her long-travel fork is on the squishy side. The big ass cushion squeaks like an old bed spring when you jounce over potholes or speed humps. A hard hand on the double-shoe front drum slows you at a predictable rate; "controllable" is a sweeter description than "weak," but that control requires a powerful paw. Anyway, Honey's lovely low CG[9] and modest torque mean it works best to simply carry speed through the corners—always with attention to those tires.

---

8  Fork oil.

9  Center of Gravity. Generally speaking, the lower, the better.

Step, shuffle, slide to your right; step, shuffle, slide to your left. It may be slow dancing, but it's still dancing, by God. And we danced and danced and danced . . .

I don't do lunch on bike trips, unless there are others along. A late breakfast can carry me all day if my machine is willing, and I just suck down water or Gatorade at gas stations when I'm "on mission." So when I hit John Day around eight that night, where I planned to roll out a bag at Clyde Holliday Park, I was righteous hungry. The Ore House on the Main vein accommodated me with a steak barbequed rare and the stout, cheerful waitress easily conned me into a colossal "individual" berry pie afterward.

With the joy of just riding and the surprising degree of comfort in a "yesterday's standard," it's hard to realize how tired you're getting as hundreds of miles quietly strip ephemeral layers of rubber off your rims. Honey had toted me across most of Oregon that first day—not one of your smaller states. Without so much as a beer in my system, I was so woozy from overeating when I stumbled out the front door that I nearly crashed Honey on a patch of gravel as we turned out from the curb. With laziness judged the better part of vacationing valor, I turned right and stopped at the Dreamland Motel, one block off the highway to the north.

Funny look from the manager preceded, "So, d'ya got triple-A or anything?"

When I parried, "Do you have a military discount?" she brightened up instantly.

"Sure, we . . . well, no.

"Not really. But I'm giving you one!" She started a receipt, scratching off about fifteen bucks.

If that won't bring a smile to bug-stained lips,  I don't know what will. "Thanks.

"What do I owe you, altogether?"

But first she wanted to talk. Her niece is a linguist, serving in Afghanistan on her second tour of SW Asia. Turns out the young lady is an officer who formerly worked on General Tommy Franks' staff. Then Tamara suddenly stopped and looked at me, taking in the road dust, smashed bugs and dirty stubble.

"Um, you are *in* one of the services . . . right?"

"Yeah. This one." I pulled out my army ID. My mug shot, post-tour and hung over in battered DCUs, is even less flattering than the reality with which she was presented.

"And you're active duty?"

"I'm a Reservist, actually, just like I was when I got called up, but my hair is still short. I wear military eyeglass frames—the round wires, not the big plastic racquetball protectors. Haven't been back long enough to get fat yet. So I fudged it with the simple truth: "Just got back from Iraq."

She looked at me for a minute. Her son, sitting in the corner, looked at her.

"Your discount tonight is one hundred percent."

"You don't have to . . ." She waved me off, handed me a key.

"Sorry it's not ground floor. I know guys on motorcycles like to be on the ground floor."

"I'm sure it's perfect." And it was: a big, exceptionally clean, non-stinking room with two queens and a kitchenette. Unbelievable. "Thank you."

By 0530 the next day, I was showered, shaved and dressed, packed, primped and primed. I knocked out a few pushups and strapped every-thing onto the bike, balanced on the left rear peg with my right toe, and stabbed at the kicker with my gimpy left leg one, two, three, four, five times: *nothing*. Hmmm . . .

Too much idle adjusting?

Checked the gas: RESERVE (hadn't fixed that petcock liner yet). Messed with throttle settings from zero to WFO.[10] Drained the float bowls, both sides, twice. Pushed Honey downhill off a slight rise in the corner of the lot, five times. Changed the left side plug. Traced wires. Prayed. Sweated like a Mississippi mule. Cussed like a Tennessee preacher over a still fire. Kicked her at least fifty times until finally, a muffled pop. Then more pops. Rest break. More kicks, some pops, and she decided to run a full 70 minutes after I walked outside with my rucksack. That's one way to warm up on an ice-cold summer morning.

---

10 Full throttle. You can figure out the acronym for yourself. Something like "wide . . . open."

I was a hundred miles down the road before I realized that I'd never tickled her prime buttons. Not even once. For the rest of the day, Honey winked at me by starting first kick, every time. And that was good, because my leg needed the rest. I should never have tossed that old t-shirt my dad gave me, the one that read, "I'm not real smart, but I can lift heavy things."

Caught final directions to the Brownlee Reservoir at a gas stop in Baker City, Oregon, where my dad lived on a cattle ranch during his high school years. It was just plain "Baker" then. Now it sports about 50,000 people and, per my service station directional patron, around 35 percent unemployment.

"I've been looking for a job myself for seven months," he told me, looking not at all bothered about it. I resisted the urge to tell him the military could always use another good man. He was at least my age, way too old for our various wars.

Richland, Oregon, is close to the Idaho border, close to the reservoir, and billed as the Entry to Hell's Canyon. I went straight on past a huge boneyard of obsolete agricultural equipment under a sign reading, "The Power of Yesteryear," and stopped at a fuel station in the hamlet of Halfway, just in time to get beat to the pumps by six HDs burbling in from the other direction. I nodded politely, snapped my shield down and went on back to the highway, unwilling to wait and not wanting to talk.

Their bikes were as new and shiny as the Harleys I'd seen in Detroit, mostly stock with a frosting of shiny gewgaws. One-percenters would call those windshielded baggers—the SUVs of the motorcycle world—"garbage wagons." Of course, one-percenters are jackasses.

The riders, bottle blonde women in XL chaps hugging men wearing Kirkland jeans and lightweight beanie helmets to preserve their follicle plugs, had what the Chinese call a "prosperous look": well padded around their chrome-tanned middles. Doubtful that any of them popped extra for the toolkit; that's what credit cards and cell phones are for.

As the army seal says: "This We Defend."

Sneer though you may about the Costco biker set, they do get out and ride. You might be faster, and you're probably cooler (keep telling yourself that; it's important), but I'll bet they post more mileage. "Real" riders work on their own bikes and memorize every racer's name from Mike the Bike

Hailwood to that Italian kid, Rossi, who smokes everybody now. These people just go out and ride, find out or remember that it's helluva a lot of fun, then go out and ride some more.

Keeping to secondary roads for nearly two thousand miles on this trip, I saw a ton of Harleys, a fair number of Wings, a handful of Beemers, zero "standards," shockingly few sportbikes. And not one bike as old as Honey, but I kept telling her she's much classier and more beautiful than a bikini-clad Speed Triple or a big-jugged queen of a Harley. Hey, some people talk to plants.

I made my gas stop at a last-chance station perched on the edge of Hell's Canyon, serving one flavor: 87-octane unleaded, perfect for Mercury outboards but less than outstanding for a late-sixties, high-compression roadburner like Honey. A well-tanned, well-fed, thirty-ish canyon coquette walked out and looked at me oddly until I remembered there's no self-serve in Oregon.

"Uh . . . mind if I fill it myself?"

"Nope."

"Got any premium hidden around here?"

"Uh, nope."

"Do you sell octane booster?"

"Ee-yep." Which brought my price for boat gas to about five bucks a gallon. Thank God for good mileage. Honey had returned a 47.2 mpg average over the first two tanks I measured, mostly in town as Bill and I shook her down. On the Great Road, she was making well better than fifty. Checked the oil, transmission (four speeds forward, as *Gott im Himmel* intended), shaft housing, and rear box. All levels good, and no gear oil blow-by on the back rim. Perhaps it's time to adjust that idle again.

And thence we went down by the riverside. Down by the riverside not to lay down my sword and shield (I may need them again), but surely to leave some things behind.

The road edging the water shows up on the map not in black (and therefore paved) nor in gray (and therefore dirt), but in brown. At its entrance near Oxbow Dam is a large sign, advising in the strongest possible terms that it is a private road, the county and state are not responsible for maintenance, and you are in every way at your own peril should you choose to take it.

We took it.

Winding along the edge of the lake, sometimes well above and often just at the water level, the Brownlee Reservoir road is no superhighway, but it is competently maintained by the power company. It is also narrow, barely graded, high-crowned . . . and virtually abandoned. We encountered three fishing boats pursuing the elusive bass, two parked trucks with empty boat trailers, and zero moving vehicles on this road.

Burbling softly through the late morning stillness, I looked to my left and saw sepia and green hills sloping down to and into the hushed waters, so calm that the negative reflection continued all the way to perfectly rendered hilltops halfway across the reservoir's surface. My grandmother's favorite verse from the 23rd Psalm came unbidden to my mind: "He leadeth me beside still waters / He restoreth my soul." I stopped and dismounted, sat on my goat hide jacket at the edge of that well of peace and looked long, and prayed hard, and remembered:

*A sergeant from Michigan, on his second tour, who didn't have to be there.* He was gunning a Stryker, running up his enlistment so he and his wife could settle back home with their kids and he could take his place as a diesel mechanic in his uncle's shop.

*A short second lieutenant who rode his bicycle all over FOB Sykes.* He loved a good joke and could take one, too. We used to jump out at him and salute, see if we could make him crash trying to return the salute. He grinned big, and laughed readily, and I never saw him mad.

*An Iraqi major, commanding a line company patrolling from Tall Afar to Muhollibiyah.* He used to freak out Americans who didn't know him by insisting on a face kiss. I got out of our up-armored HMMWV and rode standing in his tiny, weaving, grinding jeep with a squad of six IA soldiers. No roadside bombs that day.

A hundred thousand other soldiers I either knew or didn't, who either died or didn't, who believed in our cause or didn't, who were American or weren't, whom I liked or didn't, who swore an oath, and went, and struggled, and did the best they could while they walked on this earth.

I sat in the Oregon dirt and thought of those guys, and pulled a small, heavy chunk of metal out of my pocket. Once on a castle wall, it zipped into the sandbag next to my head. *Sss-SS-zzss, thwip.*

"What was that?" Steve, our commo sergeant, asked.

"SKS,[11] maybe."

"Oh. We should get down." And we should have, but I wanted to find that bastard and greet him properly. I never spotted him.

Later that evening, after the AIF sniper stopped ops for lack of night vision equipment, I dug his slug out with my Leatherman and looked at it for a long time. It wasn't the only bullet, or the first, or the last. But it was perfect, virtually undeformed by its muffled collision with bagged silica. I kept it close as a lover, and it whispered to me for months, chasing me like a ghost. It was my rosary, skeleton key, ballistic lodestone, taunting me with a papery laugh even after its author died in his barricaded window, head-shot by a better soldier than me. *Zzzzip.*

I showed it to no one, as ashamed to carry it as if it had been needle tracks on my arm.

Now I stood and held it up to let it know a place of peace before I drowned it. Then I threw it as far as a shredded rotator cuff could manage, out over the reservoir and down to the bottom forever, hushing its sibilant hiss, killing my own death.

For now.

Back underway, we putted across the one-lane Brownlee Dam bridge and climbed slowly up over the canyon rim, through Midvale and on into Cambridge, Idaho. Honey was still toting my rucksack's worth of baggage, but it felt somehow lighter.

Cambridge was enjoying a tourism mini-boom of lady bicyclists doing the Ride Around Idaho, which benefits research into cancerous female troubles. Temperatures were in the nineties, and part-time pedal pushers relaxed in the shade of a handful of bistros and cafes that I don't remember from when I lived near here.

Staying well out of their fashionable way, I downed an iced double mocha. I poured ice water over my hair, soaked down the t-shirt under my jacket and the bug-stopping bandana around my neck, which attracted a few stares. Odd looks from women dolled up in hyper-stressed orange Spandex carry low credibility for me: "WARNING: Contents Under Pressure." A wardrobe failure here, and somebody loses an eye . . .

---

11 Soviet-originated sniper rifle.

Winding through the high mountain valleys of western Idaho felt more and more like another piece of home. Passing between the peaks en route to New Meadows, I murmured briefly through Council and saw its familiar press offices staring empty-eyed over Main Street. About a decade back, they printed a book of fictional local news columns (*Kokanee and Other Fish*) under my *nom de plume* of "Gunnar Cratchit." *Kokanee* sold out its massive press run of 300 softbound copies. Eventually.

McCall, Idaho, is nothing like it was, for good or otherwise. I remember when my dad dropped through there circa 1991, pre-bankruptcy when he could fly his own airplane anywhere on earth, and it took an hour to locate the house his parents had owned, since doubled in size and transmogrified into a clothes boutique. Since then, the same has happened to the entire town.

Once the area's one assigned Idaho State Policeman (Gus; I knew him only too well) could park his Blazer on the downgrade from Brundage Mountain ski hill and issue a stack of speeding tickets as fast as he could scribble. Now you pass the 30 mph signs at a blistering 18-per behind a line of home center trucks, building contractors, new second home owners and chromed-out Hummers. Payette Lake is still there, and still probably the last place in the U.S. that meets municipal water standards without purification, but I didn't go to the water's edge for fear of trespassing over some condo owner's postage stamp of Heaven.

Stopping for a cold Coke at a street café, I stumbled back out to find a knot of people clustered around Honey. Their consensus, despite holes in the seat cover and fresh bugs over old dirt: "great looking bike!" And she is. At a distance, Honey strikes a pose as alert as a Rottweiler, strong as a Lab, friendly and eager as a beagle pup. Up close, she's more special.

Older BMWs were generally issued in black, with no more adornment than white pinstripes on tank and fenders, plus the pretty cloisonné tank badges. And, like a good worsted suit from Savile Row, lack of cheesy pretension points up deeper issues of quality. Honey's double-cradle frame wraps around a gorgeously sand-cast engine, perfectly rendered right down to its classically proportioned aluminum fins. Her substantial "comfort" seat, air-cooled engine and questing, chrome-ringed headlight put one in mind of mousy Ralph's steed in that kids' classic, *The Mouse and the Motorcycle*. It's all I can do not to sit on her seat and say, "Brrr-RRRM.

BR-*RRMM!*" and see if she'll start to move. Since it looked like one of the kids had that same idea, I cut through the crowd, cranked her up—on just the one kick, thankyaverymuch—and broke camp from McCall.

Down the Long Valley, then, through Lake Fork and Donnelly over the road I've driven before through foot-deep snowdrifts, interpolating the right of way by adding the parallel fence lines and dividing by two, to the county seat of Cascade. I can't call it the Town of a Thousand Loggers anymore since the population dropped by 50-odd souls in the last census. Their mill, once the economic heart of the valley, has been razed flat as a clear-cut. Its massive buzzsaw blades are probably backgrounds for folk art now.

But don't think that Cascade is immune to Idaho's tourist boom. If Montana is, as Wallace Stegner put it, "the last good place," then Idaho has surely been crowned the "next good place" to mint a pile of development money. Cascade Reservoir keeps their boat launch busy with Boise fishermen pursuing athletic, foot-and-a-half-long kokanee (hint: it's a fish, not a beer). Tamarack, the new mega-resort perched on a nearby mountain, holds untold revenue promise. Here then is a toast to trickle-down, and may it really happen for families who hunt to eat, not to display the glass-eyed heads of ruminant corpses.

Feedlots are practically illegal now in this valley that's hosted an annual cattle drive since the 1850s, and the zoning commissions steadily dice up minimum lot sizes to accommodate lifestyles of the rich and famous. Was it Kurt Vonnegut who described us as a nation of Realtors? Real estate agents busily buy and sell the town where I once jammed gears on a twenty-year-old Ford pumper for the Cascade Rural Volunteer Fire Department. They're probably still driving the damned thing. It'd be about Honey's age now.

Maybe it still holds water.

I parked in the old *Advocate* lot, got directions from some new gal in some new little office of some new agency, and lumbered across Highway 55 to where a good-sized, handsome guy with a brown walrus mustache was grinning at me.

"Big Jack! I knew that walk. What're you doing here, man? How've you been?"

"Well, I try to come by every decade or so, whether I need to or not . . ."

"What kind of bike're you riding this time?"

Matt is Cascade's editor-publisher, general purpose Hell-raiser, and my old boss who taught me to fly fish badly. He stood us to root beers next door to his office with too many free refills ("they know me here"), and we caught up on a lot of time and a couple of wives passed. Matt's still got a gleam in his eye, battle in his heart, and plans to make "big money, BIG money in this valley." I walked out of there already making plans to go back. Life is too short when you have friends, but it sure would be long and bitter without them.

Pocketing another piece of home, I adjusted Honey's idle again and set off down Highway 55 to where it edges the middle fork of the Payette River, one of the West's better roads when uncrowded. Every winter a half-dozen or so cars shoot off inside curves and wind up in the drink. Some can't even be recovered. That's how good it is.

On the straight stretch south of town, a carload of kids in their mom's shiny new Hyundai, frustrated by my 65 mph pace, blasted through a fractional gap between oncoming county concrete mixers. Their license plate number started with 1A (we used to say "One Asshole"); obviously Boise flatlanders fleeing the mountains after weekending in McCall. I smiled a little, behind my chin bar, and kept tiddling along.

Three miles south, the road started to shimmy. I was parked in their trunk inside of three minutes. Just for grins, I passed the little sedan between curves, boogied away and never saw that car again. I swear I heard Honey snort as we went by.

Midway down the Middle Fork is a pit stop called Banks. Get there early, and the roadside café serves terrific eggs over easy to whitewater junkies and anyone else who stops by. But it was well past lunchtime, and I turned east up the tributary creek onto absolutely the best motorcycling pathway in existence anywhere: the road bypassing Crouch, through Garden Valley and Lowman. Idaho's Highway 21 fires up the south fork of the Payette River like a corkscrew rocket and leaps over Banner Summit at 7,056 feet, dropping into a high, wide and handsome mountain valley where Stanley is the only town big enough to spot on a map. After Stanley, it pelts through Obsidian, up over Galena Summit at 8,701 feet, and cascades down through winding sweepers between the Sawtooth Mountains into Ketchum.

The late sun was still roasting the ground when I stopped at the Chevron station in Garden Valley. That station is in exactly the right place, just as I remembered from hustling a Yamaha V-Max[12] through here several years back. Slicked up in matching leathers, I wasn't packing much heavier than a credit card on that trip. A young guy with long hair, squiring a camp-packed Slash Five BMW, sneered wordlessly over the pumps at me back then. We evidently didn't see eye-to-eye on the "no bad motorcycles" theory.

Bike on centerstand, tankful of hi-test jet fuel, squeegeed the bugs off my face shield, checked the oil: standard drill. Clucked over my Michelins, which were balding quickly (rear) and badly checked (front), but holding air like champions. Well, that's what inner tubes are for—and repair kits. Found a tap and a shortie hose near the restrooms to soak down my t-shirt and bandana again, and almost snapped into hallucinations from the icy bite. That's *mountain* water, by God!

Dripping my way back to the pumps, I ran into a man who didn't ask the standard, "What year is that bike?"

"Is that the 'S' model?" Fair question, since Honey's German silver fender jewelry, identifying her as the fearsome 42-bhp powerhouse that is "R69-S," hasn't survived the years. "I really like those," he remarked in a mild voice. "Yours looks good."

"I can't take any credit," I shucked. "My step-dad's done the care and feeding for over 20 years."

"So it's not restored?"

"No, she's not. Maybe someday, when I feel rich."

"Don't do it! Listen, that bike's in great shape. It's worth a lot more with original paint. They were meant to be ridden, I think.

"I have a couple of old bikes myself."

"Really?" Disinterested, I wanted to move on. Everybody has a story, an opinion, a posterior gastrointestinal excretory pore. "What kind of bikes?"

He was driving a rusty compact pickup, painted white, with dirty flower pots in the back. His white hair wisped under his hat brim like a captive fog.

---

12 A porky muscle bike with a huge engine that handles like a greased anvil.

"Well . . ." he said, "I actually have about 60 motorcycles. Some of them are BMWs. I also have some Whizzers and old Harleys and things. They mostly all run.

"I have 75 acres up the road, grow flowers and ornamentals for the big homes.

"Mostly poinsettias, lately."

*Sixty* motorcycles?  Now there's a singular man. Also a single one, most likely.

"You should stop by sometime." That I should. I gave him Bill's number, in case he ever needs head work done, and bid him farewell. Forgot to write down his name, of course, or get a number. Or an address. Or a business name. I sure wish that weren't so typical of me.

He left the station before I got my helmet on, depriving me of the chance to show off Honey's good-natured one-kick liftoff. Seven miles up the road, I caught up with his cruddy pickup just as he turned off the highway toward a bank of greenhouses on the hillside. Guess I'll just have to ride Route 21 again sometime, and visit that fellow. I waved big, and kept riding.

Something about that road just encourages misbehavior. Despite reminding myself that there was no one around to police up my bleeding scraps if I blew a corner, despite the gathering dusk, and despite my time away from the saddle, we sailed up that closed-in-winter road like water splashing magically uphill. A twist on Honey's factory-stock steering damper cut down on the chassis wiggles induced by the forty-pound pack lashed to her rear rack, and I made the most of the dappled daylight remaining to us. It's not safe and I know it, but I always ride faster, into the twilight.

So speed-addled was I when we crested Banner Summit that I kept edging past 80 mph across the high mountain valley of Sawtooth National Recreation Area—not a good idea on a bike whose high-speed harmonic balancer went by the wayside long ago due to an endemic tendency to self-destruct every 2,000 miles. Big speed is also tough on the driveline seals. I would find gear oil hemorrhaged onto the back rim that night.

From my last gas stop in Stanley, it was a smooth drop into Ketchum, the town that is the real heart of "Sun Valley." It's a long, contemplative sunset in the summer there if you're pelting southwest toward the western limit of Mountain Time. The sun was arching orange flames over the Sawtooths, and I took full advantage of the purple mountains' majesty.

My brother Peter was waiting for me when I rolled up. I hadn't seen him in almost five years. Around five-foot-seven, he can crush bowling balls in his hands. He gave me a rib-shattering bear hug, even though I was dripping with high-altitude bug juice.

"Dude! Where have YOU been?"

"Long story, bro."

"Yeah, I guess so. Are you alright?"

"Pretty much. Getting there, anyway."

Pete's gotten to be a wheel in the Sun Valley area, way ahead of his big brother when it comes to career tracking. But he wouldn't talk business while I was there.

"Your mission here is to rest, relax, and have fun." Which, ably abetted by Pete and his general manager Jon from Brooklyn ("How *you* doin'!"), I did. There are no weekdays in Ketchum during the summer—nor, I guess, during the winter. It's a full-throttle party town. For three days straight, we sampled its wares.

On our third night of semi-pro drinking, I found a reason to get back on the bike and ride out of there. After we closed down Whiskey Jacques, the loudest place in town, yelling various good nights to people we either knew or didn't, a young man across the street took sudden and vocal exception to our presence. My little brother, to his everlasting credit, turned and walked away. I stumbled along behind him. It was his town.

But the fella wouldn't let it lay, and when he came after us, I turned and took three steps back toward him. I have conceived a strong distaste for people charging up behind me. I pawed for a weapon to stand him off, and came up with a handful of nothing.

What the hell was I *doing*, walking around without my carbine?

Once in a far-off alleyway, a drunken Iraqi policeman yanked out a 9mm Glock, just like one I have at home, one that we U.S. taxpayers bought for him. He was way too close to the soldier I was overwatching, and he came skinny-close to earning a 5.56mm reprimand before he threw up his hands and showed me his ID. Infantry soldiers assigned to that sector laughed at me: "Hey, he's one of the good guys.

"Ibrahim's cool. He's just drunk."

Later, that same cop went rogue for real. He was detained by U.S. forces after shooting up civilians in his own city. He murdered five outright that day, members of a competing tribe. Maybe Ibrahim was just drunk again.

This meth-addled local was no terrorist, just punked by his own badly managed testosterone that snapped him into junior high-style, chimpanzee-territorial mode. He probably would have jumped around, waved his arms and gibbered. Not much more. He was just trying to impress his girlfriend, but I haven't the patience to sort faux threats from real.

He twitched a punch toward me. I laid him out flat with a straight right to neutralize the threat.

From half a block up, my brother got there in two or three seconds. We recovered my specs, left the guy sleeping peacefully, and exfiltrated the AO[13] without the old t-shirt that his girlfriend shredded off my back. Acceptable losses.

The next day, on attorney's advice, I left Idaho. Abandoning plans to wash and wax the bike, I settled for a quick oil top-up of the shaft, and hasty packing. Who was coming up behind me now?

The journey home turned bleary. My hand ached, but I couldn't pull my glove on over an Ace bandage, so I ignored it. My perfectly fitted Arai helmet suddenly felt too small, and the pounding in my ears seemed to echo off its liner.

I changed Honey's oil that night in La Grande, Oregon. Froze my ass the next morning until stopping by the Pendleton Woolen Mills and scoring a thick wool offcut—for two bucks!—to use as a scarf.

I bought 2001 Reserve Merlot for Lily at Columbia Crest Winery around Paterson, Washington; crossed myself at the Stonehenge World War I memorial overlooking the John Day Dam where my granddad had kept the books; crossed the river again to buy gas at Biggs, Oregon.

After being blown around like a leaf by triple semis blasting by at 80 per, I had abandoned my original idea of droning straight back on the superslab, and instead wended west on Highway 14 along the north bank of the Columbia Gorge until breaking abruptly north through White Salmon along State Route 141 and on into the Gifford Pinchot National Forest, where I have been lost before.

---

13 Area of Operations.

Honey and I nosed our way northward through to State Route 12 at Randle without incident, except to cough out her mirror glass on a twelve-mile stretch of bumpy dirt. A real "standard" can be ridden anywhere, I think.

West from Randle to Morton, then north by northwest through McKenna, where we own a rarely visited woodlot, into Yelm and along SR 510 into Washington's capital. In Olympia, I collected the name of an excellent VA counselor from a friend who was once court-martialed by the Marine Corps while he lay in a coma. He woke up, against all predictions, and pushed their shamed faces to the wall. Now he's a medically retired sergeant, all-around crazy Irishman and beloved friend, married to another beloved friend. We ordered pizza, talked for hours. For at least the third time, Rosie and Seamus proved to be better friends than I have earned.

And so on to Seattle, to home. At ten of midnight, I dug a well-interred house key out of my bug-smeared jacket, quietly opened the door, and walked straight into the arms of my wife.

"I missed you," she said into my shoulder, holding tightly, but I could not speak. Warm is the woman who welcomes you home.

None of this may make a lot of sense now, thumb-typed with a padded aluminum splint bandaged onto my broken throttle hand, through the fog of my elastic memory, coruscated back by crisscrossed grief, panic, warmth, nostalgia, paranoia, and love.

I'm home again, back from long blue roads, from wars abroad; back to the *jihads* of internal struggle and marital strife and off-site parenting. I have a business to build, a household to husband, a heart to heal. I have a cat who rides on my left shoulder and growls into my ear when I put a foot wrong. Everything familiar is here, but I see it all new, through wondering eyes, as though I were a Japanese tourist fending off this reality with a battery of loaded Nikons.

I will carry no weapon, because I am not afraid—but I miss my rifle every day.

Being not-dead makes decisions and actions imperative. It's not me who caused the war to kill my brothers. It's not me who hides behind yellow car magnets, or picket signs; not me who asserts that we may not discuss war until it's over and the dead are counted and stacked—or that moral justice demands irrational, emotional reaction. Those protestations, those loud assertions are a luxury earned for (not by) the privileged many; earned lately by 2,000 men and women who authentically learned what it is to leave it all on the field.

I took my chances, spun the wheel, prayed every day to bring my guys back alive. They came back scuffed but whole, and I'm back, too. After a long swim under burning waters, I surfaced beyond the flaming slick to gulp cool, northwest air into my urgent lungs.

It's time to be off now. Time to get started, time to get unstuck. My war fighting days, my bar fighting days are behind me. I need to stop looking back there, head into the wind and make progress forward. I find myself once again a live man, at large in the broad world.

And once again, there's a motorcycle parked in my garage. Could be time to get that idle set just right.

AUG 05, Seattle (home)

# Silver Wing

## By Steven L. Thompson

*Cycle World*

April 1989

IKE MANY PILOTS, he was drawn to motorcycles. A half-century ago, he discovered some of the joy of flying in the freedom of riding. And in the way young men did then and do now find themselves in a certain marque, the pilot became an Indian man. He collected a garage-full when few in America seemed to care about the legacy of the machines from Springfield.

The Indians followed the pilot around the world. He always intended, as middle-aged men do, to restore them. He resurrected one, then two, and then as such things do, the projects gathered dust when life's vicissitudes intervened.

The royal-red Indians languished untouched for a decade. He did not ride them. He did not ride anything. Trapped as we all are in the interwoven, unseen webs of life, he grappled for 20 years with survival and success and failure. Midway through the two decades, more or less, he offered the proud old Indians to his son, who despaired of being able to love them or bring them to life as his father had. They were sold or given away.

And still the pilot did not ride. Until, one New Year's Day, the pilot's wife died, losing a long and bitter battle with emphysema and mental illness. Sixty-five years old, exhausted by the struggle, his own health in jeopardy, the pilot hibernated through the lonely winter.

At Eastertime, the time of renewal, his son gave him a gentle ride through the cherry blossoms. Unused to the passenger's role, the pilot was disoriented at first. But soon, something he saw over his son's shoulders changed him. After the ride, the silver-haired pilot climbed off the BMW with a look the son had not seen for decades. It was the look of their joint past, the look the son remembered when the pilot returned from flying his bomber halfway around the world. It was not the look of a tired old man. It was the look of the eagle.

*Lee Klancher*

A month later, the pilot rode again. First, as such highly disciplined men do, he restrained himself. He rode with the Motorcycle Safety Foundation, relishing the similarities to the flight training in which he'd reveled nearly five decades before, when he and his classmates had been sent off to kill the sons of Nippon in a green hell. Now the old eagle rode the work of the sons of the sons he did not kill, the Hondas and Suzukis and Yamahas and Kawasakis, and he began at last to love life.

In an eyeblink, it seemed, the pilot owned new machines to replace the Indians. The V-twin Yamaha rumbled in the ancient way he remembered, and the Honda Silver Wing Interstate spoke of the adventures that had happened to him, long ago. The adventures of eternal youth. The call of the road that never ends, the ride for life.

He knew there would be hurdles, and there were. He fell, unused to the steering of the Silver Wing, and cursed himself when his old man's body was not up to hauling the machine instantly upright. Accustomed to near-perfect performance in the air, the silver eagle agonized over his lost skills on the ground. But he persevered, in the way that such men do, and slowly, painfully, the old skills came back.

The son was concerned. Twenty-five non-stop years of riding and racing told him that his father was putting himself at great risk. More than once, he found himself about to chide the old pilot, to make him take fewer risks. And then in the way that middle-aged sons do, he suddenly remembered, with unnerving clarity, scenes long forgotten, scenes from the father-son life they'd lived.

The confidence the pilot had shown in his awkward 15-year-old son when he'd bought him a Yamaha 80 with which to take on the world. The calm acceptance of the son's burning need to hurl himself into the unknown perils of racing. The support. The endless support.

The scenes tumbled through the middle-aged son's mind, and he said nothing to the old pilot, worrying now as the father had worried then. Who am I, the son thought, to yoke a man who has touched God in the sky? Who am I to instruct a man who has stood unfailingly with courage and determination by his woman for the long, agonizing years it took her to succumb? The son could not answer his own questions.

Then the old pilot faltered in his riding quest, and the son's questions became moot. Another winter came, and with it new ravages on his father's body. Cataracts stole much of his sight. Diabetes devoured his sinews. Complications triggered complication, and the old pilot lay more than once in a sweat and chills at death's door.

As such men do, and as he always had, he fought back fiercely. They gave him a new eye, and he mastered the diabetic's lot with the same calm dignity and discipline that had saved the crews of his airplanes more than once. Now the life to be saved was his own, and he did not flinch.

The motorcycles sat unridden for weeks, then months. But as he struggled with his own weakness, as he fought to regain his health, the once-and-future pilot never failed to care for the Yamaha and the Honda as he had those ruby-red Indians, all those years ago. The son watched, and wondered.

And one day, without fanfare, the silver eagle got up from his chair and rode his Silver Wing again, as *he* at least had always known he would. His once-dimmed eyes shone as he recounted the ride to his son. It had not been a long ride, the father said. But it had been long enough.

The son listened. And it was only much later that he understood at last that his father had once again taught him a lesson. As such men always do.

# Scoring a Victory

## By Darwin Holmstrom

Previously Unpublished

FACE IT: at least part of the reason why people spend five figures on custom motorcycles is to improve their sex lives. Only a naïve neuter would argue that sex appeal does not play a role in the purchase of an expensive motorcycle. For many people, spending too much money on flashy motorcycles is ultimately an attempt to secure their immortality by helping them find partners with whom they can replicate their deoxyribonucleic acids. Yes, I'm talking about doing the big nasty, and to succeed, a custom cruiser has to increase a rider's ability to get laid. Has Victory succeeded in the Vegas? Answering this question required me to apply everything I know about Cartesian doubt and conduct a careful scientific inquiry. This was a potentially embarrassing task, but I am a professional journalist, and I scoff at humiliation.

Victory Motorcycles hit a home run with its Vegas motorcycle. The Vegas is fast, handles well, and looks great. It's even built right here in the USA. It's everything a motorcyclist could want, but perhaps the single most important question remains unanswered: can it help you score with the opposite sex?

Victory's early bikes certainly weren't much use in that department. When Polaris Industries decided to enter the heavyweight cruiser market with its Victory brand of motorcycles, it did so with a product that was both functionally and aesthetically challenged. Over the years Victory made dramatic mechanical improvements, producing a bike that was the functional equal of any cruiser coming out of America, Europe, or Japan. But stylistically the bikes still didn't appeal to a wide audience. When the best thing potential customers say about the look of a cruiser is, "That's not so bad, if you squint and look at it kind of sideways," the bike probably isn't going to do much to improve its owner's love life.

*Lee Klancher*

No one needs to get squinty-eyed to appreciate the looks of the Vegas. With a design inspired by Arlen Ness, one of the all-time greatest custom bike builders, and his son Cory, the Vegas looks great by just about anyone's standards.

Spend some time in the saddle of a Vegas, and you'll learn that not only does the Vegas look great, but it also works extremely well. As far as scoring nookie goes, the one functional drawback the bike has is that unless your potential sex partners are into getting spanked, the passenger pillion is not going to make a good impression. Owners might want to think twice about carrying passengers in states that actively enforce sodomy laws. Not only is the pillion thinly padded, but it's shaped completely wrong. It curves upward at center so that, rather than cradling a passenger's rectal region, it penetrates it. The seat is best thought of as either a marital aid or a fender protector to be placed under a duffel bag. Best keep your two-up rides short if you want to score, unless of course you've hooked up with your potential partner at an S&M club.

After picking up the Vegas from Victory's Minnesota headquarters, I parked in front of a coffee shop where a dude pulled over in his car and asked about the bike. He said he had a Vegas too, so I asked him a few questions.

Q: I see you don't have a wedding ring. Are you single?
A: Yes.
*At this point I asked him the one question that I, being terminally married, would be unable to answer empirically in my testing.*
Q: How about scoring with the opposite sex? Do chicks dig the Vegas?
A: [Thoughtful pause.] I've told some girls that I have a motorcycle, and they ask, "Is it a Harley?" When I tell them "no," they seem disappointed. I explain that the Vegas is built by an American company located in Minnesota and that it is a legitimate competitor to Harley-Davidson.
Q: Does this work? Have you scored?
A: No.

Apparently explaining the history of Victory Motorcycles didn't help this fellow replicate his DNA, though I suspect his delivery might have been as problematic as his message.

I needed to do more research, so I rode the Vegas to the annual Sturgis Rally and Races. Once there, I decided to get a professional opinion regarding the Victory's sex appeal. I went to a strip club on the outskirts of Rapid City and solicited the input of a stripper. I approached the bouncer and explained what I had in mind. It took some fast talking (and approximately $50 cash) to convince the bouncer to accompany me and a stripper outside to look at my motorcycle. I got the feeling I wasn't the

*Lee Klancher*

first Sturgis rally attendee who asked a stripper to come outside and look at his or her bike.

For this task I selected Sapphire, the only stripper in the bar who wore glasses. Sapphire seemed to like the bike and said for another $100 she'd go for a ride with me. "That's wrong on so many levels I don't even know how to respond," I said. "If I let that pillion pad do what it does for money, we're both going to get busted by the vice squad." I don't think either Sapphire or the bouncer paid much attention to what I was saying until I said the words "vice squad." Upon hearing those two words they perked right up.

"You have to leave now," the bouncer said, all traces of humor gone from his voice. I started to put on my jacket and he said, "Now!" He moved toward me in a menacing fashion, so I rode out to the end of the driveway to finish donning my gear. The question of the Victory's sex appeal still hadn't been answered definitively.

But I was a professional on an assignment, and this was a question that needed to be answered. The next day I saw a lovely woman taking a photo of the Vegas, which was parked on Main Street. She seemed a bit frightened when I ran across the street shouting, "Excuse me!" and hid

*Lee Klancher*

behind a stout-looking fellow with biceps the size of my legs. "Don't worry. I'm a professional!" I shouted in an attempt to dispel any concerns she might have, but it didn't seem to allay her fears. "I'm doing a story on this bike for a magazine," I explained. "I'm trying to gauge people's reactions to the Vegas, and I saw you photographing it. Why did you want to take a photo of it?"

The woman said, "I like the color. I like the handlebars and thought Murray would like it." Murray was her husband, the fellow with the big pipes who stood watching me interrogate his wife. "I'd be happy if Murray bought one." I asked if Murray would be more likely to score if he came home aboard a Vegas. "I believe Murray would be more appealing as a sexual partner if he were aboard the Vegas," she said. This was a positive sign, but just because the bike made Murray more appealing, she didn't say that it would help him seal the deal. I still needed a definitive answer.

At the Dodge display in Sturgis, Victory had provided motorcycles for Dodge to display in its truck. One day I found a young woman who appeared to be a professional dancer raising and lowering a Victory

*Lee Klancher*

touring bike on a hydraulic lift while a fellow who appeared to be her business manager videotaped her. It seems that the duo was filming some sort of "Professional-Dancers-Gone-Wild-at-Sturgis"-type video. I asked the young woman what she thought about the Vegas that sat in the bed of one of the Dodge trucks.

"I don't know much about motorcycles, but the Vegas looks nice," she said. "I'd rather go for a ride on this than on an ugly motorcycle."

I tried to formulate my now-stock question about the Vegas' ability to enhance its rider's desirability as a potential donor of genetic material, but at this point the young woman's business manager stepped in. He didn't think she should answer that question unless I was willing to pay her for her time. I declined, since I was already having trouble figuring out a way to expense my research at the strip club.

Later I cornered another Vegas rider at Sturgis and asked him why he'd selected a Vegas. "I bought it because the design was unique," he said. "Everybody really likes it. They're impressed with the quality, style." When I asked him if the bike made him seem more attractive to the opposite sex, he said, "I'm married. I don't score."

*Lee Klancher*

While at Sturgis I had the opportunity to ride with chopper builder Billy Lane. I asked Billy what he thought of the Vegas. "It looks like it works pretty well," Lane said, "but style-wise, it's pretty ugly. It looks Japanese." When I asked Billy if he thought the bike would help a rider score with the ladies, he replied, "I don't need any help scoring with the ladies."

Asking Billy to critique the Vegas was probably like asking Jenna Jameson to critique your sexual technique. But the general reaction of potential customers was positive. Most people seemed to think the Vegas would indeed help its rider get lucky.

Back home in Minneapolis, away from all the high-buck choppers on Sturgis' Main Street, the Vegas once again took on the air of an exotic custom. I even had one young woman flash her breasts at me as I rode around Lake Calhoun. Perhaps this bike really worked.

To explore this sex concept more fully, I took my wife for a ride, and when we got home, I scored. When I asked if the Vegas made me seem more attractive as a potential sex partner, my wife replied, "It doesn't hurt." It wasn't the definitive answer I was looking for, but it was something.

# The Invasion

## By Michael Dregni

*Motorcycle Legends*

Voyageur Press, 2004

FOR ALL PRACTICAL PURPOSES, the British motorcycle invasion began on September 13, 1948. At the time, Harley-Davidson and Indian ruled the roost in the American motorcycling world, as they had for decades and as they would for years more. They battled each other for the checkered flag on Sunday and then fought again on the salesroom floor on Monday. Milwaukee was currently up one notch over the Wigwam in Springfield, since it held the U.S. record for the fastest production motorcycle at 136 miles per hour (218 kilometers per hour).

All that was about to become ancient history.

A wealthy American motorcycle and car enthusiast and journalist named John Edgar had a jones for European machinery. He would go on to import one of the first race cars in the United States from a then-little-known factory called Ferrari and campaign it in West Coast road races. At the moment, however, he was lusting for a fast motorcycle, a motorcycle that could beat any Harley-Davidson or Indian hands down.

Edgar happened to meet up with Philip Vincent, the colorful and charismatic head of the British Vincent concern, who was in California at the time recovering from a headfirst tumble onto the tarmac during a speed run on one of his finest. Always quick to extol the virtues of his fast motorcycles, Vincent promised Edgar that the American speed record would fall to his new Black Shadow model. Vincent was also then a little-known name in the United States, but listening to Vincent's words, Edgar was ready to fall under the spell.

In April 1948, Vincent cabled his chief engineer, the irascibly brilliant Phil Irving, requesting a Black Shadow be prepped and shipped to the United States post haste.

Vincent was eager to prove his new motorcycle, since his own reputation was on the line. The Black Shadow had been conceived on the sly, hidden from even the managing director of Vincent's own company, who had vetoed plans to build the machine. Irving and Vincent factory rider George Brown had secretly converted a brace of Vincent Rapides based on lessons learned from the factory's hot-rod road racer, nicknamed *Gunga Din*. Inevitably, the managing director uncovered the clandestine project, and now Vincent's project was in jeopardy.

Irving went to work. He and his crew breathed on a Series B Black Shadow destined for Edgar. Irving ground a new cam profile designed for top-end speed, and Brown went out and rode the test Black Shadow up to 143 miles per hour (229 kilometers per hour) at the local airfield before he ran out of pavement. Happy with their tests, the cycle was crated and shipped.

## "A Gentleman of the Old School"

Now Edgar needed a rider. Enter Roland "Rollie" Free, a fearless Harley-Davidson hater who had seemingly sworn his life to battling the menace from Milwaukee. Free was an original. His mentor was O. K. Newby, the former captain of the Flying Merkel board-track race squad. Newby later teamed with Free riding a Wall of Death in Depression-era carnivals where a lion was turned loose in the barrel to take swipes at the rider as he circled the top at speed. As Free's friend Mike Parti later described him to Vincent historian Zachary Miller, "Rollie Free was a gentleman of the old school. He'd never swear in front of ladies, but he'd fistfight at the drop of a hat." Free had been devoted to Indians for outgunning Harleys on the track and countless duels on the street. He had set a handful of speed records on Indians, and combined with his distaste for all things Harley, he was the perfect man for the job.

Free looked over this strange, new English motorcycle upon its unpacking and immediately set to work. He stripped it of all unnecessary parts, junked the front fender, and threw out the large, comfortable bench seat, replacing it with a tiny pad mounted atop the rear fender. Since Edgar was friends with folk at Mobil Oil, the oil company offered its help, and twin Mobil Pegasus stickers were slapped on either side of the gas tank. (It was not disclosed until later that part of that Mobil friendship extended to mixing a special batch of alcohol fuel for the Vincent, a decidedly "non-production" fuel for beating the *production* cycle record.)

*Lee Klancher*

With the Vincent prepped, the team made its way to the Bonneville Salt Flats, Utah's dry lake bed that was the center of the world's speed record-setters. Free kicked over the big V-twin, aimed it down the straight black line bisecting the flats, and rocketed away.

Free had developed his own patented riding style for speed. Once he had the cycle into top gear, he climbed from the standard sitting position to lay prone atop the rear fender in an effort to cut aerodynamic drag. He steered by watching the black line as it unrolled beneath the cycle. This riding position was carefully plotted, as Mike Parti told Miller: "Rollie would get on the bike in front of a big mirror and have friends stand around and comment on how much frontal area he was making—like where to crouch, where to point his toes. He was looking for every little detail."

Now, on September 13, 1948, Free blasted down the salt in his racing leathers and pudding basin helmet. When he returned to the start to check the clock, his best time was 148 miles per hour (239 kilometers per hour). He had bested Harley yet again.

Free was not happy, however. His new record was fine, but he wanted more. There was something magical about hitting 150 miles per hour (240 kilometers per hour)—a ton and a half—and Free lusted for it.

Free speculated that his leathers, which had flapped about hard enough to rip a seam, were slowing him down. So he stripped them off and replaced them with his bathing suit. Wearing a blue rubber bathing cap in place of his pudding basin and tennis sneakers instead of boots, he fired up the Vincent one more time.

Roaring down the salt laid prone on the Black Shadow in just his bathing suit, the camera shutters snapped and the records fell: 150.313 miles per hour (240.5 kilometers per hour).

The result shattered Harley-Davidson's record like a home run ball hit through a plate-glass window. It wasn't just the actual breaking of the record that did it, but the publicity that surrounded it as well. That amazing British-built Vincent motorcycle was catapulted into the American motorcyclist's consciousness with its new, brazen-but-true advertising line on its promotional material: "The World's Fastest Standard Motorcycle." A photo of Free breaking the record appeared in *Life* magazine and went on to become one of the most famous motorcycle photographs ever, an example of the extremes to which those two-wheeled crazies would actually go.

John Edgar's Vincent Black Shadow was not the first British motorcycle in North America, of course. Yet by breaking Harley's record and by appearing in *Life*, it established British motorcycles in the average motorcycling Joe's mind like nothing before.

The British invasion had landed.

## To the Dirt Born

A second challenge to the sovereignty of the American motorcycle on its own turf came from a surprising quarter in a true story worthy of David and Goliath of yore.

Motorcycle racing in North America was born and bred on dirt tracks. Early races were typically held at fairgrounds, where pioneering racers lined up alongside each other to await the waving of the green flag on oval horse-racing tracks fashioned of compacted dirt. Other, point-to-point races were held on public roads closed for the day, but since most roads were unpaved in the early years of motorcycling, these too were "dirt-track" races. Racing on board tracks was an anomaly, although one of the most exciting and bloodthirsty.

*Lee Klancher*

Naturally, racing on dirt gave birth to a style of machine and riding tailored to its peculiarities. Roaring around a county fair horse track on a hot July 4th before a cheering grandstand, riders slid their steeds through the oval turns with their inside feet down as support, feathering the throttle for control. American racing motorcycles eschewed brakes as being dangerous—which they certainly were at those times and those speeds. Rooster tails of dust followed their progress, giving true meaning to the period's curse to slow-pokes, "Eat my dust!"

The pinnacle of American racing became the annual events at Daytona Beach, Florida. The flat, smooth sand that stretched to the horizons was ideal for record setting. With the addition of big, sweeping turns at each end and a return section run on a paved frontage road along the beach, an instant race oval was created that required guts to win the glory. In 1959, the tri-oval superspeedway was inaugurated with its 33-degree banked turns, and the Daytona 200 became a true road race.

Other races also spoke of North American racing styles. The Big Bear Run was a hell-bent-for-leather dash across the Nevada and California deserts. The Catalina Grand Prix, held on Catalina Island off the California coast, typified the American style of TT racing in mixing off-road, motocross segments with paved, road-racing sections in the fashion of the Isle of Man Tourist Trophy, or TT, from whence the name came. Class C racing grew up in the 1930s as a run-what-ya-brung class for production-based machines and raced primarily on paced racetracks, although American riders still rode dirt-track style.

European Grand Prix–style racing was about as different from North American racing as night and day, or as different as an iron Harley-Davidson KR was from the 30.50-ci (500cc) Moto Guzzi Gambalunga that ruled Europe in the 1950s. European racing motorcycles were built low and lean with smaller-displacement engines that were tuned to extremes. Riders rode in a crouch, keeping their feet up and using a different fashion of finesse to make speed through turns.

Italian and other European racing machines had made their way into American race paddocks in ones and twos since the dawn of motor-cycle competition. But in the late 1950s, the floodgates opened. The first arrivals were British machines, since they were the most closely paired to American standards. These were soon followed by Italian hardware that was often slotted into newly formed "lightweight" classes with speeds that sometimes bested the best Harley or Indian.

On the West Coast, a small group of European Grand Prix fans erected the American Federation of Motorcyclists, affiliated with Europe's Fédération Internationale de la Moto. The AFM held what may be the first Grand Prix–style race in the United States in April 1957 at San Gabriel, California, including entries of a privately imported Ducati 98cc (5.9-ci) Gran Sport and two 175cc (10.5-ci) MV Agusta racers. Classes were broken down for 500, 350, 250, and 175cc. The Canadian Motorcycle Association of the 1950s was also aligned with the FIM; it had an Unlimited Class for all displacements and a Lightweight Class for 250cc and less. But throughout the rest of North America, racing meant feet down through the corners as riders broadslided through curves sideways with the engine wide open.

### Turning the Racing World on Its Head

In 1958, the American racing world was turned on its head—figuratively. The historic change began, however, by turning the competition on its head—literally.

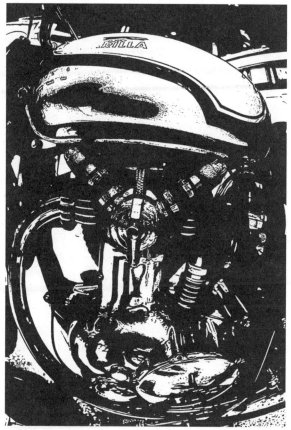

*Lee Klancher*

In 1957, an entrepreneur named Ernest Wise began importing into the United States the wares of Moto Parilla, then one of Italy's largest motorcycle makers. The arrival of the Parillas marked the first large-scale importation of Italian cycles onto American soil.

At the top of the Parilla line was the Grand Sport, a svelte 175cc (10.5-ci) single-cylinder machine with overhead valves actuated by a single cam mounted high on the left side of the engine. With alloy rims, low-mounted clip-on handlebars, rear-set foot controls, and an anatomically formed gas tank that allowed riders to wrap their bodies around it while in a low-down, aerodynamic crouch, the Parilla was a new wave in the New World.

To add insult to injury, the Grand Sport was quick. An early road test in *Cycle* magazine in 1954 clocked 95.6 miles per hour (153 kilometers per hour), although a broken-in Parilla was promised to top an honest ton!

To test the bike, however, *Cycle* magazine editor Bob Schanz first needed a lesson in the European GP riding style, and he explained for the neophyte reader how to tuck in and crouch down on a European racing machine. It was a lesson that all American road racers were about to learn.

Ernest Wise's Cosmopolitan Motors was learning other lessons. Wise and his workers were having trouble with the Parillas: They were high-strung, temperamental motorcycles, and the American tuners were shaking their heads over them. Wise lit upon the idea of importing an Italian mechanic to fettle the Italian bikes, and after cabling the Parilla factory, 27-year-old Parilla racer, mechanic, and engineer Giuseppe "Joe" Rottigni was on his way.

Rottigni was not just your typical backroom boy who happened to know what to do with a screwdriver. He was that rare combination of a racer who also knew how to tune cycles, an engineer who could also ride. Rottigni had just won the 1957 Giro d'Italia, Italy's two-wheeled version of the Mille Miglia, and he brought with him to the promised land of the United States his Motogiro-winning Grand Sport, a 250cc bevel-drive bialbero Parilla, and a crate chock full of "special" parts.

There was one problem, however. When Rottigni arrived in 1958, he spoke no English. That was a minor point, though, and he quickly organized Cosmopolitan to get its Parilla line up and running as well as spearheading the new Cosmopolitan Race Team. As one Parilla racer remembered, "Joe was the gear that drove Cosmopolitan." Rottigni aided Cosmopolitan's Parilla dealers and privateer racers, tuning racebikes, running his own Grand Sport, and winning races in Canada that brought Cosmo fame and fortune. Ernest Wise's son, Larry, began advertising the victories in *Cycle* and other magazines to spread the good word about Parilla, some of the first motorcycle ads in America to promote the old proverb, "Win on Sunday, sell on Monday."

It was at one of these races that Rottigni and his Parilla would turn American racing to a new light. The first race of the AMA season following Daytona was the national held on the winding race course run through the forests of Laconia, New Hampshire, on June 16–22, 1958. It was a race that changed American motorcycling.

## Shattering the Status Quo

Before the race began, Rottigni was disqualified. On the starting grid, the judges pointed out that Rottigni's pudding-basin racing helmet was illegal. Rottigni spoke no English, so Larry Wise spoke for him. A conference ensued. After an argument with the judges, Rottigni pointed out that many of the other racers also had the same type of helmet. He was allowed to start.

The helmet debate was a silly skirmish—but it also told volumes about the times and environment in the U.S. racing fraternity. Word of Rottigni's prowess had gotten around, and strings were being pulled to keep him out of the race. Harley-Davidson was at the height of its campaign against foreign imports into the United States, which were challenging Harley on the racetracks and on the showroom floors. The debut of the Parilla at Laconia, along with one of Joe Berliner's first Ducati 175cc racers, was the first time many people had ever seen an Italian motorcycle. Walter Davidson himself was at the race, and he certainly had powers within the AMA to defend the old ways.

That status quo was about to be shattered.

Rottigni was finally allowed to line up on the front row for the Lightweight Class IV race against Cliff Guild's 200cc Triumph Cub and Hal Burton's 200cc Jawa. Rottigni's 175cc bike was obviously special. It wore low clip-on handlebars and rear-set footpegs in the days when American racers used high bars and put their feet down in the turns flat-track style—whether they were racing on dirt or pavement. And Rottigni's one-piece leathers received special, awed mention in the *Motorcyclist* report.

From the drop of the flag, Rottigni set the pace—until the first turn, that is, where he was immediately knocked down. Larry Wise remembered the historic race: "[Rottigni] really introduced GP style racing in this country. The Americans were 'flat tracking' their way around the road race courses. They would dive far into the turns, and slow almost to a stop at the apex and downshift, all the while broadsliding with their foot down. Rottigni would downshift before entering a turn and pick a line and slow before actually entering the turn. The other riders would come along flying by him but his engine revs were up and he would come rocketing out of the turn sometimes running over an outstretched foot of a broadsliding rider he was pursuing. . . .

"In the first turn he incredulously saw a rider broadsliding toward him even as his 'line' had him committed to a collision course. After the crash as the whole pack passed him and the other rider, he started the bike and started to go. He soon passed the field and opened a lead followed closely only by Cliff Guild on the factory Triumph. After halfway he crashed again on an oil slick at the bottom of Laconia Hill, and the whole pack passed him again. He straightened the bent levers and pedals even though his hands were torn and bleeding. This was in front of the main crowd of spectators, and they were wildly cheering for him now. At the finish line he had caught most of the riders except for two and finished third with blood streaming from his torn hands, covering the machine."

The winner of the race was Guild, with Burton second. But the true winner was Rottigni. As *Motorcyclist* recounted Rottigni's feat: "It was quite apparent that he was the fastest man in the field, as well as the most seasoned. . . . Had the race gone a few more laps it would have been interesting to see if Rottigni could have again captured the winning position." In trying to catch the leaders, Rottigni had set a lap record for the 250cc class on his 175cc bike.

And after the checkered flag had been waved, even Walter Davidson came forth to shake Rottigni's bloody hand.

### "You Meet the Nicest People on a Honda"

At the dawn of the 1960s, a surprise attack on the world's motorcycle market came from a quarter few people could ever have guessed at.

This new invasion struck North American shores orchestrated by one Jack McCormack, who would go down in history as one of the most influential figures in motorcycling since the early pioneers, such as George Hendee and Oscar Hedstrom, and Bill Harley and the Davidson brothers.

In 1959, however, McCormack was a former salesman for Johnson Motors of Los Angeles, the Western states Triumph distributor. He had left JoMo to sell buttons for his father's firm, but he still made his sales calls on a 650cc Triumph TR6, his business suit ruffled by the breeze.

*Lee Klancher*

McCormack simply loved motorcycles. He was not a Marlon Brando clone in a black leather jacket, though. McCormack sported an all-American crew cut and looked like Mom and Dad's dream prom date for their sweet sixteen daughter. He rode motorcycles, though, and that was enough to draw dirty looks as he rode down Main Street.

McCormack had heard word of the new Honda motorcycles that were just starting to be imported from Japan. These were different machines from the Triumph and other Brit bikes that he knew so well. The Honda cycles piqued his interest.

Following World War II, Soichiro Honda had adapted his mechanical expertise as an aftermarket maker of pistons and rings and built an empire crafting motorcycles and automobiles. He first used 50 and 100cc gasoline

284    THE DEVIL CAN RIDE

generator motors from World War II aircraft to power bicycles. He next formed the Honda Motor Company in Hammamatsu to build his Model A, a motorized bicycle.

But Honda had a dream. His goal was to build a true motorcycle that would rival the best of the British machines. After a succession of clip-on engines and diminutive motorcycles, he jumped in 1955 to building the luxurious, 250cc (15-ci) overhead-camshaft Model D, which he nicknamed the "Dream." This machine signaled a technical leap that brought Honda up to date with—if not surpassing—many makers of the day.

By 1955, Honda boasted a gigantic factory complex that cranked out some 500,000 machines annually. Motorcycles bearing Honda's name were sold throughout Asia, and the firm was expanding its market into Australia, Africa, the Middle East, and Europe. Honda was the largest motorcycle maker in the world—and most Americans had never even heard the name. All of that was about to change.

## The Promised Land

In 1959, Honda entered the promised land, the U.S. market. The beachhead was a nondescript storefront at 4077 Pico Boulevard in Los Angeles, where the American Honda Motor Company was trying to figure out how to sell its nifty Honda 50, the Super Cub, to the American public.

Enter Jack McCormack, who talked his way into the national sales manager post for Honda in 1960 with dreams of popularizing motor-cycling in an anti-motorcycle world. McCormack was one of several Americans to be hired by the foundling importation business, whose Japanese managers spoke only halting English; others included former racer George "Frenchy" French, Bob Hanson, Don Graves, and Doug Moncrief. McCormack outfitted each of his small crew of salesmen with a Chevrolet El Camino, the half-car, half-pickup-truck vehicle that could carry up to six Super Cubs. The "El Camino Brigade," as they were known, set out across the West to sign up dealers.

Knowing firsthand that motorcycling had a bum rap, the first thing that McCormack did was to not call his motorcycles "motorcycles." "We did everything we could to keep from calling the Honda 50 a motor-cycle," he told motorcycle historian Phil Schilling. "We called it a two-wheeled compact, a family fun vehicle—anything but a motorcycle. We

*Lee Klancher*

stayed away from talking about performance or about anything other than fun."

That was all a part of his strategy of selling a motorcycle to people who hated motorcycles. McCormack also knew that he could not sell the scooter as transportation in the United States; he envisioned the buyers of his wares as the all-American family looking for a fun runabout.

McCormack and Honda also had another image problem to overcome. Japan was still the bad guy of World War II in America's eyes, and many Americans simply would not buy Japanese products. To others, "Made in Japan" meant *poorly* made. The sole other Japanese motorcycle line then being sold in any numbers in the United States was foisted surreptitiously on unknowing buyers. Throughout the late 1950s, Montgomery Ward sold mail-order motorscooters with the glamorous model names of the Nassau, the Waikiki, and the Miami. Beneath the Monkey Ward nameplate, however, these were Mitsubishi C-74 Silver Pigeon scooters, proudly made in Japan by the former builder of the infamous Zero-san fighter plane of World War II.

The El Camino Brigade set up Honda franchises anywhere and everywhere they could. Some Old School motorcycle dealers signed on the dotted line to sell the new machines, such as Floyd Dreyer of California, who went on to become the operator of the oldest U.S. Honda dealership. Other Super Cubs were sold through unlikely venues, such as farsighted automobile dealerships, hardware stores, even men's clothing outlets and barbershops. McCormack established 125 "dealers" in the West before pointing his El Caminos east.

Then, McCormack had a further vision: He wanted big money from Honda to spark an advertising campaign to bring Honda's "non-motorcycle" in front of all of America. Honda accordingly upped his promotional budget from a mere $20,000 in 1960 to an astonishing $150,000 in 1961. McCormack put the money to work, running full-page ads in *Life* magazine at $40,000 a pop.

In 1962, McCormack and his crew had a brainstorm that came in the form of a marketeer's dream—the perfect advertising slogan. Someone at American Honda came upon the rallying cry, "You meet the nicest people on a Honda." With help from the firm of Grey Advertising of Beverly Hills, the ads began appearing in magazines everywhere, from *Cycle* to the *Saturday Evening Post*.

With a simple slogan, McCormack's sales force removed the stigma that a switchblade was the chief tool you needed to ride a motorcycle. Suddenly, from out of the days of *The Wild One*, the image of the motorcycle got a haircut, a shave, and a new set of respectable clothes. Almost overnight, the name "Honda" became nearly synonymous with *motorcycle*—or at least synonymous with good, clean, crewcut motorcycling fun.

Still, few of the old school of real motorcyclists ever thought Honda would sell any of its oddball little machines. McCormack, however, had lofty goals—and confidence. When one Honda salesman was asked—rather snidely, of course—by a Triumph dealer how many Hondas he thought could actually be sold in the United States, the Honda rep responded, "5,000." This confidence bordered on the audacious if not arrogant to the

Triumph dealer, who was fighting tooth and nail to sell 2,500 Triumphs annually in the West. Then the Honda salesman clarified his statement: "Five thousand *per month!*"

As with the early Volkswagen Beetles in the United States, Honda dealers began selling motorcycles like grocery stores sold milk. In 1959, American Honda sold some 2,500 machines; in 1961, it sold 17,000. By 1962, Honda was selling more motorcycles on Harley-Davidson's home turf than the Milwaukee company itself—in fact, Honda was selling more machines in the United States than all of the rest of the industry combined. In 1963, Honda sold an amazing 90,000 in a year when the entire American motorcycle industry sold 150,000. Not only did Honda now control 60 percent of the market, but it had almost singlehandedly tripled the size of the total market. McCormack's El Camino Brigade had done good.

## The Right Place

Honda was in the right place at the right time. It entered the United States just as the recreational market was set to open wide with Baby Boomers reaching driving age and the country flush with leisure time. Honda also helped to make the market, bringing inexpensive, reliable, easy-to-use little motorcycles that were the perfect toy. First-time motorcycle buyers made up 65 percent of Honda's customers, just as McCormack had envisioned. Most of those buyers were between 16 and 26 years old—and 10 percent were female. The statistics were startling.

Some old school motorcycle dealers of the day grudgingly approved of Honda's success. After all, the overall market was expanding as people bought Honda Super Cubs, then moved up to a 250cc Honda CB72 Hawk or a 305cc Honda CB77 Super Hawk. Some day, the dealers reasoned, these people would want a real motorcycle, and they would come calling. The old school dealers would have their Triumphs, Nortons, and Harleys polished, gassed, and waiting.

When that day came, however, Honda unveiled a "real" motorcycle of its own. The four-cylinder CB750 of 1969 boasted power and performance, brakes that actually braked, electrics that truly turned things on and off, and engine casings that kept the oil inside the engine. In a few short years, Honda's CB750 rewrote the rules.

# Do You Believe in Fairies?

## By Michelle Ann Duff

*International Journal of*

*Motorcycle Studies*

November 2007

LEGEND HAS IT that a giant living in a land that is now known as Ireland battled regularly with another giant living to the northeast across a narrow sea. One day, in a fit of anger, the Irish behemoth scooped up a handful of dirt and threw it at his distant counterpart, but the projectile fell short of its target and landed in the sea between. So large was the handful of dirt that a small island was formed. Many years later, Vikings inhabited this small island and established a large community that lasted for many years. Today, in gentler times, this little island is known as the Isle of Man. Steeped in folklore, fables, and fairy tales of mystical little people that bring fortune to believers and despair and destruction to nonbelievers, the Isle of Man is a green jewel bathed by the indigo waters of the Irish Sea. Its lush countryside is what most North Americans envision England to be, with stone fences separating patchwork fields of green and gold, rolling hills speckled with grazing sheep, fieldstone farmhouses in distant farmlands, castles reflecting Viking history, and quaint thatched-roof cottages with well-groomed gardens. A breathtaking coastline, more reminiscent of the rugged rocky bays of Newfoundland, Canada, abounds with little villages rimming pretty coves, deep fjords, and sheer rock walls falling steeply into ocean-blue waters. For years the island's main industry, tourism, flourished, but now, with the world's vacation destinations at anyone's doorstep, tourists no longer flock to the island as a favoured holiday spot. As a tax-free haven the island's financial district does a booming business, and banking has now taken over as the island's main source of income.

The Isle of Man is also famous for the Isle of Man TT Motorcycle Races held annually since 1907. The Isle of Man Mountain Course is unquestionably the most demanding of all motor racing circuits, with a single lap of 37 3/4 miles of public roads closed for racing. From Douglas,

289

the Island's capital, the course winds its way up the west coast of the island, through little villages and picturesque glens, past country farms and churches to Ramsey, the island's second largest city. From Ramsey the course turns south and climbs the mountain road to an elevation of 1,500 feet before dropping down to Douglas once again. Over 200 corners and a multitude of bends and kinks, bumps and jumps, humpback bridges, telephone poles, traffic lights, traffic circles, curbs, telegraph poles, brick walls, and grass banks line the entire circuit. The course's beauty and immensity cannot be appreciated unless witnessed personally.

From 1960 to 1967 I had the honour to represent Canada in these races. In 1962, it was my third visit to the races; it was also the first year I felt comfortable and confident with my level of knowledge of the course. That year I had also been invited to ride bikes owned and developed by a major dealer/sponsor from England. Not only would I be riding potentially better machinery, but it would save untold wear and tear to my personal race bikes, which had been left on the mainland awaiting my return. Because these sponsored bikes were the unofficial factory entries, I was obligated to use Dunlop racing tires, as per factory agreement. Up to that time I had been using Avon tires, but the switch to Dunlop rubber seemed of no consequence.

These new Dunlop tires came straight from the company's experimental department. The front tire had a normal round profile, but the rear tire possessed a decidedly triangular shape. Dunlop's racing manager explained the theory behind the design.

"In a straight line," he said, "the peak of the tire puts less rubber on the road. With less rubber there is less rolling resistance, which gives you more speed. Lean it into a corner, the triangular sides increase the amount of tire in contact with the road. This lets you lean the bike over farther. So, you can go around the corner faster and accelerate sooner. Simple!"

It all sounded terrific, but was it?

These tires proved excellent during practise. In fact, they didn't feel much different than the Avon tires I had been using. So, I just accepted the Dunlop rubber and got on with the job at hand.

"And, don't forget to say hello to the 'Wee Fairies,' " said Gladys, the owner/operator of Rose Villa, the boarding house where I was staying. I was on my way to the airport to pick up my mother flying in from Toronto via London to be with me for the races, and I would have to drive over the little Fairy Bridge where the "Wee Folk" supposedly reside.

"Yeah, sure," I replied, a silly grin on my face.

The little bridge, about 5 miles from the airport, was situated just beyond a tight right/left S bend and could easily have been missed. Had I not been warned of its exact location, I would have driven past without giving the expected courtesy and would have been damned for the entire race week. As I approached the S-bend I reduced my speed and crept around the corner. An inconspicuous sign indicated the Fairy Bridge. I slowly crossed over the tiny bridge, and, tipping my imaginary hat, "Good morning, Fairies," I said. "Lovely day." To say I felt foolish was a gross understatement, but, fortunately, nobody witnessed my embarrassment.

I stopped the van just past the bridge and walked back for a closer look. The terrain underneath the bridge appeared to be nothing more than a small culvert, its stream of spring waters long since dried up, and seemed such an unpretentious palace for such important people. I could only assume they knew something we mere mortals could not begin to comprehend. At that moment, a local tour bus came down the road. I stood and watched with anticipation. I assumed the driver would be a knowledgeable island resident, and if he did not acknowledge the Fairies, I'd know I was being taken for a fool colonial. As the bus neared the bridge, I watched the driver carefully. Sure enough, off came his cap, and I could make out his lips, puckered in silent words. I'd swear it was the beginnings of "good morning" but could not be sure. Now, I was really confused. Stories of untold vexation and general bad luck during TT practise and race week from riders who scorned the existence of the "Little People" had me all but believing.

On the return trip to Douglas, for fear of awakening the Fairies' wrath, I warned my mother about the bridge and the expected courtesy, and in unison, smiling at each other, we wished the Fairies a good morning.

During the 350 Junior TT Race on Wednesday of race week, the races took the life of Tom Phillis, an Australian rider. He and his family had been staying at Rose Villa, the same boarding house as me, and I was witness to the aftermath for his wife and two young children. It had a sobering effect on many people involved with the races, especially those at the Villa. An intimate gathering of friends and officials at a church on Thursday, to honour our fallen comrade, dampened enthusiasm for many of those in attendance, including me.

On Friday the coveted Senior TT for 500cc machines took place. I felt obligated to at least go through the motions because so many people had put a great deal of effort into getting me to the starting line.

On a racecourse as long and as narrow as the Isle of Man TT Mountain Course, for safety reasons, the customary mass start was not employed. Riders start in pairs: numbers 1 and 2 start first, followed 10 seconds later by numbers 3 and 4, etc., until the entire field has departed. The event is a race against the clock more than it is against other riders. Lap times that year were just over 21 minutes in length. An added bonus with a staggered start: spectators are able to see action just about all the time.

With a riding number of 17, I was to start 80 seconds behind the leading pair. Riders funneled up to the line in relative order awaiting their turn, all engines silent. (At that time, all European races employed a push start with dead engines.) Numbers 15 and 16 were flagged off, and, along with number 18, I took my place in the twin starting boxes. Gone were the usual pre-race butterflies, replaced by an air of indifference, my thoughts still pensive, remembering the events of the previous day. On a small platform to my right stood the starter, a small Union Jack held high in his right hand. A hand-sized clock in his left hand ticked off the seconds. I had already pulled the Matchless' piston back against the compression stroke to give the engine three forward strokes to build up momentum before another compression stroke happened. Fuel and chain oiler taps were on. I pulled in the clutch and concentrated on the starter. Almost casually, the flag fell. I heaved the heavy bike forward, taking five steps before releasing the clutch. The engine turned and immediately fired into life. I swung myself into the seat and accelerated away toward the top of Bray Hill to begin the six-lap, 225-mile Senior TT.

On a racecourse as intricate as the Isle of Man TT, concentration is paramount. A moment's lapse can cause instant repercussions. So many sections are blind, and trouble is not often seen until it is too late. Within a few miles of my start, the course had fallen into its learned pattern and rhythm, with all my thoughts on the job at hand.

At the end of lap three, I pulled into my pit to refuel, change goggles, and have a mouthful of water. I came to a stop with the fuel cap already open, and my father, who was acting as my pit crew, inserted the fuel hose and began filling the tank. I reached over and took the clean goggles that lay across the top of his head and replaced the bug-splattered goggles I had been using. As I climbed off the bike and pulled the piston back against compression again, I shouted, "How am I doing?" My father had just finished filling the fuel tank and clicked the gas cap closed. He shouted back as I pushed off to begin my fourth lap. It took me a moment or two to digest what he had said. On the plummet down Bray Hill at about 140 miles per hour, I shouted to myself, "Third! No, it can't be. Not me." But it was true. My previous best position at the races had been fifth, and that had been due to many other riders experiencing mechanical failures. It seemed out of character for me to be in a podium position.

At the end of lap three, Phil Read, a British rider, and I were officially tied for third place to one hundredth of a second. The previous year, Read had won the 350 Junior Race, so for me to be in such select company was indicative of how much my riding had improved in the last year. Read and I were averaging just under the 100-mile-per-hour mark. On my second lap, I lapped at an average of 100.36 miles per hour to join the elusive "ton-up" club, its ninth member, and shortly thereafter, Read, with a later starting number, had done the same. Unknown to either of us at the time, the rider who had been second had retired with engine problems on that lap, so, in fact, Read and I were tied for second place.

All subdued concerns from the previous day's memorial service forgotten, I rode with renewed enthusiasm. Halfway around on lap four, at Sulby Bridge, unofficial timing placed me 15 seconds ahead of Read. However, on a racecourse the length of the Isle of Man TT, the latter half of the circuit could easily have been Read's better half, and this startling advantage I appeared to have could have been lost. We were never to know, however, for my 500 G50 Matchless came to a sudden stop with a broken crankshaft, on the climb up from Ramsey Hairpin. I tried in vain to restart the engine in the hope my initial conclusions had been in error, but a tortured grinding of metal on metal was the only response out the open exhaust.

I threw the useless pile of organized metal, plastic, and rubber against the wall at the track's edge just the other side of Waterworks Corner. In disgust, I plopped myself down on the stone wall with my feet resting on the bike's seat. Read, now in sole possession of second place, motored past a few moments later and waved. I sat, fighting back tears for what might have been, cursing my bad luck. It was at that moment that I glanced down at the rear tire. I couldn't believe what I saw. I looked again, questioning what my eyes recorded. Big chunks of rubber, many an inch in diameter, were missing from the treaded face of the experimental tire, and the canvas showed through in numerous places. I stared in horror at the mutilated tire and considered what lay just up the road from where the crankshaft had broken: the Mountain Mile, the Black Hut, the Veranda, the three lefts before Windy Corner, the 33rd Milestone, and the drop through Kate's Cottage to Creg-ny-Baa, all fast and demanding corners requiring a good rear tire. It could have been instant death, or worse still, permanent mutilation, should a tire have blown on any of these corners. I wonder to this day if the tire would have finished that lap, let alone another two at nearly a 100-mile-per-hour average had the crankshaft not broken? Looking again at the tire, I knew for sure it would not have gone the distance. The metallurgy failure had been a blessing. But what had caused the crankpin to fracture? It was not a common failure.

Back at Rose Villa, Gladys suggested another possibility: "Perhaps it was the Island's Wee Fairies who came to your rescue." The possibility had crossed my mind, but for fear of sounding foolish or slightly demented, I had not suggested it or, for that matter, seriously thought about it.

Whatever explanation best suited the situation, it had prevented serious injury or my possible demise, and I was glad to be sitting in the warmth and comfort of Rose Villa, in relative good health.

Although I still professed a degree of skepticism concerning the existence of the Island's Wee Fairies, later that evening, following the ceremonial prize giving, I drove alone out to the Fairy Bridge and verbally expressed my gratitude—without embarrassment.

# Index